SCENES THROUGH THE BATTLE SMOKE.

REV. ARTHUR MALE.

Frontispiece.

SCENES THROUGH THE BATTLE SMOKE.

BY

THE REV. ARTHUR MALE,

ARMY CHAPLAIN AT LUCKNOW, AND IN THE AFGHAN AND EGYPTIAN
CAMPAIGNS.

PROFUSELY ILLUSTRATED BY SIDNEY PAGET.

London:

DEAN & SON, 160A FLEET STREET, E.C.

LIST OF ILLUSTRATIONS.

REV. ARTHUR MALE . . . . . *Frontispiece*	
	PAGE.
LIEUTENANT-GENERAL SIR SAMUEL BROWNE . .	5
DEATH OF BIRCH AND FITZGERALD	11
LIEUTENANT HART WINS HIS V. C.	61
MAJOR O'MOORE CREAGH, V. C.	72
REV. ARTHUR MALE AND FRIEND RUNNING THE GAUNTLET AT JELLALABAD	153
CHARGE OF THE GUIDES AT FUTTEHABAD . . .	186
DEATH OF BATTYE	198
INCIDENT AT SURKH PUL	239
BURIAL OF QUILLEN, RIFLEMAN	264
ARABI PASHA	284
THE KHEDIVE	286
GENERAL LORD WOLSELEY	306
REV. A. MALE AND SHEPPARD	357
LIPSCOMBE AT KASSASSIN	385
SIR HAVELOCK-ALLAN AT TEL-EL-KEBIR . . .	441

CONTENTS.

Chap. Page

I. The Attack on Ali Musjid—Sam Browne's Strategy —Guns in Action—Charge of the Sikhs—Maclean Struck Down—Death of Birch and Fitzgerald—Col. Ball-Acton's Coolness—The Afghans "Hold the Fort"—Burial of the Dead at Nightfall—The Trio of "Specials"—The Afghan Flight in the Darkness —At Dawn the Fortress found Deserted—England's Flag Unfurled—The Army Chaplain and his Duty . 1

II. Lucknow at the Time of the War—Who goes to the Front?—The Parson Scores—Preparations and Start for Afghanistan—Cawnpore and its Memories of Blood—Delhi and John Nicholson—Umritsur— Lahore—An Anglo-Indian Hotel—Runjeet Singh— The Delays of Red Tape—All Officers on "Cabul Scale"—A Staunch Horse—Christmas *en route* to the Frontier—Villiers of the *Graphic*—The Christmas Ghost—The Start—Crossing the Indus by the Attack Bridge of Boats 21

III. Turbulent Peshawar—An Indian Dâk Bungalow— The Lonely House on Jumrood Road—A Picturesque Scene—The Peshawar Bazaar—Church Mission Work—An Encouraging Subscription—The Missionary's Ambiguous Epitaph—Poshteen and Sable Cap—My Patient (!) Camels—A Wild Country

Chap.		Page

—Boorj-i-Hurri Singh—Fort Jumrood—Soldiers' Rations—Alert in the Camp 40

IV. Hart goes for the V.C.—A Gallant Act wins it—"Sappers" can Fight—The Immortal Gordon—Too late for the Convoy—Wild Grandeur of the Khyber Pass—Unpleasant Travellers to Meet—"*Salaam Alaikoom*"—The Marwara Battalion, and its Officers—Mess Arrangements—The Parson's Glass—Afridi Shots from the Hillside—A Death Struggle by Night—Precautions for Safety . . 59

V. "Bright Chanticleer" from the 51st Bugles—A Path through the River—Dangerous Road—Afghan Village—The Guns peep over the Wall—Perfume of the Dead Camel—A bitter Night at Lundi Kotal—Graves joins me—Dakka Fort—Basawal—Jellalabad—Havelock's "Saints"—Arrival in Camp . 79

VI. Twelve or fifteen Regiments in the Big Camp—Arrangement of the Lines—Square Meal at the Headquarter Mess—The "Loving Cup" or Mess "Night Cap"—A quiet Stroll through the City—Annals of 1842—The "Illustrious Garrison"—Piper's Hill—A Hunting Rifle gets the Range—An old Veteran's Second Visit to Afghanistan—The Rains come—Sand Storms and Rain Storms—Villagers Help us for Rupees—Walls and Trenches—Night Tempest—The Rain floats Villiers 9

VII. Sunday Morning Parade—The Soldier worships God—No longer the Scum of Society—He merits Respect and Sympathy—Religions of the Army—Voluntary Services at Night—Soldiers' Bible Class and Tea Meeting—The "Sing-Song"—Sergeant Moon's Topical Song—Tenth Hussar Band—"As pants the Hart" 114

VIII. The "Red Cross" Quarters—The Sick Soldiers'

Chap.		Page
	Friend — God's Acre—Solitary Graves — Looting Afghans shot by Sentry—The Wolf and the Ghoorka—Visit to the Ameer's Gardens—Tea-drinking with the Khans—Church Construction on a Novel Scale—The Commander-in-Chief comes up —Tytler Charges the Shinwaris with his Lancers— Three Expeditions Start	. 130
IX.	A Second Visit to the City—A Startling Adventure —The two *Ghazis*—Running, or Walking, the Gauntlet—Murder of the Kahars—Swift Vengeance descends on the Murderers—The Tale of Fanatic Ferocity—To be Shot when well enough—Closing the Gates of Paradise—Attempt to Capture Azmutullah Khan—I Volunteer with the Cavalry .	. 147
X.	Squadron of the Tenth March out by Night—The Fatal Ford—Messengers of Death—Napier Swims for his Life—Taking out the Bodies—Nineteen Buried together—Harford's Funeral—The lonely River-side Grave—Thurlow's After-fate . .	. 165
XI.	The Seventeenth Mess—Wiseman's Prejudice—Expedition against the Kujianis—Gallant Battye— Five Thousand Kujianis well Posted—Stewart's Stratagem with the Guns—The Kujianis are "Drawn" — Advance of the Leicester Men — Wiseman Attacks the big Afghan Standard Bearer, and is struck down—Corporal Clarke's gallant effort —Manners-Wood nearly Killed—Battye Shot— Mahommed Khan Defends his Body; but is Killed —Vengeance of the Guides—Night Scene—A Solemn Vow—The Warrior at Rest . .	. 182
XII.	Forward ! towards the Jugdullak Pass—Strange Wounds—Night Packing—Reveille at Half-past Twelve—The Lost Subaltern—Night March to Rozabad—Fort Battye—Neemlabagh—Arrival at Safed Sang—My Quarters on the High Ridge—	

Chap.		Page
	Yakub Khan Prepares to Come in—The Meeting—General Daud Shah—Yakub's Afghan Highlanders, Kilts and all—He Rides Through Three Miles of Troops — Queen's Birthday Celebration — Treaty Signed May 26th	203
XIII.	A Dark Page in our History—Slaughter of 16,000—The Remnant at Bay—A Solitary Survivor—Burnes's Cantonments—Relics of a Lost Army Discovered—The Burial of the Bones—A Villainous Escort—Strange Stone Bridge—Ghilzai Man-Stalking—A Narrow Escape—A Mother's Plea for Mercy . .	221
XIV.	Return to India in Intense Heat—Cholera Wave Sweeping up the Pass—An Unfortunate Start—"Budmash" Mules—The First Stage Down—An Al Fresco Bath—Jellalabad once more—Thirty Miles a Day—The Cholera Touches us—God's Acre—A Strange Thirst-Quencher—The Cholera Camp—A Sad Spectacle—We Shift our Camp in the Night—The Grip of the Sickness on me—A Hard Ride to Save my Life—The March of Death Begins	245
XV.	The "March of Death" continued—My Gay Escort—Tracks of Death—Fallen by the Way—The Lonely Grave—A Gallop for Life—The Perils of the Pass—Good Escort Work—A Halt at Basawul—The "Rifles" En Route—The Dead Colonel Borne Along—My Escort Done Up; Get Fresh Men—Dakka Fort—Shadow of Sickness and Death—The End of my Twenty-five Miles' Gallop—Rest at Last, and Life—A Staunch Horse, and his end—Men to be Buried—"Dandy" Transport—The Nemesis of Laziness—Lundi Kotal Hospital and its "Padres"—Last Stages—Farewell to the Ghoorkas—A Tough Old Veteran—Home Again—The Later Dark Page—Russia and Afghanistan—England's True Responsibility in connection with India . .	263

Chap.		Page
XVI.	Clarions of War in the East—Causes of Egyptian War—Mohammed Tewfik Viceroy, and Ahmed Arabi Pasha—An Alien Government—England's Interests in the Nile Valley—The Suez Canal—Naval Demonstration—Massacre of 11th June—The Egyptians will Fight—Bombardment of the Forts—Charlie Beresford and his little "Condor"—Incendiarism in the Town—Deeds of Blood all through the Country—Beresford's Police—Military Expedition from England—My Summons—Sir John Adye—Getting my Kit—"Tommy White's"—Little Tailoring Mistakes—My Friend's Dilemma—Detailed to Sail with the Headquarter Staff	282
XVII.	Embarking for the War—The Headquarter Staff Boat—The "Wolseley Ring"—Selection by Merit—Some Distinguished Names—Convict and Brigand Style—Board Ship Lecturing—"Gib," and First News of Bloodshed—Final Preparations—First Sight of Alexandria—Near Inspection—Dark Horrors—The Guards in Service Kit—Horse Dealing under Difficulties: I Score a Point, however—Wolseley's Ruse—A Feint on Aboukir Bay—Seizure of the Suez Canal—We Steam towards Ismailia	302
XVIII.	Ismailia—Landing of Troops—Difficulty with the Horses—Merry Jack Tars—I take one for an Arab—"Baines's"—Bivouacing—The Palace Hospital—My Quarters—Greek Looters and Swift Justice—Highlanders Fighting at Chalouffe—Lang Swims the Canal—Plan of Campaign—Arabi Cuts off our Water Supply—The Fight of the 24th of August—British Tenacity—Long Odds against us—Hickman's Two Guns against Arabi's Twelve—Gunner Knowles's Pluck—Reinforcements—Night Bivouac	320
XIX.	The Fight to be Continued—Captain Hallam Parr and Lord Melgund Wounded—An All-Night Journey	

Chap.		Page
	through the Desert—Cruel Marching—Schreiber's Guns—We Lose our Way—Halt!—A Soft Bed—Morning Dawn—The Egyptians Bolt—Cavalry Fight at Mahsameh—Guns in Action—Major Bibby Shot—Charge by Squadrons—Enemy's Fire Effective—A Ghastly Group—Effects of a Shell Explosion—Waiting for a Surgeon—A Scare—All's Well that Ends Well—Commissionaire Sheppard and his New Leg	338
xx.	The Fight at Mahsameh Continued—Terrible Thirst—Final Dash—Description of a Cavalry Charge—Trooper Browning Halves (?) an Egyptian—The Crafty Mahmoud taken Prisoner—Rush for Water—The Polluted Canal—I Carry Despatches—A Lonely Desert Ride—The Solitary Old Troop Horse—The Duke of Connaught's Disappointment—Wounded Transported in Boats—Sun Blisters—Naval Officers' Escapade, and its Result.	359
xxi.	Our Indian Contingent under Herbert Macpherson—O'Brien and his Cooking Pot—Graham Seizes Kassassin Lock—Arabi Strikes out at our Advancing Column—First Fight at Kassassin—Bad Odds—A Struggle all Day—The Attack Pressed at Evening—Drury Lowe Brings up the Cavalry—Moonlight Charge—Baker Russell Leads—Lipscombe's Victory—Plucky Hospital Men—To the Front in a Steam Pinnace—Biscuit Bag Defence—A Big "Scare"—My Night Ride through the Desert—Animated Bushes—A Near Shave for the General—The Press Den—How the News was Flashed to England	375
xxii.	Tedious Waiting—Short Commons of Water—A Handy Sausage Machine—Arabi Aroused—Cavalry Reconnoitring—Graham's Reconnaissance—September 9th—Second Fight at Kassassin—Shells as an Early "Eye-Opener"—Pennington's Plucky	

Lancers—They Check the Advance—Egyptian Guns Search our Camp—Volunteers under Fire—The Enemy Four to One—Our Cavalry let Loose—Wolseley Comes Up—Arabi begins to Fall Back—Marines Capture Two Guns—Stanhope's Muscular Feat—The Lines at Tel-el-Kebir—Gribble Found—The Dead Lancer—Nine Hours and no Breakfast—Shall we Rush the Entrenchments?—Wolseley Returns to Camp—Bengali Courtesy—Field Hospital Scenes—Both Legs Lost—The Dead Riflemen—A Chaplain Knocked up 397

XXIII. Wolseley Carefully Reconnoitres—Arabi's Strong Position — Details — His Numbers — The Odds Against Us—Quiet Sabbath in the Desert—I Take Down a Sick Chaplain to Ismailia—Railway Service—Sepoys Eager for the Fight—Hospital Arrangements Perfect—The Convent Sisters—Netley Nurses Arrive—The Hospital Ship *Carthage*—Death of the Rifleman—Everyone Keen for the Front—The Highland Brigade Veterans—No Boy Soldiers—Laying in Stores—Off to Kassassin Again—Force Gathered—Ready ! Aye Ready ! 415

XXIV. The Battle of Tel-el-Kebir—The Lull before the Storm —Orders Out for an Advance—Last Letters—Fall In !—Disposition of our Forces—St. Vincent and his Final Fate—The Advance—Halt !—Onward March—Wyatt Rawson Steers by the Stars—Brookes of the "Gordons" goes in with a Spade—Silent March through the Darkness — Day Breaks—Terrible Opening Fire—Arabi's Arrangements—The Highlanders in First—Havelock-Allan Rushes the Ditch—A Narrow Shave—Egyptians Fight Steadily — Graham-Stirling and McNeill — The English and Irish Brigade at it together — The Marines Lose Heavily—Death of Strong—Wardell Falls : but is Avenged by Luke 428

CONTENTS.

Chap.   Page

XXV. The Guards Peppered—Father Bellord Wounded—Forward! the Guns—Scotland for Ever!—First Gun Breaks Down—The Bridge—The Naval Brigade Work their Gatlings—The Indians and the Seaforths Shoulder to Shoulder—The Butcher's Bill—The Track of the Storm—Succouring the Wounded—Revolver or Water Bottle—Trenches Full of Dead—The Unread Letter—A Fatal Shell—Arabi's Army a Mixed Multitude—Words of Christian Burial in the Great Redoubt—Young Graham-Stirling—The Colonel's Promise—The Gallant McNeill—Scanty Dinner Rations—Wounded Egyptians—A Fierce Amazon—A Wounded Woman's Gratitude—Evening Burial—Strong and Kayes—A Smart Telegraph Trick—Wolseley's Wise Measures—A Dash on Zagazig and Cairo—Rout of the *Bedaween*—The Irish Lads' Love of Loot—I Sleep on the Field . 446

XXVI. After the Battle—Dash on Zagazig by the Indians and 72nd—The Cavalry Ride to Cairo—Surrender of the Citadel—Arabi Pasha a Prisoner—Wolseley Arrives—Scenes in Hospital and on Board the *Carthage*—The Tainted Battlefield—Strewn with Dead and Debris—I go on to Cairo in a Cattle Truck—The Donkey Boy at Midnight — Luxury of a "Square" Meal and a Bed—Mosquito Pests—Return of the Khedive—Illuminations and Rejoicings—The Fête at Ghezireh—*Bedaween* seek Wives among the Highlanders—A Little Blunder—The "Holy Carpet" Procession—Explosion at the Cairo Railway Station—Arabi's Trial and Sentence—What We Learned from the Trial—England's Mission in Egypt—My Meeting with Gordon—Is He Dead?—Testimony of Two Campaigns to the Pluck of Our Soldiers, and the Splendid Work of the Medical Department—The Chaplains' Department—The Echo of Wyatt Rawson's Words—The Call of Stern Duty to Every Man 464

SCENES THROUGH THE BATTLE SMOKE.

CHAPTER I.

The Attack on Ali Musjid—Sam Browne's Strategy—Guns in Action—Charge of the Sikhs—Maclean Struck Down—Death of Birch and Fitzgerald—Col. Ball-Acton's Coolness—The Afghans "Hold the Fort"—Burial of the Dead at Nightfall—The Trio of "Specials"—The Afghan Flight in the Darkness—At Dawn the Fortress found Deserted—England's Flag Unfurled—The Army Chaplain and his Duty.

"WE shall advance to the attack at daybreak to-morrow morning. It is too late now to expect any answer from the Ameer to our *ultimatum*. And we must see whether the Afghan obstinacy will bend when our 40-pounders batter at the gates of Ali Musjid fortress."

A little group of Indian officers are standing together on some rising ground just outside Fort Jumrood, and looking forward where, some half a mile ahead, the rocky gorge of the Khyber Pass opened in all its frowning grandeur. Every man of them a bronzed veteran; the ribbons on their *khaki* undress uniform speaking of many a fierce fight. The first, a bearded man, with upright, well-knit frame, and with left sleeve empty, has just spoken. Sir Sam Browne, V.C., is well-known as a gallant officer of the old Mutiny days, and of the terrible Sikh campaigns before them. He can tell of Chillianwallah, and of the many fights around Delhi; and of Sirpoorah, where, at the head of his wild horsemen, he slew in single combat the big rebel standard-bearer, losing his own left arm, but gaining his "Cross." No name so well loved among the men of the native cavalry corps of the Punjaub; for "Sham Broon Sahib," as they call him, can ride straight, and strike hard and home even now, when he leads them.

Near Sir Sam stands Appleyard, short, wiry, keen-eyed. And sturdy Macpherson, destined to lead his brigade, on his chestnut pony, many a weary march among the Afghan passes and mountains. And Tytler, too, than whom the Queen-Empress never had a truer soldier in her service. He has little to say, but much to note, and when called on carries out his operations with dash as well as skill, and with invariable success.

"I want you, Tytler, to take your brigade over the hills here on our left, making a wide detour; and taking up position, if possible, at this spot marked Kata Kushta," said the General, pointing out the locality on a map which he held in his hand, "you will thus be in the rear of the fort, and effectually cut off the retreat of the Afghans, should they be driven back or attempt to make off. You will march at nightfall, and, favoured by the darkness, you ought to make the position by daybreak.

"And will you, Macpherson, start with the 1st Brigade four hours before dawn, and occupy the Shagai heights, which you see marked here on the enemy's left? The hills on our right will thus be cleared of any possible opposition, and Appleyard's Brigade will be able to operate along the valley, and towards the Afghan position itself."

Very briefly the orders were given, and the officers most concerned moved off to perfect their arrangements and carry out the orders of their chief. Tytler's Brigade, including the 1st Battalion of the 17th Foot, a regiment which had trodden Afghan heights nearly forty years before; the 1st Regiment of Sikhs, and the Guides, marched when the night shadows fell. Macpherson, with the 1st Brigade, which comprised, among others, the 4th Battalion of the Rifle Brigade and the 4th Ghoorkas, started a few hours later.

The next morning, Thursday, November 21st, about six o'clock, Sir Sam Browne, with Appleyard's Brigade, altogether numbering some six regiments, four native and two European, and accompanied by a mountain battery, and a battery of 40-pounders,

LIEUTENANT-GENERAL SIR SAMUEL BROWN.

drawn by elephants, entered the rugged gorge of the Khyber, and marched steadily forward towards Ali Musjid. The golden glory of the Eastern dawn flooded even the gloomy recesses of the Pass, as the men, European and native, pressed on, braced up somewhat by the keen air of the early morning. Presently, emerging from the narrower defile, the scenery changed. On both sides there rose a succession of undulating hills, until away in the distance, a mile and a half or so, one could see Fort Ali Musjid strongly placed on a rocky plateau, some 600 feet above the bed of the river, which flowed in breaks and shallows along the valley below. Impregnable indeed it seemed, by its very position, frowning down from beetling crags, while a nearer observation revealed something of its strength of fortification and armament. It was built of hard mud, faced with stone, with regular towers and bastions, and mounting numerous guns. The slopes, both above and lower down, bristled too with *sungahs*, a special form of Afghan defence consisting of strong walls of stone, behind which dense bodies of men took up position, Now and again guns were mounted here too.

General Browne halted the men for awhile to allow the elephant battery to come up. For although these huge animals made no trouble of dragging forward the heavy 40-pounders, still much difficulty was experienced in threading the narrow hill-paths, which were alone available. The halt was not for long, however. Presently the bugles sounded the attack; and as the last echo reverberated among the mountains the 81st Regiment and the 14th Sikhs could be seen throwing forward a line of skirmishers to clear the adjoining hill-sides, while Manderson's battery— I.C. R.H.A.—came galloping around the bend of the hill, and, getting into position, opened fire on the guns of the fort. In an instant the Afghan gunners returned the fire, and with good effect; for the range of the various points along the Pass had been carefully taken by them before the fighting opened. And now the crash of the shells as they exploded, and the constant rattle and roll of the rifle fire made valley and mountain side alive with deafening reverberation. The men pressed on with impetuous valour; but the wild defenders of fort and *sungah* were nothing daunted. Gun answered gun, while crowds of Afghan warriors could be seen rushing out to man the outer entrenchments, and even streaming over the hillside. Suddenly the welcome sound of the big 40-pounders—a deep-toned hoarse booming—could be heard behind. The elephant battery had at last arrived and taken up position, and was now playing upon the strong fortress to some tune. Gradually the enemy's artillery fire was silenced, or partially so, and the gaping defences began to show patent signs of the rough handling they had received.

But the roughest and most sanguinary part of the work was yet to come. The *sungahs* must be rushed, and the fortress itself stormed, if this key of the road to Cabul was to fall into our hands at all. Some of these *sungahs* were strong indeed, formed of huge boulders held in great strength by the Afghans; and in one instance mounting three guns, which were by no means silenced. Right gallantly Captain Maclean rushed on towards one of them, followed by his fiery Sikhs, who knew no fear. But an Enfield bullet struck him down, though not fatally; while seven of his non-commissioned officers and twenty rank and file fell killed and wounded around him. Lying under the shelter of the *sungah* where he fell, the gallant leader shouted back for the supports. And Major Birch, heading the 27th Punjabis, brought them forward, under the fiercest fire from rifle and battery. Down went Birch, shot dead, his face towards the foe, and round him thickly fell his men. They wavered; then fell back, with the remnant of Sikhs, and the wounded Maclean. Birch's subaltern, young Fitzgerald, would not brook that his chief's body should lie there exposed to the wanton ferocity of the fanatics, who were used to mutilate with such unnameable barbarity. He called for volunteers from his own Punjabis to bring in the body of their leader. But alas! the Afghan fire still fiercely swept the slope, and there was no response. Turning to the Sikhs, who were forming up again near by, their one officer lying desperately wounded, he shouted for some of them to follow him; and fifteen gallant fellows rushed forward to climb again the slope of death. Up they went, step by step, one and another falling here and there. Halfway up Fitzgerald was struck, but with heroic resolution he still pressed on, intent on his task of rescue. He reached the body of Birch, raised it in his arms, when a bullet again struck him, and he fell dead; the two friends thus side by side in the sleep of death, almost within touch of the Afghan guns. Alas! very few of the gallant fifteen returned alive. They fell almost to a man. Just now Manderson's Horse Battery came clattering down the very bed of the river itself. Over the boulders and through the deep pools went horses and guns, seeking a position of vantage where they could unlimber and shell the

DEATH OF BIRCH AND FITZGERALD.

To face page 10.

sungahs. But the fire from rifles and batteries poured down with redoubled fierceness, both on retreating Punjabis and Sikhs, and on battery too. Here a cannon shot, hurtling through the air, took off the head of a gunner—" one of the best men in the troop," as his commanding officer said; and there several other men and horses fell wounded before the terrible raking hail of bullets from above. Still the guns secured a position. The heavy battery came up, and a mountain battery as well. And acting with the 4th Brigade, which included the gallant 51st Regiment, the " K.O. L.I.'s," as they are called, our men, undaunted, resolved to sweep the fierce warriors from *sungah* defences and fortress alike; or perish on the slopes which stretched away above them. To this end Colonel Ball-Acton, second in command, was ordered to lead a wing of the 51st across the stream to the left. This he did with admirable coolness, his old horse " Bismarck " being apparently as calm and unmoved as his rider amid the storm and crash of bullet and shell. On they went, and began to climb the slippery hillside in support of the native troops. For a moment the Afghan fire seemed checked. But ere this final, and, perhaps, decisive movement could be developed and carried out the shadows of the night descended, as they do in Eastern lands, all too suddenly, and the bugles were heard sounding the "Retire." Even as the men, Punjabis and Sikhs, fell back unwillingly, the Afghans, recovering, swept again the slope with parting volleys, and many another was added to the list of killed or wounded.

The after-scenes of a battle-field are never pleasant. When actual fighting has ceased, and fierce passions are somewhat allayed, men have time to pause and to think, and then the saddest thoughts gather in upon one. On this occasion, however, there was scarce time for mental rest, or pause or thought. The fierce struggle was to be renewed at dawn; for the position must be ours at all costs. So every man turned to the question of supper and bed. But some things must needs be done first. The quiet dead were lying around. They were comrades with us this morning. What now? At least must their remains be gently put to rest in the narrow bed which awaits us all. A little funeral party hastily formed up, composed of men from Manderson's Battery, to bury their comrade. As gently and tenderly as possible the mangled remains were composed to rest. In the pockets just a few coins were found, and a letter from the poor lad's sister—written amid the pleasant surroundings of the country home, now sharing with the stricken soldier the carnage scenes of the battle ground, and almost, too, the alien grave. And thus one and another were consigned to the quiet resting-place of mother earth's bosom. And the living looked round for some soft spot where they might take a lighter sleep.

This was no easy matter. Easy to search, but not so easy to find. Occasionally a fortunate doctor by virtue of his office and work could secure the shelter of a *dooley*, or hospital stretcher, with curtains around, where, though not a wounded man, he might sleep the sleep of the just; but for the most part every man lay down on the lee side of some friendly boulder or bush, and, wrapped in his blanket, if he happened to have brought it, dreamed of home and feather beds and " square " meals; and, waking, found it but a dream. Thus did three correspondents—the redoubtable Archibald Forbes, the facile-penned Phil Robinson, and the genial, tough old warrior and " illustrator," William Simpson, who had already done more than a quarter of a century's work as " special artist; " and seemed able for another quarter at least, if duty called him to it. There the three lay, scarce more animated than mummies, and largely resembling them in appearance, gathering strength by sleep for the coming day's fatigue and fighting.

But happily there was to be no more fighting—there. Tytler's movement had been carried out with that gallant officer's usual skill and success; and his brigade was securely occupying the Kata Kushta position, in rear of the

Ali Musjid Fort, and effectually cutting off the clear retreat of the Afghans. Such retreat nevertheless was attempted by Gholam Hyder, the Ameer's general, directly he heard that his path of safety and flight to the rear was threatened, if not blocked, by a hostile force. Under cover of the night-darkness and through a perfect knowledge of the hill paths he at first led his panic-striken force in safety. But the darkness at last proved his foe. For, after just avoiding the lines of the "Rifles" and the "Ghoorkas" belonging to Macpherson's Brigade—some twinkling watch fires betraying their proximity in time—he marched his men into the very arms of the 17th Regiment, who, with the "Guides" and the 1st Sikhs, were on the alert all night; and very large numbers were captured.

This, then, was the surprise which awaited our weary men when they awoke from their brief slumber on the morning of the 22nd. A Cashmiri merchant, who had been a prisoner in the Fort for some days, at the risk of a bullet from one of our sentries, brought the news just at daybreak; telling how a wild panic had seized the garrison, and they had fled, leaving guns, tents, food, and property as they stood. Indeed, those who had escaped Tytler could now be seen streaming away across the distant hills towards Lalpoorah and Jellalabad. Early in the morning the General and his staff toiled up the steep ascent, and entered the battered fortification The Union Jack was run up on the ramparts, and this key to India's gateway was once more securely in British hands.

* * * * *

And how comes it that I, a minister of religion, should be thrown into association with scenes of blood and carnage such as those which I have attempted here to depict? Simply because the English nation, when it sends its gallant soldiers into the field, credits them with something more than mere physical frames to be kept strong and in good fighting trim. "Tommy Atkins," while he has a strong arm to strike for his country, has a heart also to feel and sympathise. He is a *man*, not a machine; and has needs other than those which can be met by the daily meat ration, the third of an ounce of tea, or even the rum ration. "We like to know that we've got a parson with us in the field," said a man to me one day in plain, blunt words, "we don't like when we get knocked over, to be buried away in a hole, like a dog, without a prayer." And so the British people, recognising these deeper needs of her soldier sons—needs which may not be always apparent on the outside, but which are none the less real, has her Chaplain's Department in connection with the army. And there are never wanting men who in this path of duty are proud to go forth under her standard, not to fight, unless indeed some stern necessity should arise— then they can—but rather to enhearten the men, and keep them in touch with that higher duty which embraces and covers all the lesser but essential duties of their soldier life. The men are none the less unshaken in discipline, and plucky in fight, because of their Sunday morning parade service; or the quiet word of comfort and friendly sympathy spoken in the hospital tent; or the knowledge that if they fall, words of Christian prayer will be reverently spoken by their grave side, as they are laid away to rest in the far-off land.

With the causes or righteousness of the Afghan War, I have nothing to do. The fall of the fortress of Ali Musjid marked the opening of a campaign which brought to me many strange and stirring experiences in the path of duty to which I have above referred. Thus I have depicted it first of all. But many a weary month was to elapse, and many a rough time was to fall to my lot, before even this first Afghan episode of chaplain work was to come to an end.

CHAPTER II.

Lucknow at the Time of the War—Who goes to the Front?—The Parson Scores—Preparations and Start for Afghanistan—Cawnpore and its Memories of Blood—Delhi and John Nicholson—Umritsur—Lahore—An Anglo-Indian Hotel—Runjeet Singh—The Delays of Red Tape—All Officers on "Cabul Scale"—A Staunch Horse—Christmas *en route* to the Frontier—Villiers of the *Graphic*—The Christmas Ghost—The Start—Crossing the Indus by the Attack Bridge of Boats.

INTENSE excitement prevailed in Lucknow—the historic city, with its mutiny memories—when it was known that very shortly in all probability we should enter upon another of our "little wars;" this time beyond the North-West Frontier. Desultory fighting was the chronic condition of this frontier. The Jowaki tribesmen were never accustomed to remain in a state of quiescence for long together. The corps of "Guides," cavalry, and infantry which our people had raised among the frontier population were always at work, administering well-earned thrashings to their brethren over the border. But as soon as they had, to some extent, recovered from the said chastisement, they were sure to be at their old tricks again. Many of our best Indian officers found their school of training in this wild frontier fighting ground.

But this, which was rumoured as likely to come to pass, was a different thing altogether. A country which was supposed to have flirted with Russia, and snubbed England, was to be straightway invaded, and England's dignity was to be vindicated, even within the walls of the Ameer's palace at Cabul, if need be.

Everybody knew that Shere Ali had fortified positions, serviceable guns, an army which was to some extent disciplined—trained, as some supposed, by Russian officers,—and yet imitating the English army to the length of having its Afghan Highlanders, tartan kilts and all. This would be no frontier fighting assuredly, but the invasion of a scarcely-known country, and with an adequate force. Who would have to go? That was the question. And as Lucknow was a big military station, having in its cantonments a large garrison of English and native troops, numbering some six or seven regiments, infantry and cavalry, with batteries of artillery to boot, it was naturally felt to be a question which affected Lucknow very vitally.

Presently, the papers announced that war was duly proclaimed, and the Ameer's territory actually invaded; while Lucknow had not been called on to furnish a single man or horse to aid in the work of conquest. Every regiment which had been called out was the object of envy among us then, even though it might only have gone across the border, and was never at the front at all. Every march and movement was followed with intensest interest. And the progress of the three columns through the Khyber Pass, over the Peiwar Kotel, and through the Bolan

Pass, was prognosticated with the most thorough and all-sufficient military skill by the latest young "griffs" who had just joined their regiments from home.

One chill morning (for we have such mornings in the cold season in the north-west of India), I was sitting in my verandah busy with my *choti hazri* or early breakfast, and busily scanning at the same time the columns of the *Pioneer*, which recorded the first movements which had taken place, when the Post Office peon, with his scarlet *cummerbund*, suddenly stood before me, making his presence known by the utterance of his usual formula. "*Dâk chithi, sahib;*" and holding out to me a big official envelope. It did not take me long to open it, and to my utter astonishment I found that I, of all, was the fortunate man of the Lucknow cantonments. For it was a communication to the effect that I was to proceed to Lahore, where the Commander-in-Chief's camp then was, there to await orders with a view to proceeding to the front.

We do not set out now to join troops, and enter on campaigning, as they used to do in the proverbial "good old days," burdened only with a carpet bag; although I have seen a man's kit bag, containing all he had, and all he needed, scarce bulkier than a good-sized portmanteau. Still we like to do a little better than this, if opportunity permit. Consequently I used the two or three days at my disposal, before I needed to start, in gathering together, as I thought, a useful assortment of necessary articles; most of which I afterwards left behind me at the base of operations, as useless *impedimenta;* and which I had the pleasure of picking up again as I returned to India, after the toils and vicissitudes of the campaign were over. Some of my own men of the 13th Hussars were specially solicitous for my comfortable well-being; one constructing for me a very huge pair of fur gloves, with the hair inside; and another kind friend coming forward with a cap, "fearfully and wonderfully made," with large lappets to cover the ears. I laughed at the time at the absurdity, as I thought. But I did not laugh afterwards, when in the Afghan passes the glass registered from ten to twenty degrees of frost; and officers and men, forgetting what was grotesque, were only concerned to get a little warmth into their finger ends and ear tips by any means within their reach.

In a few days my preparations were made as far as necessary; for I knew that at Lahore I should be able to complete what was needful; farewells were said; and along the East Indian Railway I was being carried swiftly northwards towards the city of Runjeet Singh, the old Sikh "Lion of the Punjab." Away past Cawnpore, with its bloody memories of '57: the "Massacre Well," enclosed now as hallowed ground, and guarded by an angel figure, marvellously sculptured, which stands overshadowing with outstretched wings the actual spot, as if weeping for the "great company of Christian people, chiefly women and children, who met their deaths hard by." Away northwards, skirting by

Meerut, where the mutiny broke out on that fatal Sunday; and through Delhi—which afterwards became the rebel stronghold—and which they held in their grip so tenaciously, till the gallant John Nicholson, at the head of his brave lads, snatched it from them, and in doing so broke the back of the mutiny in those parts. Ah! he was a man! one of pure spirit, amid the horrid scenes of carnage by which he was surrounded.

> Brief, brave, and glorious was his young career;
> . . . . He had kept
> The whiteness of his soul—and thus men o'er him wept;

for he fell in the streets of Delhi even as the shouts of victory rang in his ears. On again through Umballa, where in '69 the Earl of Mayo, the then Viceroy, received this same Afghan Ameer, Sheer Ali, in friendly *durbar*. And through Umritsur, where the "Golden Temple" and the "Sacred tank" mark the headquarters of the Sikh religion; and the holy dwelling-place of their chief

Guru, or high priest. Until at last, after I had been travelling thirty-six hours on the stretch, the train steamed into the station at Lahore very early in the morning. Glad enough I was to get out of it. For despite all that is said about the comfort, and even luxury of Indian travelling, it becomes a trifle monotonous after a day and a half of it. The next anxiety was to obtain quarters for oneself. This I found to be a matter of some difficulty. The presence of the Commander-in-Chief's camp, and the transference of all the headquarter staff and military offices from Simla and Calcutta to the plain just outside Lahore, had brought such a rush of people, official and non-official, that all the usually frequented hotels were crowded out. The next best thing, therefore, was to patronise some decent native hostel, or rather some hotel for Europeans, but under native proprietorship and management. It seemed to me that the pressure put upon the city by the unwonted influx of visitors had taxed its resources to the very utmost. Things looked worn out all round. The native porters at the station were weary. The horses of the public *garis* or carriages were attenuated. And I noticed that as my steed got up a feeble gallop in the vain effort to convey me speedily to the Punjab Hotel, the very harness was supplemented here and there with pieces of cord and string, which threatened at every tug to give way incontinently, and leave me stranded on the roadside. Arrived, however, without fatal accident, mine host of the "Punjab" managed to find me fairly comfortable if not luxurious quarters; and after a much-needed "tub"—the universal panacea of every Anglo-Indian—I felt quite fit first to discuss breakfast, and then set about the duty which had brought me to Lahore.

I found this hotel, like all others, crowded with men either going up to the front or trying to get some appointment which would take them thither. Two or three had actually been over the border; and, returning for some reason, had strange tales to narrate of the wild country and the wilder tribesmen, who lined the Khyber Pass, skulking behind the boulders, far up on the hill side, waiting for "pot shots" at those who marched below; and especially paying attention to any who might be going up without sufficient escort. These tales I fear we sometimes received with incredulity: at any rate *cum grano;* and they served rather to whet the appetites of the eager spirits who were quite willing to go and see for themselves. The tales were quite true, however, in the main, as some of us had afterwards cause to know.

There is no city in Northern India more interesting than Lahore; none more rich in records and memories of the past. In old time the seat of the mogul Emperors, it became later the Sikh capital. And here old Runjeet Singh built his fortress and drilled his army to such a pitch of efficiency that, under Gholab Singh, his successor, it nearly proved itself a match for Lord Gough's troops in the Punjab War. It was here, also, that Runjeet was the proud possessor of the famous Koh-i-noor diamond, which he wrenched from Shah Shuja the Afghan, and which now belongs to our own Queen, the Empress of India. Neither the monuments of Shah Jehan, and Jehangir, and Runjeet Singh, nor the beauties of the Shalimar Gardens, however, were sufficient to attract me now, as I wended my way out towards Meean Mir, where the military camp was pitched. I had fondly imagined that a day or two at most would be sufficient for the settlement of all preliminaries ; and that then I should go forward to join our men in the Afghan Pass. Had I not letters of introduction to Sir Neville Chamberlain, the man of seventeen wounds, from his brother, my own general at Lucknow? Alas! I found that there was verily "red tape," and plenty of it, in military arrangements, as in legal, and many days elapsed before the longed-for orders to proceed came to hand.

This waiting time I employed to profit in gathering together a serviceable kit, and sending back much that I had brought with me that was unserviceable. Officers and men were to be strictly on Cabul scale, as it was called. What that meant for the men I can scarcely tell. For officers it certainly meant the barest necessaries, and no more, one tiny tent, which, with all its paraphernalia, was to weigh only 80 lbs., and all else, including camp equipage, bed, table, chair, cooking utensils, and personal baggage, to come within the limits of 120 lbs. When a man's house, and all within it, has to scale under 200 lbs., he cannot be said to live in luxury. Thousands of camels had been purchased as baggage animals. And for yourself, the best carrier was a strong, sure-footed horse. Such an one I managed to secure in the outskirts of Lahore. And many a time I had cause to thank Providence that I fell in with that staunch beast. He belonged to the Herati breed, and when I bought him was only half broken in; well set-up, strong-boned, and with a spirit of his own, as I soon found. But that same spirit stood me more than once in good stead, for he was always game, most so at the pinch ; and saved my life, as I believe, on one or two occasions of peril. Dear old horse! He could not brook the quiet drudgery of Lucknow work, when I got him back to India, and only seemed himself again when, on some field day, plenty of blank cartridge was cracking and banging around him, and he imagined he smelt the battle from afar. Now he lies beneath the sod—dying, as he ought, by a trooper's carbine; but his memory will ever be green to me.

We were a merry party at that same Punjab hotel, though naturally inclined to chafe at the delay in sending us forward. Around the fire at night we often sat after dinner, and wondrous yarns were spun, sometimes far into the small hours. It was the coldest of the cold weather—near Christmas time—and thoughts of home and the dear ones we had left behind were often with us. Our experiences in this dismal Indian hotel stood out in grim contrast with the bright jollity of the festive season in our own country over the sea.

Just now a new comer appeared among us.

He was a bright-faced, cheerful young fellow, who was evidently, like ourselves, intent on getting to the front, but in what capacity we could not at first divine. He did not belong to the service, and yet he knew pretty well as much as the men who did belong to it, about soldiers and the soldier life. Campaigning, too, seemed not altogether a new experience to him; though India, with its peculiar customs and ways, evidently was. The mystery of his identity was solved, however, one morning when an orderly sowar, a wild Mooltani cavalryman, on this occasion bestriding a camel, came riding up to the hotel with an official communication from headquarters, addressed, "Frederic Villiers, Esq., special correspondent of the *Graphic*."

No wonder he knew something of campaigning. Had he not served already in the Russo-Turkish campaigns, and climbed the *glacis* of Plevna, slippery with the blood of those who were falling fast around him? To-day he is a man of eight campaigns in all parts of the world; but even then he was no novice at his work. This casual meeting in the far north-west of India was the commencement of a friendship between him and me which has endured through many a year since. Strange indeed have been the experiences which we have had together amid the wild passes of Afghanistan, or the great deserts of Egypt.

But my friend was new to India and its habits. And among other things he did not know that when a man travelled there he almost literally "took up his bed and walked." That is to say, he always carried a bundle of blankets and pillows with him, as a necessary portion of his baggage; for when you take possession of your room in the hotel, you invariably find a small bedstead and bare mattress for your sleeping accommodation, and but little else.

One night we had been tarrying by the fireside, according to custom, hearing and telling tales. Villiers had modestly enough given us a yarn or two about Skobeleff on his white horse, and the Russians. Another man had been unfolding some of his experiences of wild fighting on the frontier and over the border, for he was a native cavalry officer; and a third had whetted the appetite of the hunting men with his *Shikari* tales of bears and elk shot in far Cashmere. So the night had fairly worn away when we turned in for a few hours' sleep, and were soon wrapped in our blankets, and folded in the arms of Morpheus too. At least I was. For the god of dreams was verily with me that night. Whether it was that I had eaten too hearty a dinner, or the thrilling tales of the fireside had excited my brain to unusual activity, I cannot tell, but this I know—that ghostly and ghastly visions began to rise before me. It was a bitterly cold night—some degrees of frost outside—and every available rug I had piled on my bed. But even then I seemed not to be able to sleep. Outside I heard close to my window the weird tones of the *Chowkeydar* as he shouted to his brother-watchmen, and struck his iron-bound *lattee* on the ground. Then the horrible yells of the laughing jackals broke upon the still night air. And for awhile, disturbed by these and other sounds, I lay between sleeping and waking. All was pitch dark. The jackals and their hilarious yells died away in the distance, and the *Chowkeydar* subsided, probably to sleep in some distant corner of the compound, when my eyes, seeming to pierce the darkness, lighted on what seemed a gaunt, white form slowly and noiselessly moving from a distant corner of the room. Whether it was form or only vision I could not tell. No sound issued from it. Only aimlessly it seemed to be floating about my bedroom. I simply lay and gazed with starting eyes. A cold perspiration began to break out upon me. And now the shadowy form came nearer. And what seemed, in my horror, to be a bony hand was slowly raised towards me. I could not shout for my tongue clove to the roof of my mouth. I only gazed, and gazed in speechless horror . . . when I was recalled from ghostly visions to hard fact by the voice of poor Villiers, as with chattering teeth he gasped out, " I wish you would lend me a rug, old fellow; it's awfully cold to night." Ignorant of our habits and customs, he had brought no bundle of bedding with him, but had hitherto made shift with his ordinary travelling rug. But this night was too severe; and, unable to sleep, he had made his shivering pilgrimage to my room in hopes of getting some extra covering. His gliding form, by no means shadowy in its proportions at any time, my excited brain had transmogrified into a ghostly visitant.

A few days after, "red tape" having had its way, we received our marching orders, permitting us to go forward as far as Peshawar, the great frontier station, where our troops were gathering in large numbers for a long winter campaign; shortly to be sent forward to join one or other of the three columns which had crossed the border. The railway only then reached as far as Jhelum. Thence I was despatched by *Dâk Gari* or post. This was a rough, strong conveyance in which you could lie down and sleep, and dragged at full gallop by a pair of country ponies, which were changed every six miles or so. On we went, hour after hour, crossing the great Indus river by its creaking and swaying bridge of boats at Attock in the dead of night. Very fine indeed was the scenery on the way. The country was wild and broken, spurs of the neighbouring mountain range stretching right down to the plains. Some twenty-seven hours of this hard galloping brought me into Peshawar, where I put up at the already overcrowded Dâk Bungalow.

CHAPTER III.

Turbulent Peshawar—An Indian Dâk Bungalow—The Lonely House on Jumrood Road—A Picturesque Scene—The Peshawar Bazaar—Church Mission Work—An Encouraging Subscription—The Missionary's Ambiguous Epitaph—Poshteen and Sable Cap—My Patient (!) Camels—A Wild Country—Boorj-i-Hurri Singh—Fort Jumrood—Soldiers' Rations—Alert in the Camp.

PESHAWAR! Ah! what memories it has! Records of the old past! Deeds of turbulence and outrage! And no wonder. For it is situated right on the very edge of the Afghan frontier. And things are not much better to-day. Over the borders come the truculent Afridis, who by no means confine their black-mailing to their own mountain land. They raid all around, sometimes even stealthily creeping on a dark night into the very midst of one of our own out-pickets, "knifing" a sentry, perhaps, and carrying off two or three rifles, which is their most coveted *loot* of all. The town has always been wild. The old Emperor Akbar founded it. Runjeet Singh afterwards conquered it, and built a fort and magazine. It is, of course, our most advanced station. And to keep people and things in anything like order, no less than five thousand troops are permanently stationed here. In the Mutiny days it was "touch and go." Ten thousand natives, and only a quarter that number of Europeans, were in the cantonments. By a skilful and rapidly-executed operation, which was rightly designated by Sir John Lawrence a "master-stroke," Herbert Edwards and Brigadier Cotton suddenly disarmed the natives, and the critical period passed, the doubtful chiefs in the States around at once coming to the English aid. A magnificent grand trunk road, commenced in 1836, stretches right away from Calcutta, a distance of 1,423 miles, over which our troops used to march in the days of good old "John Company," before the "iron horse" puffed and snorted along the railroad to the amaze and sometimes horror of the simple villagers. Many a good regiment has traversed the whole distance, taking five months to do it. Now things are changed, and at the time I write this, even the hundred and fifty miles or so of *Dâk* travelling has become a thing of the past, the railway reaching now to the frontier itself.

There needed a good deal of "shaking down" to be done in the *Dâk* Bungalow before the crowd of men who had taken possession could pretend to the slightest comfort. These *Dâk* Bungalows are an immense convenience in India. They are built by the Government at intervals along their main roads for the accommodation of the English traveller as he does his weary journeys stage by stage. A very small fee is charged; and the native who looks after the place is able to provide at least something to eat. The usual thing when you drive up is to summon this native official, probably an old *khansama* or native butler, and ask what he has to give you to eat. The first answer is invariably,

"Anything your honour may wish for." You then proceed to order perhaps some mutton chops, when the *khansama* expresses regret that there happens just then to be no mutton. And thus it is with other things you suggest. Until at last, wearied and irritated, you cry out, "Then, what have you?" And a light flashes across that native's face as he replies, according to invariable custom, "*Murghi Sahib : bahut atchcha murghi.*" "Fowl, Sir : very good fowl." And so you give orders for "fowl, very good fowl, as quickly as possible." No need for the latter clause of the injunction. As you tumble into your "tub" to wash away some of the dust and travel stain, you hear sounds which indicate a profound agitation among the attenuated cocks and hens outside. You had perhaps noticed them as you drove into the *compound*. You had observed how those wily birds flew with marvellous vigour to the roof of the bungalow directly they saw you. Of course they did. They knew well the programme which was to follow. And now vigorous efforts are being made to dislodge them. With the aid of various missiles and long poles they are brought down to earth; and our friend the *khansama*, assisted by his numerous family and others, is seeking to capture some devoted bird. But the chase is a stern one. For legs and wings have been invigorated by long exercise and many a fight for life, as you afterwards prove when you begin to carve. But at last some wily stratagem succeeds. The fowl is captured, slain, plucked, and cooked, and waiting for you on the table in something like forty minutes. And this is what we call "sudden death" in India. And recognising that this fowl worthily constitutes a race by itself, it has been christened "*murghi dâk-bungaliensis.*"

Talk about a gathering of the clans! Verily there was one at Peshawar. Officers from Madras in the south, and from Calcutta in the far east; from the Central India Horse, the irregular regiments, the Ghoorkas, the Beloochees, and the Punjabis—all intent on getting forward, either to join their regiments or on Staff employ; all bound by military "red tape," and compelled to tarry and fume to their hearts' discontent. Our bungalow sheltered as many as possible, and the one or two poor apologies for hotels were filled from floor to ceiling, which is not saying much.

The Government regulations affecting these dâk bungalows prevent you abiding there more than three days at a stretch, if others are waiting to come in. And as there seemed prospect of further delay, I cast about for accommodation elsewhere. Nothing was to be got apparently. So, finally, I solved the difficulty by simply renting a tiny house which was empty, far out on the road to Jumrood. This, no doubt, was the reason of its being vacant. It was much to near the haunts of the Afridi rascals, and too distant from our military guards to be a pleasant residence at night. However, there seemed nothing else available. So I transported my camp kit to the empty domicile, and made myself as comfortable as circumstances would allow. In one of the outer rooms lived my factotum, and my syce or groom. In the front, before a scanty wood fire, my tiny camp table was placed, and hard by a *charpoy* or small native bed. Outside my horse was picketed. And as this also was a piece of *loot* which the hill robbers coveted much, I kept him not far from the door of my room. How the jackals howled around the place at night! And how many times I crept out, revolver in hand, imagining that I heard a stealthy footfall, or discerned, in the shadowy moonbeams, a creeping form! It was a fair beginning of true Afghan camp life, with many of its nocturnal dangers and anxieties.

The Peshawar Bazaar—whither I wandered one day—presented a most striking scene. Full of fanatical Mohammedans at all times, it was a place of some peril for an Englishman alone. Among these Mohammedans occasionally *ghazis* would be found—men who had devoted themselves to death in order to slay an "infidel." The accomplishment of their purpose ensured them certain passport to

Paradise, however swift their passage thither might be. Only a little while before, murderous outrages had taken place; one on Colonel St. John, and others on some soldiers of ours. As I passed through the motley gathering of Afghans from Cabul, Afridis from the neighbouring hills, tribesmen from near and far, and Punjabis from the country around, I kept my eyes and ears well on the alert. Every man was armed to the teeth. Even those who squatted around the little stalls where their goods were exposed for sale seemed to think it necessary to hold in hand, or, at any rate, have hard by them, the long *jezial* or gun, which is one of the common weapons of the country. The Cabuli men were very picturesque in their appearance. Picturesqueness does not always go with dirt. But it did in this case. With long black, flowing locks and fresh-coloured faces, strong-featured, and even Jewish in cast, they were swathed, rather than clothed, in coarse cloth which had once been white, but long, long ago. Probably they had dressed themselves in Cabul, and no change or removal had taken place since. Through the rugged defiles of the Jugdulluk and Khyber Passes, and over the narrow mountain paths, had they led their train of camels, heavily laden with the dried fruits which are the produce of these northern countries. What was the war to them? What cared they for political causes so long as they could get their wares to the Indian markets and make good sales? There they stood with their loaded camels in the Peshawar Bazaar; their *cummerbund* or waist scarf, holding in tight embrace half a dozen or more most murderous weapons in the form of long Afghan knives. I shall have more to say about these Afghan knives later on.

While at Peshawar I took a survey of the large Church Mission premises, and was glad to find that extensive work was carried on under the able guidance of Messrs. Hughes and Jukes. Sir Herbert Edwards, a grand Christian soldier, is said to have founded this Church Mission enterprise when he was

Commissioner here. An indication of the general estimate held by outsiders as to the probable success of Christian Mission work in this city may be found in one item of the subscription list which went round. It read thus:—" One rupee towards a Deane and Adams revolver for the first missionary." As a matter of fact, one missionary was actually shot as he sat in his verandah, in the dusk of the evening, by his own *chowkeydar* or watchman, whether by accident or intentionally was never certainly known. Just off the road, on the way to Jumrood, one sees the solitary grave. On the stone which stands at the head is a somewhat ambiguous inscription, which runs thus:—

SACRED

TO THE MEMORY

OF THE

REV. — SONNENTHAL.

He translated the Scriptures into the Afghan tongue, and was shot by his own chowkeydar.

"Well done, thou good and faithful servant."

There is not much work done outside Peshawar; though Mr. Jukes some time ago essayed to enter Kaffaristan, through one of the mountain passes, a tract of country which is most jealously guarded from European foot. He never succeeded, however, and was happy in getting back to Peshawar with his life. Strangely enough, though, when talking with a man one day far up the Pass, I learnt from him of the existence of a tiny Christian, or semi-Christian community, in the city of Cabul. They were permitted to worship after their own Christian fashion by the Ameer, and had existed for many years. They had no *padre* to minister to them; but were accustomed to bring their children down to Peshawar at certain periods for baptism by Mr. Hughes. I purposed to find out more about this interesting little Church, but never had the further opportunity. The Garrison Church, where our own soldiers were marched, was a totally different place— the chaplain being excessively High—one whose extreme ritualism greatly irritated the Brigadier in command of the station, who being a Scotchman, was, of course, a strong Presbyterian.

At last, after many days of weary waiting in Peshawar, orders came for me to go forward. And right glad I was to get everything as ship-shape as possible for a start across the border on the morrow. A curious kit I had too. There was a bed, native fashion, consisting of a wooden framework and canvas, capable of being rolled up. A chair and a table—all collapsable and exceedingly miniature. A couple of iron *degchees* or cooking pots, and a kettle. Some enamelled iron plates and cups, plus a big tumbler, which was a luxury, and although of fragile glass, survived the strange chances of the campaign. These, with two or three knives, forks, and spoons, constituted my furniture. My personal baggage was contained in a couple of small leather cases. And the Cabul tent, some seven feet square, and weighing, poles and all, about 80 lbs., completed my total belongings. So intensely cold was it just now that we found it necessary to wear over our ordinary uniform a native *Poshteen* or Afghan coat, made of Bokhara sheepskin. The leather of this garment is tanned quite soft, and neatly embroidered. This is worn outside. Inside is the long hair of the sheep, and a wonderfully warm garment it is. It was necessary to get them even for the servants, who could not otherwise stand the cold. I saw also that several of the native cavalry regiments had had them served out. To the *Poshteen* I added a soft, round, fur head-piece, in the form of a sable cap, and felt myself equipped amply against any frost or snowstorm with which even the dreadful Khyber could furnish me.

* * * * * * * *

"*Syce, ghora taiyar hai?*" "Is the horse ready?" I shouted to my groom.

"*Han Sahib khub taiyar hai.*" "Very much ready, Sir," he replied, hinting in his answer at a long delay which had taken place.

It was about one o'clock in the day, and for three mortal hours I had been struggling valiantly to conquer the idiosyncracies of the patient camel. About ten o'clock that morning two of these strange but useful creatures had been sent to me as baggage animals. A native, who was supposed to know all their peculiarities, and they are legion, was sent also to take care of them. The first thing was to get them to sit down. This was successfully accomplished by certain tricks known only to camels and camel drivers. Then having tied up the knee in order to prevent the quadruped from suddenly getting up, in the midst of some critical loading operation, we went to work. *So did the camel*, on which we were first operating. He commenced at once grumbling —a kind of cross between a gobble and a growl. This did not excite any apprehension however, as to grumble is the patient camel's chronic habit. It is his usual accompaniment to the process of loading or unloading, feeding or not feeding, giving water or taking it away.

Everything alike excites the camel's huge disgust. So we proceeded a little, and had succeeded in getting a part of our load, as we thought, safely secured on the pack saddle, when lo! the eccentric animal, with a gobble and growl of more than usual vehemence, thinking he had had enough of reclining, began calmly to rise. First, the hind legs, which had been tucked under, commenced to expand themselves and stretch out, which movement produced a mighty lurch forward, and the articles aloft began to tremble. Then the forelegs followed suit and expanded, till the camel stood up in all his native dignity, towering far above us. This was too much for the cargo. There was a further ominous trembling. The cords began to give way. And down came clattering pots and kettles and baggage of various kinds, and were strewn in dire confusion around us. Job had many camels I believe! I wonder whether he ever had anything to do with loading them! Two or three times was this process repeated; the second camel when we dealt with him rising just as inopportunely as his brother had done. But we grew subtle as we proceeded. We learned a trick or two from the camels themselves. And after three hours' work, during which experience for all future time was gained, we were ready to move, and the signal was given to start. Around the nose of each camel a thin kind of halter was fixed. The camel driver or *oont-walleh*, as he was called, seized hold of that attached to number one; while that of number two was deftly fastened on to the tail of number one. And the comical procession began, moving out of Peshawar, along a road that was never too safe. Dreary enough it was, too! No trees, no villages, no cultivation of any kind. Patiently the camels plodded on, but very slowly. My horse was eager enough for a gallop, for he had had a long rest after his march up, and had been eating his head off for some days. But it might not be. The "convoy" had gone on early in the day, and the protection which it would have afforded us was therefore not available; so it was wisdom quietly to proceed, keeping one's eyes and ears open, and trusting in Providence. On we went, then, passing on our left Boorj-i-Hurri Singh, or the tower of Hurri Singh, until after some eight or nine miles we came within sight of Fort Jumrood. In appearance it is somewhat imposing, perched up on some rising ground. But in reality it is only built of mud, and would be knocked to pieces in ten minutes if ordinary nine-pounders got to work on it. Around the fort a large courtyard had been utilised by the Commissariat Department. And here I found Major Sir B. Bromhead in charge. How that man did work, to be sure! He was here and there and everywhere on his swift-trotting camel.

The first thing was to get my tent pitched, and then to make out my "indents" for rations. The scale for these was, of course, fixed, and was as follows:—Bread, 1¼lb.; meat, 1¼lb.; potatoes, 1lb.; rice, 4oz.; salt, ⅔oz.; tea, ¾oz.; sugar, 3oz.; and firewood, 3lb. Certain rations were also served out for the native servants and the horse;

and the camel man "indented" for himself and the beasts he had in charge.

My servant, who was no longer young, and never at any time probably very bright, took some little time in getting his kitchen establishment in working order. There it was, just behind the tent! The old fellow had scooped out a hole in the ground, placed two or three stones around to make a little wall on three sides, and on the top of all had planted the cooking pot. Inside the hole some of the commissariat firewood was packed together; and a spark having been obtained, he was puffing his cheeks out in a vain attempt to excite a blaze. It came at last, and the cooking proceeded merrily, resulting eventually in what the Irishman would probably term an "illigant Oirish shtew." Though it might be none too elegant to cultivated eyes and satiated appetites, yet it did very well for the occasion; for in campaigning times we do not "live to eat," but rather "eat to live;" and provided the food be wholesome, we find *fames optimum condimentum ;* such sauce being usually available towards the close of the day, if not before. I certainly enjoyed my first meal outside Fort Jumrood, and served in most primitive fashion, infinitely better than many a one that I have since eaten from well-appointed tables.

The stars were twinkling in the sky, and the air was keen and frosty as I turned in for the night, and tried to fall asleep, amid the multitudinous sounds of a big camp. Around me the unspeakable camels were still grumbling, even in their dreams. Dogs were barking on the outskirts yonder. And ever and anon the hoarse challenge of the sentry—"Halt! Who goes there?"—told me that our men were on the alert, in this wild spot.

CHAPTER IV.

Hart goes for the V.C.—A Gallant Act wins it—
"Sappers" can Fight—The Immortal Gordon—
Too late for the Convoy—Wild Grandeur of the
Khyber Pass—Unpleasant Travellers to Meet—
"*Salaam Alaikoom*"—The Marwara Battalion, and
its Officers—Mess Arrangements—The Parson's Glass
—Afridi Shots from the Hill-side—A Death Struggle
by Night—-Precautions for Safety.

"I'M going in for the V.C. to-day."

These were the first distinct words which struck upon my ear as I tumbled out of my rough *charpoy* bed in the early dawn of the morning after my first night in Jumrood Camp. Strange words, thought I; not boastingly uttered either. Half jocosely. And yet there was a ring of determination in the boyish voice. Young Hart, of the Engineers, it was, who had just turned out of his tent near to mine, and who shouted out the encouraging sentiment laughingly to another fellow who was performing his camp ablutions in a brass *chillumchee*, which his bearer had prepared and placed in front of him. "I'm going in for the V.C. to-day." Well! I thought, as I listened to the grumbling of the camels, and the incessant clatter of the camp servants while they loosened the tent pegs with the heavy mallets, I hope you'll get it. And he did get it. The words, so lightly spoken, had a prophetic element, as well as a ring of determination in them; for Appleyard was just taking a force up the Terah valley, and this force Reginald Hart managed to accompany. The acme of his hopes was certainly not attained on that very day; but it was in that very expedition. And thus it came to pass. It was the custom for the mail to be carried by a mounted man, with a couple of *sowars* or native cavalry as escort, for it was a dangerous duty. Thus the three galloped along at top speed, men and horses being relieved at each military post. On this occasion (January 31st) the force to which Hart was attached had just marched in, and were settling down at one

LIEUTENANT HART WINS HIS VICTORIA CROSS.

such post, when from afar—a full half a mile or more—the mail and its escort could be seen galloping along the dry river bed, which formed the only approach. Suddenly from the hills on either side, armed Afridis rushed down into the defile, and their long sword-like knives flashed in the air as they attacked the devoted three. In the camp the alarm was raised, and men prepared to go to the succour. But Hart, swift-footed as the Greeks of old, and celebrated in the athletic annals of Woolwich, was already well on his way. Down went one sowar before the fierce attack of the Afridis. But Hart had reached by his side; and as he lay prone upon the ground, and sore wounded, he stood over him, and with deft skill warded off blow after blow till further help came, and the rascals were driven off with more than they bargained for. It was a right gallant deed, for it saved the man's life, and deservedly the Victoria Cross was afterwards awarded to the young lieutenant of Engineers. Neither was it the first episode of this kind which had happened in his life. Off Boulogne he had boldly plunged into the sea to save a life; and the Humane Society's medal had thus been already won by him. More than once did I come across this gallant fellow afterwards; indeed, we travelled down to India our last stage together, he riding and sleeping peacefully on the roof of my *dak ghari* because there was no room inside, where a corpulent medico was doubling up with me. And yet once again on an occasion, to which later on I shall have to refer at greater length—a somewhat stirring episode—when in the great, lonely Egyptian desert, and at the witching hour of night, a rush of Arabs was momentarily expected on a solitary post where Hart was. There I heard his voice ringing out cheerily, and encouraging the men to pile up their bags of biscuit to form some slight defence. Now and again I have heard among the fireaters a word of half-contempt launched against the "sappers." Scientific soldiers, they! Not much good when hard fighting is to the fore! Not much good, indeed! There are some of them at any rate who can use revolver as well as theodolite, and wield sword as skilfully as measuring chain ; and surely the undying name of Charles George Gordon at least has brought lasting glory to the corps of the Royal Engineers. But after this digression we must hark back to Jumrood Camp. I had just turned out, or was about to do so, when I heard the words which led me to detail the above incidents. I was not long in completing the preliminary operation and all subsequent proceedings. Camp toilet is very quickly accomplished. Plenty of water was available, and cold enough it was; and a good splash in it sent all the blood coursing and tingling through one's veins. But for the most part razors were voted a general nuisance, We had no drawing-rooms to visit on that or many subsequent days, and no fair ladies to look with critical eye upon our stubbly chins. We were entering upon a period of high liberty, and the "proclamation of independence" began at once to be visibly manifest in the astonishing hirsute appendages which were shooting out on every side. Many an erstwhile natty soldier became for the nonce a veritable brigand.

By happy accident I had met with an old friend Wallerstein of the 24th Punjab Native Infantry. Therefore as soon as possible I wended my way through lines of camels and marching troops to the hospitable mess of the Punjabis, where I was to breakfast before I started on my journey. What fine fellows these Punjabis are to be sure! They could fight splendidly. And whatever might have been said as to the more than doubtful sympathies of some of the rank and file in another Punjab regiment, sympathies which brought us into difficulties more than once, no word was ever alleged against the stern loyalty of the "24th." They at any rate would follow their colonel, the veteran Norman, wherever he might lead them.

Before I went off for breakfast I gave my old bearer strict orders to strike tent at once, and to get the camels loaded up as soon as possible. I knew that the Convoy would be starting shortly ; and as the road was very unsafe on account of the Afridi hillmen, who were prone to lie concealed behind the boulders on the cliff side waiting for stray travellers, discretion as well as valour suggested that I should not miss their company. But the best concerted schemes of mice and men " aft gang agley." To my chagrin, when I got back—the Convoy being about to start in a few minutes—I found things very much *in statu quo*. After a liberal allowance of mild abuse had been dealt out all round, and especially to the bearer, who turned out to be a very incapable old fellow, we set to work in earnest. Down came the tent, and down went the camels on their knees. Not indeed in any act of devotion ; but rather to receive their daily allowance of baggage burden ; which they hastened courteously to acknowledge with the usual gobble and growl. We were not deterred by this, however, and though one wicked rascal looked around at me with a particularly malicious leer, showing his huge, ugly teeth as I neared his flank, we carefully piled article after article on his assortment of humps and made all tight. Then for a start. But, alas! all this had taken a long hour: and by this time the Convoy was far ahead. So there was nothing for it but to follow on as best one could.

After a little bit of open but rough road you begin to pass into the shadow, the solemn gloom, of the Great Khyber; and the wild grandeur of the mountain pass simply defies language to describe. On actually entering it, it seems as if you were passing the giant gateway of some immensely rugged country where earthquakes and convulsions had torn the solid ground, and heaped the mountains in grotesque immensity on either hand. There they are, towering away in rough cliffs and ragged peaks sometimes a thousand feet or more. Now and again, indeed, so narrow is the pathway that it appears as if rather the towering height which had once barred onward progress had been simply cleft by some omnipotent hand, leaving a tiny crevice through which the traveller, oppressed with awe at the Infinite Power which has manifestly wrought here, merely threads his way. Presently the Pass widens a little. Then, a quarter of a mile ahead, you see it narrowing into a second black gateway. And from this gateway a mountain torrent some two or three feet deep dashes forth, bounding along in endless eddies, and with many a cavernous roar, over the broken rocks and boulders which would block its waterway.

Quietly I made my way along, taking in as many of these details of grandeur as was compatible with a careful vigilance on either hand. Presently the path wound upwards higher and higher, on the very face of the cliff; so narrow, too, as to become somewhat ticklish on horseback, as a false step would most probably precipitate both horse and rider some two hundred feet into the gorge below. This cliff side I found to be bored with an astonishing number of caves, in which, no doubt, the hill robbers, the Afridis, found sure refuge, and whence they issued forth on their work of plunder and murder. One or two of them I saw, and as it was my first acquaintance with these gentry they were to me particularly impressive. Wild, lawless ruffians they were, with long, black hair and almost typical Jewish features. Their dress was filthy, and they were armed with the native *jezail*, and the usual assortment of knives in their *cummerbund*. I eyed them, and they eyed me too.

"*Salaam Alaikoom!*" I said, hastily summoning up the usual Persian salutation among Mohammedans, "God's peace be on you!"

In surly and disappointed surprise they gave me back the usual Mussulman response, which could not according to their religion be omitted, and passed on. So did I—as quickly as possible. For as I saluted them I gave a surreptitious touch with the spur to my horse on the off flank and he gave a bound forward. I looked back, and saw them halting and watching me, and apparently not very well pleased with themselves that they had let the "infidel" go on his way without levying black mail.

After more than an hour of this rough travelling, having infinite bother in getting my camels over the more precipitious parts, a sudden bend in the mountain path brought me in view of what might be called the Ali Musjid gorge. There it was far below me, with the broken stream rushing along the bottom, and the apparently impregnable fortress perched high up on the solitary crest of the great hill, with the fragments of broken-down *sungahs* still marking the old outworks, and telling of the fierce fight which had so lately been raging on the declivities in front of them.

Descending the last hillside I fell in with a troop of Bengal Lancers. Gay enough they looked with their fluttering pennons and picturesque costume. Their big mustaches and whiskers, curled upwards, gave something of a wild, fierce expression to their countenance; and the strong-boned, wiry, sure-footed animals on which they were mounted picked their way with perfect safety down the rough hill path. Both men and horses seemed admirably suited to the mountain warfare in which they were now engaged. With them we went on till we reached the camp, part of which was pitched literally in and immediately around the bed of the stream. Here I fell in with the Marwara Battalion, hailing from the big Rajputana State, lying to the south-west of Delhi, and a very fine, well-set-up body of men they seemed to be. Many of the villages of their native State were depopulated by the drought of 1868 and 1869; and it is said that then fully a million people, two-thirds of the whole population, fled to other parts. Now, alas! its plains are comparatively deserted, flocks and herds all are gone, and its rich uplands are for the most part wild and uncultivated. These men, however, did not seem to have suffered from any famine, at any rate for some time past.

I had a note of introduction to one of the officers attached to this battalion, Creagh of the Staff Corps (who won his Victoria Cross later on in the campaign); and was by him most hospitably entertained at their mess.

MAJOR O'MOORE CREAGH, V.C.

And a very merry party of men I found assembled there when the dinner bugle sounded. It is usually so, especially in these native regimental messes. The Indian Staff Corps attaches its men to the different native battalions of our Indian army, and changes were very frequent, in order that these men might gather experience of a varied character and in various parts of the country. Thus you generally found a mixed company. And though a native mess may lack the cohesion and settledness which belong to that of a European regiment, soldiers so quickly shake down and chum up with one another that this is not so great a drawback, while the variety of past experience adds an interest and colouring to the chat of the mess table. There at the head sat Colonel Boileau, a veteran, who came of a family of soldiers. Many a year had he been in India, and it seemed probable that he would leave his bones there, as some of his brothers had done before him. And near him young Durand, a smart, soldierly fellow, just joined from the Central India Horse. Afghanistan has some spceial interest to him, too. Was not his father a "political" at the old Court of Cabul thirty-five years before? and is not his brother in the way to be the same not long hence?

The necessary contingencies of campaigning preclude the possibility of transporting the mess plate, glass, or crockery, or, indeed, anything else in the way of the most ordinary luxuries. So it was the custom for every man to bring his own knife and fork, crockery, and drinking cup or glass, together with his camp chair. And a comical assortment indeed appeared on the table. Most men went in for enamelled iron requisites, both plates and drinking vessels, but not all; and I came in for a little chaff in connection with my tumbler. Not because it was glass, but because of its shape. It *looked* of modest capacity; not very tall, but nevertheless very broad, and the same all the way down. Hence it was capable of holding a good long drink of whatever character. This was at once observed by my jovial hosts, and remarked upon. The laugh was quite on my side, however; and it was generally conceded that the parson had scored. It was astonishing how clever the native cooks were in turning out a decent mess dinner! The materials at their command were but scanty, consisting almost entirely of commissariat rations, but the result was a credit to their powers of contrivance. Soup that was decidedly good; an *entrée* or two that were passable; a *pièce de resistance*, in the shape of a huge chunk rather than joint of beef; together with a pudding of some sort, constituted a meal that was not to be scorned by hungry men, whose appetites had been keenly whetted by the strong mountain air.

We were chattering away gaily enough when the sharp crack of a rifle sounded away up the hill side. and reverberated among the rocky defiles.

"Ah!" said the Colonel, "they have begun early to-night." In a moment or two the tall, soldierly form of one of the Marwara men appeared at the tent door, and, saluting the Colonel, reported—

"*Goli mara hai, Sahib, pahar men.*" "A shot has been fired up the hill."

This was pretty evident. And so the Colonel, simply ordering that the picket on that side should keep a sharp look-out, dismissed the man, and we returned to our chat. It was quite the usual thing, night by night, as soon as darkness set in, and the glimmering lights of the camp could be discerned, for these fellows to come down as near as they dared to our line of sentries, and from behind some convenient boulder or the shelter of some hill cave to draw a bead on the mark thus afforded. Of course the mess tent was most brightly illuminated; for the table was made quite brilliant with no fewer than three tallow candles stuck in three several nine-pounder shells (blind of course) which had been found in the fortress above; thus the mess tent received most of the attentions of the hill marksmen. Fortunately their aim was bad, and no great damage followed.

But these men have other tricks of their trade. With their lithe forms they are accustomed to wriggle their tortuous course unseen along the ground, sheltered and concealed by every tiny bush or boulder. In this way, eluding most cunningly even the keen-eyed native sentries, they were known to creep into the very tents when the men were sleeping, to plunder, and even murder. A sergeant of the 51st, for instance, lying wakeful and restless in a tent under the very nose of a sentry, flung his hand careless over the side of his *charpoy*, and it alighted on the bare skull of one of these creeping robbers, who had got in and was lying there waiting for further opportunity. In a moment both men sprang up, and for a brief instant there was a life and death struggle. The Afghan, armed with his keen heavy knife, cut and slashed to free himself; while the sergeant, unarmed, and hampered with his heavy greatcoat, in which he was lying, could only hold on and shout for assistance. In rushed the guard, but out at the other side rushed the robber, breaking from his captor's grasp, whom he left behind bleeding from many a wound.

I thought it well as far as possible to avoid the repetition of such an episode, in my case, and so pitched my tent within the shelter of a square *sungah*, which would serve to stop any flying bullet and at the same time offer material resistance to any wriggling corporeal form which might essay an entrance.

Now and again the sharp crack of a rifle broke the continuity of some happy dream of home and brighter scenes ; but for the most part I slept behind the Afghan *sungah* as peacefully as within the big antique fourposter at home, till the shrill bugles sounding the "reveille" turned us all out to begin another day of march and toil.

CHAPTER V.

"Bright Chanticleer" from the 51st Bugles—A Path through the River—Dangerous Road—Afghan Village—The Guns peep over the Wall—Perfume of the Dead Camel—A bitter Night at Lundi Kotal—Graves joins me—Dakka Fort—Basawal—Jellalabad—Havelock's "Saints"—Arrival in Camp.

HARK! What sounds are those that strike upon one's ear just as the dawn is breaking? There they go, echoing and reverberating among the rugged hills which are clustered around Fort Ali Musjid. Surely they are the strains of the old English air, "Bright Chanticleer." Jauntily enough the old song trips along, sounding strangely out of place in these wild Afghan defiles. But the English are wonderfully conservative in their tunes as well as in their tastes. They carry them whithersoever they go. And so it is the never-changing custom of the gallant "Fifty-first" to rouse themselves in the morning, and all who may be their comrades for the time being, with this ancient English air. At home among their own people, or abroad among foes, their band salutes the rising sun, immediately "reveille" has sounded, with these cheerful strains.

I listened awhile as I lay in my tent down in the Khyber Valley, and then turned out, and set to work with my preparations for going forward on the toilsome march, for I did not forget the delays and difficulties of former occasions.

The camp was already astir. There, high up on the height of the Shagai hills, were pitched the tents of the "Fifty-first," and thence came the strains of the English air, for the band was still playing, or rather a few members of it. My camel driver was busy mixing up the usual modicum of *bhoosa*, consisting of chopped straw and other things, which was to be the early morning meal of his patient charges, and to the usual accompaniment of their gobbling growl too. The syce was grooming the horse, and the old bearer was making the fire burn merrily for breakfast preparations. I thought, well! we shall be in good time this morning at any rate. No fear of missing the convoy to-day. And it was highly important that we should not miss that convoy. They had told me in the mess the night before, and, indeed, I had heard it elsewhere, that this particular bit of the Pass leading on from Ali Musjid to our next post at Lundi Khana was the most dangerous of the whole stretch. Owing to its suitableness to their purpose it was infested with those gentry whose usual salutation was, "Your money or your life," often varied with, "Your money, goods, and life too." I had no desire to make their nearer acquaintance; so getting all ready, breakfast over, and camels loaded, I waited the signal to start with the convoy.

But where was it? I saw plenty of bustle and loading up in the camp. Camels innumerable were being manipulated, and the noise was indescribable. But there was no sign of any considerable armed guard forming up. I made inquiries here and there among those most likely to know, and I could only learn that the convoy had most probably started, and was a little distance ahead. So I whipped up my animals and men, and went off in hot pursuit; though that is scarcely the expression to use when camels are involved. The stolid beasts plodded along, thinking not of Afridis on the road, but solely, no doubt, of the burdens on their backs. The first part of the way from Ali Musjid was very bad going indeed. No road had yet been made, and the only path to follow was literally the river bed. Rugged and gloomy enough it was! Before us frowned the second black gateway of the Pass; when the defile seemed from a little distance so narrow that you might span it with your arms from side to side. The depth of the water through which we had to pass varied very much. Now my horse, which fortunately was a most sure-footed one, was passing almost dry-hoofed over some huge boulder, or through the stream where it was only a few inches deep. Then he was plunging into some three feet of rushing water, much to my personal dis comfort; and to the utter wetting of his accoutrements, and of things in my saddle-bags. The difficulty of getting the camels with their loads through this rough bit was immense. But at last patience, or at least perseverance, conquered, and we were fairly through; and after some two miles of what might be called cat-climbing, we emerged upon a tract of country which was fairly level, though still rough, with the usual crop of rocks and stones.

All this occurred while we had been looking anxiously for the convoy. We surely ought to have overtaken it by this time! For, being a large body, with a string of loaded camels, it would only be able to move very much more slowly than we. But no convoy hove in sight. The country around looked desolate and lonely. No sign of life—bird, beast, or man—except that which we ourselves presented. And, indeed, so we would have it. For failing the convoy we had rather be alone—much rather.

But it was not to be. First a solitary

Khyberi came loafing along, with his long *jezail* over his shoulder. He eyed me suspiciously, but paid a good deal more attention to my two loaded camels. I was nothing but a worthless man to be killed, and there was an end of it; though, certainly, my horse and the revolver I was compelled to carry might be acceptable. But the camels and their burden! Ah, there was *loot*. Who knows what might be hidden away in those modest leather bags. For an instant or two he paused. So did I. And we looked one another up and down. Meanwhile the beasts of burden, with their possible *loot*, passed on, and the chance was gone. I was not sorry to see the back of the fellow, *jezail* and all, disappear around a bend in the path.

But more was to follow. The country began to open out a little. We were crossing a stretch of barren plain, when we suddenly came upon what I had been taught to know was an Afghan village. There it was—a big, square, mud-built fort apparently, with a tower at each corner, and walls about fifteen feet above the level of the ground outside. It was not a fort, however, though fortified thus. But within those mud walls was a collection of little huts, thickly clustering together, and sheltering perhaps two or three score Afghan families. I was by no means pleased to see it. The solitude was far preferable. But there was the Afghan village before me—a grim fact. And what might be going on within its mud walls I knew not; for there was no sign of life for a minute or two. I thought it wise at once to execute a movement which with a large body of men is somewhat intricate and difficult, but which with the limited forces under my command on this occasion was not so hard of accomplishment—a left half-turn—in order that I might, by getting into the centre of the open plain, give the village as wide a berth as possible. As I proceeded to do this I saw the village wall immediately opposite me suddenly dotted with men, one here and another there, holding their guns lightly over the wall, and keenly scanning me and mine.

I did not half like the look of those guns. It is so easy to loose off suddenly. And despite the fact that I should be bringing my property into prominence, pointing to the possibility of *loot*, I thought it wise to provide as far as possible for my safety, and that of my men, in case of any such contingency arising. So I brought on the camels quickly, and took up position with the other men on the far side of them. I apprehended that their bulky bodies, loads and all, would afford an excellent rampart against any chance shot. And I do not think I did unwisely. For no sooner had my tactical arrangement been completed than a shot was fired. From which point it came or whether it went I did not tarry to inquire, but pushing on as rapidly as dignity would allow, I was soon out of sight of the Afghan village and its undesirable inhabitants.

Now and again, as I passed through some of the narrower and rougher parts, I came upon the carcase of a dead camel. Oh! those dead camels! Words fail utterly to describe all one's feelings under the circumstances of such meeting. It is *one* thing to pass Rimmel's shop in the Strand, but another thing to pass a defunct camel! Quite! It is not a thing to be talked of; you can't describe it; but you can never forget it. There is a lingering sweetness, long drawn out, which persistently clings to one for long after. The mortality among the poor beasts was simply appalling. What with the cold, and the roughness of the way—for they were not mountain camels, but came chiefly from India—they died in scores daily. It is stated that no fewer than fifty thousand perished during the campaign. And to see a camel die is one of the most pathetic sights in the world. The poor creatures dies in harness, carrying his load till he can carry it no longer, and then lying down and patiently waiting for death. Slowly moving its head from side to side, great tears sometimes falling from eyes that look so expressively sad, it droops lower and lower, till at length it rises not again. Nothing could be done apparently to help and recover them when in this condition, and the most merciful thing was to put them out of their misery with a bullet. All along the way there lay numbers of these carcases, polluting the air with the foulest odours.

When I reached Lundi Kotal, which I did late in the afternoon, I found the convoy, which I had so eagerly pursued, had not come in. Indeed, I found afterwards that it had not left when I myself started from Ali Musjid. No wonder we never caught it up. It arrived some hours after us.

Perched up on the top of a mountain ridge some 3,700 feet above sea level, Lundi Kotal was one of our coldest posts. Do what we would at night, it was impossible to keep warm in the tent. Everything available in the way of covering, even to the very clothes one took off, *Poshteen* included, were piled on one's bed; but all to little or no purpose. My teeth seemed to chatter all night; and in the morning I found the horse's bucket, which had been filled overnight, frozen almost to the bottom.

I was very glad here to find a *compagnon de voyage* in Graves of the Artillery, now a staff corps man and one of the transport officers on the line of communication. He was going forward like myself, and we were glad to chum together. He was a most ardent and skilful sketcher. The next morning we climbed down from the Kotal to a magnificent gorge below. Here we found at the cleft and shattered mountain base a pretty grotto sheltering a clear pool, with the most lovely maidenhair fern growing in profusion all around. Graves fell to work at once, and produced a very effective sketch.

Before we reached Dakka Fort, which was our next station, we had a little more experience of the roughest hill-climbing. Once again the path, narrow and dangerous, wound along the very face of the almost sheer cliff. In one spot we saw that one of our own nine-pounder guns had toppled over, team and all. There, far down at the bottom, we could discern the bodies of the horses; while the ponderous gun had been stopped by some obstruction, and lay on its side three parts of the way down.

The fort at Dakka was the usual mud construction, consisting of an outer wall enclosing an inner yard, in the centre of which was a single rough building. Around the wall, however, was a row of little rooms, with a wide verandah, capable of accommodating a large number of men. They were indeed the barracks of the Afghan force, which were necessarily stationed here by the old Ameer to keep in some kind of subjection the turbulent Shinwaris and the obstreporous Khan of Lalpoora, who dwelt on the other side of the river, close at hand.

The cold here was excessive, almost more than at Lundi Kotal; although Dakka is only some 2,500 feet above sea level. We were very glad to get on next morning to Basawal. At this place I had my first reminder that campaigning is not picnicing, and that it means hard and trying work. The excitement, and the keen air too, prevent you sometimes from realising it; but the constant toil in marching throughout the day, with little or nothing to eat from early breakfast to late dinner, and even then your food being of the scantiest and poorest description often, cannot fail to tell, especially on the raw campaigner. Faintness and other unpleasantnesses were to me painful reminders of these facts at Basawal; and I turned in early, resolving on no breakdown at this early stage. The next morning I was all right again, and gradually I got hardened to my work, so that these little episodes of hard mountain marching and scanty food troubled me no more.

Barikab was our next halting-place, a very small post where only a few men are stationed. After our rough dinner a good big fire was made in the open, and in true camp fashion the officers (we only numbered about six, all told) sat around it spinning yarns till past ten o'clock. Some of these camp-fire stories were truly tremendous.

The last march, to Jellalabad, which was to be our final halting-place, was a very long one—more than eighteen miles—so we had to set off betimes. A detachment of the 10th Royal Hussars, the Prince of Wales's regiment, had been halting for the night at Barikab, so I joined them in the onward march of the morrow. It was the first time I had come in contact with any of this splendid regiment, our crack cavalry corps, I suppose; and very smart fellows they seemed to be. The men were very proud of their designation and their Royal Colonel; and a strong *esprit de corps* animated all ranks. Little did I think as I rode out with them— the officer in command and his "sub" making the march far from wearisome with pleasant chat—of the sad scenes which were soon to be associated with many of these same gallant fellows. Some in the ranks were destined never to come back from the far-off alien land. The two officers were to escape only by the very narrowest margin: one from knife of the Afghan, the other from drowning. Now they all rode along merrily enough, these lads from their homes in the old country, thinking of the dear ones they had left behind; but recking little of what might be in the future for them. How mercifully the big curtain of ignorance veils that from us! To know too much of what awaits us on the morrow would paralyse our efforts of to-day.

Mile after mile was passed by stony ways and across rough, barren plains. The letter bags passed us on our way, clattering along under escort of two sowars of the Bengal Cavalry, Verily a load of treasure was being carried in those bags; for exiles in the far-off land appreciate above all else the letters from home.

Presently Jellalabad came into view, dimly seen on the distant plain. We could just make out the high walls of the city, and the mulberry-tree gardens clustering around. I thought of the gallant defence made by Sale, assisted by Havelock, and Broadfoot, and others, in the old 1842 campaign; of Havelock's "Saints" of the 13th Somersetshire Light Infantry; men who were so nicknamed for godliness of life; but were always dependable and called on when a stern bit of work was to be done. Their saintliness never impaired their fighting powers, when they went out to face Akbar Khan's wild horsemen on the plains outside the walls of the city. Many a memory of deed and legend clustered around those old walls, some of which we shall try to gather up presently.

Our big camp lay outside the city, some mile and a half from the gates, on a great stretch of sandy plain. We could see the lines of white tents covering a considerable area. It was known that this detachment of the 10th was coming in to join; and when we were some two miles from the end of our march a group of young officers who had ridden out to meet us came in view galloping along the stony way. Then followed much handshaking and general salutation; exchange of news—some from the depôt, some from the camp—until it might almost seem as if men were being welcomed home rather than received into a companionship of hard living, stern fighting, and constant peril. Still there was the satisfaction, both to them and to me, of having accomplished safely one somewhat perilous stage of the campaign and reached a goal where we might rest awhile, even though it be on the sandy desert plain of Jellalabad.

CHAPTER VI.

Twelve or fifteen Regiments in the Big Camp—Arrangement of the Lines—Square Meal at the Headquarter Mess—The "Loving Cup" or Mess "Night Cap"—A quiet Stroll through the City—Annals of 1842—The "Illustrious Garrison"—Piper's Hill—A Hunting Rifle gets the Range—An old Veteran's Second Visit to Afghanistan—The Rains come—Sand Storms and Rain Storms—Villagers Help us for Rupees—Walls and Trenches—Night Tempest—The Rain floats Villiers.

BUSY, if not gay, was the scene on the sandy plain a mile this side of the great gate of Jellalabad. Here the First Division of the Peshawar Valley Field Force had its camp. And here Sir Sam Browne, who at present was chief in command of the expedition, had gathered his Staff about him, and was awaiting the progress of events, for all sorts of strange rumours were afloat, sometimes dealing with Shere Ali's flight into Russian territory, sometimes hinting that he had yielded and was coming in to notify his submission, and latterly with greater truth telling of his despondency and fatal sickness. For a mile or so across the plain the white tents of this big camp could be seen stretching, giving shelter to some twelve or fifteen regiments, European and native. All arms were represented, infantry, cavalry, artillery, and engineers. On the far extreme yonder were the lines of the 4th Battalion Rifle Brigade, side by side with their constant comrades in arms—the 4th Ghoorkas. These were flanked by the 17th (Leicestershire) Regiment, and the 20th Punjabis. Nearer in came the lines of the 10th Royal Hussars; then the Artillery—one battery of Horse ("I.C."), one of Field ("E. 3"), and the heavy, Elephant, Forty-Pounder battery ("13.9"). At the extreme opposite of the camp were located the Sikh regiments, the 1st and the 45th, or Rattray's; as also the "Guides" Infantry and Cavalry, and the 11th Bengal Lancers. While in the very centre, flanked on the one side by the Engineers, the Sappers and Miners, or "Suffering

Miners" as they were jocosely dubbed, and on the other by the 51st King's Own Light Infantry, was fixed the Headquarter Camp. Here were to be found Sir Sam, with his Staff, and the heads of Departments. On the one side of the little cleared space, Smith, the A.A.G., and Sanford, the A.Q.M.G., and others. Across the way, Davidson, the Deputy A.A.G.; Gibbon, the senior medical officer; Hunt, the Commissary General, and the two chaplains—one parson being opposite the other. Far away, down at one extreme corner of the camp, was the little hospital enclosure, with its lines of tents flying the red cross flag. Many a touching incident and many a sad episode did I witness within the shelter of those tiny hospital tents!

My horse seemed to share his master's rejoicing at having at last reached some kind of a resting place. This he testified by all kinds of madcap pranks as we made our way to the Headquarter Camp, plunging about and leaping the ditches as if he had only just been saddled, instead of being at the far end of a nearly twenty miles rough march. Ten, twenty, or thirty miles were much the same to old " Yakub " in those days.

We settled down soberly, however, presently. The spot for my tent was assigned, the camels came along with their burdens, and in an hour or so everything was fairly ship-shape for a lengthened tarrying in this spot, till the march of events should summon us to move forward, or else return to India.

A great comfort it was to sit down to what might be called a good square meal in the Headquarter Mess that evening. Officers, cf course, are dealt with in the matter of "rations" exactly as the men in the ranks are. "Share and share alike" is army regulation. But the members of a mess generally club their rations, and hand them in bulk, meat, vegetables, &c., to the mess cook, who does the best he can with them. Here, of course, is a wide field for the individual skill and ingenuity of this most important functionary. And many a tasty dish have I partaken of the ingredients of which it were hard to name.

These were the old days of the rum rations. Every man had his "tot" served out to him daily. I think every steady soldier, whether teetotaler or not, regarded this as an altogether unnecessary stimulant, and very few regretted its disappearance from the list of daily items. In these days, however, it existed, and sure enough at the end of mess dinner a most wonderful concoction used to make its appearance in a large tin can. The collective "tot" of the mess, deftly mingled with sugar, lemons, and much hot water, appeared to constitute in the main this "loving cup;" but there was a method in mixing, or else some secret addendum, known only to one or two members of the mess, who kept the knowledge to themselves, and always manipulated the concoction in some obscure corner of the tent. But there was no harm done. The Headquarter Mess was an abstemious one to a degree; and when the tin can had gone the round it afforded but a very small modicum, in which, with many a tender thought, each man pledged the dear ones in the old country. Then we turned in : and in our dreams quickly bridging the vast space intervening between us and our friends in England, ignoring mountain passes and wide rolling seas, we were standing by their side again. But alas! the morning reveille shrilly sounding over the plain recalled us to the hard realities of war and camp life.

It was not to be supposed that lying so near as we did to the historically far-famed city of Jellalabad we did not desire to inspect it a little more closely, and examine various points which memory and legend made deeply interesting. During my first day, while I was busy getting tent and surroundings into something like permanent order, a man presented himself, and hearing that I was a "padre," announced himself as a "munshi," and expressed a desire to teach me Persian. I turned into my tent and had a chat with the man. What he was I could not quite make out. Certainly not an Afghan, pure. Probably a mongrel, half an Afghan and half a Hindu. He could speak Hindustani, however, after a fashion; and this served my purpose, and we got on very nicely. He had lived a good while in Cabul itself, and told me about the little so-called Christian Church which existed there; the members worshipping in some underground vaults, under the very walls of the Ameer's palace, and with his cognisance and permission. I made a mental note to inquire more closely into this when I reached Cabul, if we ever did advance thither. The point of more immediate interest just now was Jellalabad, lying a mile or so ahead. And this I arranged to visit next morning under the guidance of our mongrel munshi friend.

The early beams of the morning sun were making even this wild, barren country glorious as we set out on our enterprise. I slipped into the pocket of my great coat *a little friend in need*, in case of any serious danger or dire necessity arising, against which I devoutly hoped, and passed along through our camp and by our line of sentries into the open country beyond, facing the city. On our right lay the Cabul river sweeping along with swift current between narrow strips of cultivation. Away to the left, some ten miles or more, stretched the range of the Safed Koh, or White Mountains, throwing down spurs of rugged hill almost to our camp. Well-named, the White Mountains, surely— white with their wintry covering. And how grand they looked just now. Every snow-capped peak was tipped with golden glory, as the beams of the morning sun flashed and gleamed upon them. And before us and around were the very plains, sandy and rugged, which had witnessed such deeds of valour some thirty-seven years before. For it was on these plains that the British garrison of Jellalabad, scanty but "illustrious," war-worn and famine-stricken, but dauntless unto death, stood face to face with the wild hordes of the traitor Akbar Khan, fresh from the massacre of the Jugdulluk Pass. There, standing shoulder to shoulder, as Britishers know so well how to do in the pinch, they smote and shattered the forces of their savage foe, scattering them like chaff before the wind. Well done, the Somersetshire Light Infantry! Deathless glory covers thy laurels for that same deed!

Crossing this plain of fight and fame, we saw right before us the Peshawar gate of the city. It was from the turrets of this gate that Sale's sentries looked forth and descried Pollock's avenging force marching across the sand to their relief. As we passed through it, I tried to realise the scene of thirty-seven years ago. The city appeared to be divided into four quarters by two long narrow streets or bazaars which intersected one another about the centre, and terminated at each end by a great gateway. The one by which we entered was called the Durwaza-i-Peshawar, or Peshawar Gate, because it looked down the Pass towards Peshawar. At the opposite extremity was the Durwaza-i-Kabul, or Kabul Gate, looking over the sandy waste to Kabul. The intersecting Bazaar had its north end looking out on the river, the Durwaza-i-Pheel Khana, or the gate of the elephant quarters. And at the southern extremity the Durwaza-i-Jati, that is, the gate of the Jats or Hindus, indicating the quarter where these traders most did congregate and live. Most of the houses and shops were light constructions of wood and mud, and part of the central street was actually covered in—no great difficulty, inasmuch as it was very narrow. I found that already this part had been dubbed by some wag of the force the Burlington Arcade. With great interest I traversed the old walls, and thought of the time in '42 when the elements and nature seemed to fight against the "illustrious garrison" as well as the wild tribesmen, for an earthquake one night shook the town, destroying bastions and parapets, and reducing both the Peshawar and Kabul Gates to a heap of ruins. But the dauntless garrison, to whom it seemed as if difficulties were only made to be conquered, turned out and reconstructed them, with infinite toil, under the guidance of the indefatigable Broadfoot. And only just in time, for within three days an overwhelming Afghan force appeared, and completely invested the fortress and town. Standing on the wall adjoining the Hindu quarter, and looking away to the south-west, I saw a solitary rocky hill, some distance off, but completely overlooking the place. This hill was known as "Piper's Hill," from the fact that when the Afghans were besieging Jellalabad one wild fellow used to come thither daily to pipe and dance in derision before the beleaguered garrison. Many a man tried to end the insult and the insulter with a bullet. But the old-fashioned "Brown Bess" was no use at the distance. One day, however, an officer, getting hold of a hunting rifle of better range, drew a bead on the piper, and for ever ended his piping and dancing. Not far from the Peshawar Gate, the spot where General Elphinstone was buried was pointed out. Poor old man! Never strong enough by disposition or will for the task before him, and worn out with old age and disease, he broke down utterly, and died; and here he lies buried far from kith and kin and home.

Strangely enough we had in camp an old veteran, Major Bailey, who had seen some half-a-century of service, and who had actually served in this former Afghan campaign, and was one of the aforenamed "illustrious garrison." Many a strange yarn he spun of those old experiences of hard, stern fighting every day, and many a spot of interest he was able to point out inside the walls. I did not find very much to purchase at the little native stalls, one of the chief objects of sale being Afghan knives of all shapes and sizes, and, indeed, every shopkeeper seemed to be armed in the usual fashion—knives in *cummerbund*, and *jezail* in hand, to guard his paltry goods.

Before we left I took a peep from the Kabul Gate, and recalled Miss Thompson's well-known picture, "The Relics of a Lost Army." There was the same old beaten path across the sandy waste over which Dr. Bryden and his feeble pony, both man and beast almost dropping from fatigue and wounds, made their weary way to the shelter of the city: he, the sole survivor of our annihilated army. It all lived again very realistically in my imagination as I looked forth from the gate.

When I got back to the camp I found that I had unwittingly done a perilous thing. It was not safe to visit the city except in parties. Only a short while before, one of the wild fanatics had fallen upon one of our native soldiers, who, at the time unarmed, was making some purchases at a bazaar stall, and tried to kill him. The would-be assassin was seized and sentenced at once to death by the military authorities, a sentence which was confirmed by the *Kadi* or Mussulman judge of the city. There were plenty of *Ghazis* among the people, however, who were quite ready to take the chance of similar death if only they could slay an infidel, as they called us. So I mentally resolved not to run quite the same risk again.

About this time the weather, which had

been hitherto sharp and cold, began to threaten rain. One or two premonitory signs had already appeared. Since we knew that if it once began to rain it would continue to rain to some tune, it was necessary to make provision betimes for any such emergency as might arise.

My tent had been simply pitched upon the plot of ground assigned; and there it stood, without any defence either from rain, sandstorms, or bullets; which last were not infrequent visitants during the night.

Three things appeared necessary, and for the accomplishment of these three things I got a small gang of Afghan villagers and set them to work. Very willing indeed were they to do as little work as possible for as many rupees as they could extract from the English Sahib, and equally ready to cut his throat the next minute if the opportunity presented. Truly they were a sweet lot! I kept my eyes well about me while they were working at my place.

The first thing was to dig out the inside of

the tent, some eighteen inches down, leaving a narrow parapet all round. This reduced my interior area from about eight feet square to seven; and in this seven feet square apartment, what with camp bed, washstand, table, chair, baggage, and saddle, one had not much room for perambulation. But the sinking of the ground gave me a little more room in height, and also afforded some slight protection as I lay in my tiny low cot from any flying bullet.

The next thing was to close down the bottom of the tent all around with carefully prepared mud; and also to dig a little trench to act as a drain. By these measures two dire evils were partially averted; one arising from sand storms, the other from rain storms. When the former swept over the camp the sand and dust penetrated even the tiniest crevice; and in a few moments every article inside the tent was hidden, and you yourself too under a coating of fine sand; hair, ears, eyes, all filled. A pleasant thing for a man's temper! When the latter burst upon us like a water spout, a dug-out tent afforded an admirable arrangement for the formation of a cistern. But the little trench around helped to obviate this.

The third item in our provision against emergencies was the building of a stout mud wall, some three or four feet high, to surround the tent on all sides, leaving, of course, a narrow entrance in front. This was an excellent defence against occasional flying bullets, but more useful still to save the tent from being carried away bodily in some wild tornado of wind, such as now and again visited us, sweeping down the sides of the mountains, and across the sandy plain where we were, with immense force, carrying all before it that was not anchored down pretty firmly.

All this was accomplished—the internal digging out, the trench around, and the mud wall—while the servants were sheltered under a matting construction in the rear of the enclosure. And not a day too soon! That night the rain descended—sheets of it—and the tempest swept over us, bringing catastrophe in many corners of the camp. Here a tent was down, having completely collapsed, and almost smothered its occupant. There in the Cavalry lines the pegs to which the horses were tethered had loosened, and there was very nearly a stampede among the steeds.

Poor Villiers, of the *Graphic*, was once more in a comical predicament. His little mountain tent had been pitched not far from the Headquarter Camp. Inured to dangers and inconveniences of all kinds, in previous campaigns, he had not troubled to provide against any here. No trench was dug around. Fatal neglect! As he lay that night muffled up in his blanket, sleeping the sleep of the weary war correspondent, the rain descended, and the flood, first as a gentle insinuating stream, began to creep into his tent and about him, until at last he woke to find himself lying in a swamp half a foot deep. Poor fellow! he had to turn out in the stormy night and find shelter in the Post Office tent near, where I found him next morning working away as unconcernedly as if all the night through gentle sleep and calm repose had visited him. Calm, imperturbable men these war correspondents are, taking most things as a matter of course!

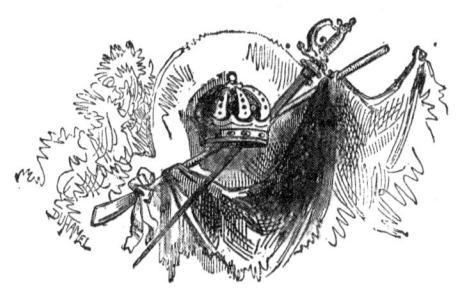

CHAPTER VII.

Sunday Morning Parade—The Soldier worships God—No longer the Scum of Society—He merits Respect and Sympathy—Religions of the Army—Voluntary Services at Night—Soldiers' Bible Class and Tea Meeting—The "Sing-Song"—Sergeant Moon's Topical Song—Tenth Hussar Band—"As pants the Hart."

SUNDAY morning in camp! Ah, you say, very different from Sunday morning at home in England. Yes, of course, it is necessarily very different. No church-going bell sounding over hill and dale, and summoning the simple villagers to some ivy-covered church on the hill side, or clanging through the quiet streets of the big town, where the orderly groups of people, all in their Sunday best, are wending their way to some old time-honoured temple. Certainly these accompaniments of the English Sabbath day are all wanting. But if you suppose for a moment that amid the bustling realities of active war, the stern and multifarious duties which belong to a campaign, the Sabbath is forgotten, and the worship which belongs to the day ignored, you are very much mistaken. " Tommy Atkins " is no heathen. And one of the privileges which belong to his profession is that he is allowed to worship God according to the dictates of his own conscience. No man need be a worse man morally for going into the army. Many a man has become a better man. Indeed, speaking from large experience and personal observation, I have always regarded the army as a great school of training and discipline; where the man who, in civil life, lacking the restraints and helps which belong to army discipline, would, through sheer weakness of character, rapidly degenerate into a worthless fellow, receives the very aid that he needs, to give him some moral backbone, and is thus made into a very decent man, and when he leaves the service becomes a respectable citizen. Whereas, if a man be radically bad —bad through and through—he soon finds his measure taken in the army. It is a bad refuge for him, and ten to one he is soon drummed out with ignominy, as unworthy to wear the Queen's uniform. The time for regarding the ranks of the British Army as filled with the scum and off-scouring of society has gone by ; and the scorn with which some people affect to regard our soldiers can only arise from ignorance, or groundless prejudice. From close contact with the British soldier, and a personal experience extending over many years, I can honestly say that some of the grandest qualities which go to make a noble character in man, I have seen over and over again exemplified in him. Who so unshaken in discipline, so patient in suffering, so ready for any sacrifice or service in the cause of Queen and country ! Many of the lads die in the alien land and are laid in some far-distant grave, where no mother can come and weep at her boy's quiet resting-place. Have they not nobly earned the kindly interest and sympathy of the people at home, for whom they thus toil and march and fight in every part of the world? In the name of all that is just, putting aside the question of kindliness and charity, let us hear no more of scorn for our soldiers. It is an injustice and a folly.

In the army there are now four recognised religious denominations—the Church of England, the Presbyterian, the Wesleyan, and the Roman Catholic. When a man enlists he is questioned as to his "religion," as it is called; and he is compelled to make choice of one of these four parties, which choice is then recorded, with other items, against his name and number. He can, of course, afterwards "change his religion," as the men term it, by explaining his reasons to the officer commanding his regiment. The Sunday parade service, at which attendance is compulsory, unless a man be on guard or otherwise fulfilling some duty, is never by any chance omitted, if it be at all possible to hold it. Usually it takes place in the morning, often soon after dawn, though sometimes I have known it "in orders" for the afternoon.

On the previous day arrangements, as to time and locality, are made at the office of the Adjutant-General, and all such particulars inserted in the General Orders for the day, and are, therefore, known throughout the force, however large or widely scattered. Sometimes, indeed, it happens that owing to the wide disposition of a large force, portions of which may be miles apart, several parade services are held at various points, the chaplain going from one to another in succession until he has reached all the men of his "persuasion."

Thus, on Sunday morning, the Church of England party would be seen marching away to some central spot in the camp, headed, most probably, by one of the regimental bands. There, by the side of the simple lectern, consisting of the big drum, perhaps, the chaplain would await their coming, and around him, in hollow square formation, the men would presently be drawn up facing inwards on three sides, himself and any of the staff who attended the service forming the fourth. And there, under the broad canopy of heaven, the true sacrifice of worship has risen from many a sincere, honest heart, hidden under the scarlet tunic or the blue jacket. A parade service was no opportunity for a long sermon. Straight truth, put into plain words, " able to be understanded of the common people," and kept within the limits of fifteen minutes or thereabouts, was what well suited the soldier. He does not object to hard hitting, but you must be quick about it, and it will not be the less effective. Happy the chaplain who is able to let his men have the chance of a good sing. They dearly love it. I had specially printed and prepared a large number of very thin, pamphlet-like hymn-books, containing a score or so of well-known hymns, and sufficiently portable to be carried around and distributed at each service in a few moments. I never heard anything grander, I think, than the vast volume of musical song that used to rise and swell from hearts sincere at our Sunday morning parade service. And surely the ministry of song may be credited with some strange subtle power to touch the deep-down chords in men's hearts, and help them up to better things, when stern denunciation of sin and the most pleading voice of a man may fail.

Thus also the Presbyterian party would be marching towards another quarter of the camp, the pipers of some Scotch regiment swinging along at the head and discoursing their weird music, so dear to the heart of the Scotsman.

And yonder the Wesleyan party, too, would be gathering in its appointed place, including most likely all the Nonconformists of the force.

And then in some secluded spot the Roman Catholic chaplain would arrange his simple altar, and around him would be gathered the devout worshippers who held his creed. Parade service usually lasted about three-quarters of an hour. No wisdom was shown by the chaplain who prolonged it beyond that limit.

Most of the chaplains held a voluntary

service in the evening, which the men might attend or not as they chose. A good number of men used to come; and generally a very hearty and earnest service was the result.

While we lay here at Jellalabad it was my custom, in accordance with the wish of some of the men, to hold a short religious meeting —somewhat after the fashion of a Bible reading—almost every evening. This was held, not in the open air, for it was then very cold at night, but in a large tent attached to one of the regimental hospitals. I was very much amused at the zeal of one of the apothecaries, who, good-hearted fellow that he was, used to boil up a great *degchee* of tea, to serve as a kind of loving cup for the men ere they dispersed. This little meeting rapidly became very popular in the camp. Let us not for a moment hint that bribery and corruption in the form of the tea *degchee* was the influence which stimulated the men and brought them together. But so it was that at the appointed hour a goodly number might be seen in undress quietly wending their way towards the apothecary's tent, every man of them armed with his tin canteen for drinking purposes. At first the men sat about on the ground, or on boxes, taking up a good deal of room. But as our numbers multiplied it was needful to economise space, and the following ingenious method of seating was adopted:—Tent pegs were driven into the ground at intervals, two pegs being crossed so as to form a forked rest; and on these were placed long ten-foot dooley poles—the poles on which the dooleys, or stretchers for carrying the sick were slung. These were fixed row after row, and although the result was not quite like a well-cushioned armchair, the accommodation was marvellously enlarged, till the tent interior was a living mass of men. How our numbers increased, and the ambition of our men, too, resulting in a kind of church building of their own, I shall have occasion to narrate later on.

But there were other methods of spending

the evening pleasantly, for all sorts of contrivances were set to work to make the weary hours pass. One of the other chaplains used to read every night to the men whatever of interest he could lay hold of, they gathering around him smoking their pipes and listening with a good deal of appreciation.

But the great evening's entertainment was the "sing-song," as the men dubbed it. A big space, amphitheatrical in shape, was roughly dug out, and so arranged that many hundreds of men could find some sort of sitting accommodation; while in the centre was a flat space, called by courtesy the platform. Somebody was master of ceremonies, though little ceremony was observed beyond that of calling out the name of the singer or reciter, as he appeared. First uprose a stalwart young officer, Hamilton, of the Guides Cavalry, who gave a song in good style. A gallant fellow he! But a few weeks more, and he was to lead his men in charge against the fierce Kujianis at Futtehabad—his chief slain by his side—and he sweeping through the masses of the foe to save the life of a native officer and win his Victoria Cross. And then a few more months were to pass, and with Cavagnari, Kelly, and Jenkins, he was to meet a soldier's death, after many a deed of "derring do," in the gateway of the embassy at Kabul. All this, however, was in the future, and was now mercifully hidden from knowledge. Then young Gunner Burke, of the Artillery, sang a comical ditty telling of a tempestuous voyage in a barge from Deptford to London Bridge, which provoked broad grins, especially from the Cockneys. After him a Post Office official, who had to accompany the force, and who hailed unmistakably from the Emerald Isle, sang of the little "Cruiskeen Lawn" and of "Shan Van Vocht, and other equally Republican songs. He was succeeded by Sergeant Moon, of the 10th Hussars, who gave a very clever topical song of his own composing, dealing with the circumstances in which we now found ourselves, and with poor Shere Ali, and the Oxus river boundary, and

Russian sympathy, and so on. A very good song it was, and well put together, testifying both to Moon's literary and musical skill. And the men responded to every point, political or otherwise, with huge guffaws and cheers. But now, last of all, a modest young corporal of the same gallant regiment stood up to add his part to the evening's entertainment. He was but a boy, smooth-faced, and not too robust looking, and, indeed, I remembered to have talked with him in hospital not so long before. But as his sweet, clear, baritone voice, gentle-toned at first, rang out over the plain, I noticed a hush gradually falling upon the assembly. The loud laughter is stilled, and the men are sitting smoking and silently gazing at the singer, who can just be discerned by the flickering light of the single lantern. And why the hush? Ah! the great quietness has fallen upon the spirits of those rollicking men, because the words of the song have wafted their thoughts away from the wild Afghan land to the old home in England.

It was only a simple old English ditty called, I think, "The Vacant Chair." But as the words of the chorus came around—

> "We shall meet, but we shall miss him,
> There will be one vacant chair,"

there were only a few who could join quietly in it, and those with a certain tremor in their voice. They knew well enough that there would be a vacant chair in many a cottage home in England ere this campaign closed: the place where the soldier son used to sit, but which would know him no more.

And then with a verse of the National Anthem joined in with loyal enthusiasm, the "sing-song" used to close.

It was pleasant to see with what heartiness the officers threw themselves into these recreations of the men. One of them—Mercer, of the 4th Ghoorkas—was particularly clever in devising amusements for them. I have now by me a curiosity in the form of a programme printed here in Afghanistan, I should think with a portable printing press, giving the details of an *al fresco* entertainment of a most wonderful character. It was a sort of *pot pouri* of pleasant things—songs, recitations, musical selections by the Ghoorka and Rifle Brigade Bands, humorous sketches and comical delineations from some, who were evidently not quite new to the boards—and under the distinguished patronage of the general commanding. There was no difficulty, of course, with the musical part, as every regiment had its band in camp—even the Sikhs with their *tomtoms* and curious kind of native bagpipes. There was one exception at first. The 10th Royal Hussars had left theirs behind them in India. Having reached Jellalabad, they had sent at once for the instruments. But there was some unaccountable delay, and the "shave" in camp was that in transit they had been looted by the Afridis in the Khyber Pass; and that the unearthly howls and groans, the shrill echoes, and the various uncanny sounds which broke the stillness of the night, and were heard by our men down the Pass, were really due to the futile attempts of the wild hill men to extract music from the trombone and other big "brasses" of the 10th Hussar Band.

Ah! but it was all a joke; and the apprehension of looted instruments only a "shave." I was passing through the lines one evening on my way to Headquarters to turn in. The "second post" had just sounded, bugle after bugle taking up the echo through the camp. Then the quiet stillness of night followed. But after a few moments of pause gently and sweetly the strains of the tune taken from Spohr, and set to the hymn,

"As pants the hart for cooling streams,"

broke upon the night, followed by the Troyte which is sung to "Abide with Me," and then the National Anthem.

It was the recovered band of the Royal "Tenth." And this was their nightly custom —a custom introduced when poor Valentine Baker commanded them, at the express wish of his wife—and one which is carefully maintained to this day. Very soothing were the sounds which thus fell upon one's ear, almost the last, as one turned in. And the men lying in the tents around were none the worse for the suggested prayer, which was linked with the plaintive strains of the 10th Hussar Band as they echoed over the great camp.

CHAPTER VIII.

The "Red Cross" Quarters—The Sick Soldiers' Friend — God's Acre—Solitary Graves — Looting Afghans shot by Sentry—The Wolf and the Ghoorka—Visit to the Ameer's Gardens—Tea-drinking with the Khans—Church Construction on a Novel Scale—The Commander-in-Chief comes up—Tytler Charges the Shinwaris with his Lancers—Three Expeditions Start.

AT the far end of our camp, near the lines of the Rifles and Ghoorkas, conspicuously waving above the tents was a well-known flag—a red cross on a white ground. Everyone knew what it meant. And towards that red cross flag many a poor weary lad was borne with shattered limb or fevered body; for it was our hospital. In the foreground was a little cleared space. Here was the big tent where the drugs were kept and the dispensing done. There a quantity of special commissariat stores, called "medical comforts"—arrowroot, beef tea, and even port wine and brandy; and, farther along, the lines of white tents, all arranged in convenient order, within the shelter of which the sick lads found quiet rest, nursing—careful and efficient, if a trifle rough—and all that the best medical care and skill could give them to bring them back to health again. The kindness of our soldier-doctors is proverbial, and the way in which they spare themselves no toil in their skilful care of the men is beyond all praise. But let us lift the door-hanging of this nearest tent and peep inside. Here are the rows of little cots which are used with our marching army all the world over. Every cot, alas! is occupied. At the head of the patient is fixed a hospital " sheet," with a record of all facts about the sick man which it may be necessary to know; his name, his number, and his regiment; his religious denomination, that his own chaplain may be able to find him out; his disease, with the doctor's orders as to medicine and diet. All these items are recorded, and the variations marked from day to day. As you look at the record, you see perhaps man after man suffering from enteric fever. That often means that, through the exigencies of the campaign, bad water or unwholesome food has been pertaken of by the men. Every care is taken to avoid this, but sometimes it is impossible, and this disease runs like an epidemic right through the force; or perhaps it is rheumatic fever in case after case, pointing to exposure, damp ground to lie on at night, and so forth. Yonder, at the end of the tent, lies one whom the fever has gripped strongly, and he is muttering in his delirium. From the broken babblings that fall from his lips it is not hard to know where his fevered thoughts are. He is at home once more. Village scenes, and cottage homes, and green fields are now around him. And as his voice drops to tender tones, a word falls from him which tells that the soldier-lad, in his extremity and pain, seeks again the shelter of his mother's arms, as when a little child. Poor lad! he will never see her more. And she will look in vain for the home-coming of the soldier-son in whom she had such pride. A big, strong hospital-orderly raises him with strange tenderness; and presently the babblings cease, and the weary head sinks in calm sleep.

Here is one evidently recovering from some sharp sickness. The gleam of new life is in his eye, though the face is drawn and wan from the conflict he has had. Sitting on the edge of his cot is one of the chaplains. Quietly they talk together, and the face of the sick man brightens more and more. There is evidently the touch of sympathy between them. The Chaplain knows his man, and how to get at the best part of his heart. There are kindly inquiries about the home and the old folks there. And perhaps, as the man is sick and unable to sit up and write, the Chaplain becomes his scribe, while he in plain, soldier terms dictates his letter to the old mother in the village home, or the sister, or perchance to the "nearer one still and the dearer one yet;" for almost every soldier has his sweetheart, and he doesn't for-

get her either while he is far away. And
then with cheery words of encouragement
and a little good advice the Chaplain goes on
to some other sick lad in the tent. This
work among the men was certainly one which
needed special fitness and special equipment.
True it is that a man must be born to it first
of all. For if there be not some innate fitness, some disposition or power which puts
one in touch with the soldier nature at once,
it is useless to try and grow into it. There
is a quick and ready discernment on the part
of the soldier himself, and he knows in a
moment where there is true sympathy
animating the work, and where there is the
mere perfunctoriness of hard duty. Equally
true is it that experience teaches the army
chaplain a great deal. He learns every day.
And to true sympathy and wise experience
the soldier readily responds. He opens his
heart and lays bare his very nature to one
whom he learns to regard as his friend and
counsellor. Many a sad tale of sin, and many
a story of sorrow have I listened to amid the

quiet stillness of the hospital tent ; and many a time have I thanked God that I have been placed where I could do something towards lightening the sorrows of the poor fellows, or helping them to bear their burdens.

A soldier's funeral is always an impressive sight ; and even with our wild surroundings in Afghanistan, and despite the sad frequency of the event, there was always something that touched our heart as the little procession wound slowly through the camp on its way to our cemetery. The solemn strains of the band ; the party of comrades with arms reversed ; the riderless horse (if it were a cavalryman's funeral) led quietly behind the body, with boots in stirrups, and crape on the bridle ; and then the burying away in that far-off grave ; all made it more solemnly impressive to me there than even it is at home here ; for here at least the dead man will lie among his kindred and his countrymen, but there the feet of strangers only will presently tread around his resting-place.

Near to our camp at Jellalabad, in a little

cleared space scantily shaded by a group of tall trees, we had prepared our tiny "God's acre," and around it a broad mud wall was thrown. Alas! how soon it was well occupied. For the sharp and sudden changes in the weather, the intense cold followed by the chill rain, and then the equally intense heat, produced a good deal of sickness among the men; and at one period almost every day Handel's "Dead March," or the strains of the Vesper Hymn on the fifes, with the roll of the muffled drums, used to sound solemnly through the camp about sundown. As indicating the kindness and sympathy of the soldier's heart, I noticed that often a man would spend hour after hour in caring for his comrade's grave; sometimes covering it with white pebbles in some pretty design; sometimes making a kind of white cement with which the surface was covered, and where tender words of sympathy or farewell were inscribed. One such inscription of which I heard in another campaign was very touching. The man had died right out in the desert, and there he lay in his lonely grave over which were these words:—

> "No brother near to see him die,
> No sister dear to say 'Good-bye,'
> In a far-off desert land
> Rest in peace!"

I always used to think that these graves which we left behind us were the saddest footprints of our retiring force.

While we were here at Jellalabad we were constantly having visits at night from natives intent on *loot*. On certain sides the sentries were doubled and kept a sharp lookout; but still these gentry continued their predatory incursions into the very midst of our sleeping men, and carried off valuables. They were usually very clever in eluding the sentry; writhing their course along the ground until inside the line, and then their path was a comparatively easy one. Still they did not all escape. On the contrary, several were shot. But this did not by any means deter others from making similar incursions, and running the same risks. Other nocturnal visitors, too, we had. One night the stillness of our headquarter camp was broken by the crack of a rifle, and as I lay in my tent I distinctly heard the thud of a bullet in the ground far too near to be pleasant. It was not easy to understand it, as there had been no sound of a preliminary challenge. But the mystery was solved the next morning when I saw the dead body of a huge, gaunt wolf lying not far away, its great teeth grinning horribly in death. It seems that the beast had come down, probably from the neighbouring hills, in the night, and made an inspection of the camp while in search of food. While coolly lobbing along the very centre road, he was seen by a little Ghoorka sentry. At first, in the darkness, the native mistook him for some huge dog. But presently, discerning more correctly, he fired at the beast, but unfortunately missed him. This was the bullet that I heard. In an instant the savage creature turned and sprang towards the throat of the plucky little fellow, who stood his ground, receiving his enemy on the point of the bayonet, for there was no time to load again. He succeeded in killing him, but not before he himself had received an ugly scratch on the throat. The wound was dressed, and nobody thought very much more about it for a time. But three months after, that unfortunate Ghoorka died of hydrophobia. The wolf was an old one, diseased, perhaps; at any rate, there was poison in the scratch. This was the third wolf within a short time that had thus come prowling about the camp at night.

On the other side of Jellalabad were some remarkable gardens surrounding a kind of country residence of the Ameer. A few of us went down one afternoon to visit them, and a very bonnie sight it was. The gardens were shaded by a large number of poplar-like trees, planted in groups; and there we saw vast parterres of English flowers— strangely enough, roses and the common stock predominating. It was a very refreshing sight to English eyes. We found that some of the Khans of the country were then resident in the country house in the centre of gardens, so we ventured to make a call on them. They were very pleasant and hospitable, though necessarily our conversation was within somewhat narrow limits. We were served with tea, evidently after the Russian style, in tiny delicate bowls rather than cups. By the aid of Hindustani, a few words of which the Khans appeared to understand—Persian words chiefly—and many signs, we got on fairly for half an hour, and then made our bow. They were interested in our English revolvers, and in return showed us their Afghan swords, pointing out the fine temper of the steel and the exquisite workmanship both on blade and hilt. These Khans are associated mostly with the Shinwari, Kujiani, and Ghilzai tribes, who are continually giving the Ameer a good deal of trouble; for they can bring thousands of fighting men into the field, and well they know their own power.

Though there were rumours almost constantly to the effect that we were about to move towards Kabul, we tarried on the sandy plains of Jellalabad day after day. We had a taste of all seasons and weathers; the keenest cold, floods of rain, and then the fiery blasts of early summer heat. The men were getting very impatient. Sickness had done its worst among us, pneumonia after the chill rains carrying off a great number.

Some of the men who used to attend my Bible class and other meetings came to me one day with a strange request, which at the time amused me very much. "We seem to be stuck here," said they, "perhaps all the summer; why should we not build a church?" I laughed heartily at the proposition, for although we had been necessarily a good deal inconvenienced by having no definite place of meeting in common with the other chaplains and their men, the singular lack of material of any kind seemed to preclude the possibility of any building operations. Of course there were no bricks which we could use, nor anything with which to make bricks. Stones, indeed, there were in abundance, for if ever there was a country on the face of God's earth which seemed to produce a plentiful harvest of stones, there it is beyond the Khyber Pass. These, however, for our purpose seemed useless; we therefore set our wits to work to devise some other arrangement. We concluded that we could not in anywise build up, but that it might not be so difficult to dig down. Already a good deal of excavation in connection with the tents had taken place. Why might we not adopt the same contrivance on a larger scale and dig out our church? First, it was necessary to sketch, in amateur architect fashion, a rough design of the groundwork of the church. This was not difficult. Moreover, it was, as far as I can describe it, pure Gothic in style. Then a number of strong fellows set to work with pick and shovel, and commenced to excavate the seating and aisles according to the delineation on our plan, digging down about a foot and a half. In a very short time this part of the work was completed, and seating accommodation was provided for more than a hundred men, with lectern at one end—in fact, the groundwork of a little church in all respects complete. Then remained the question of walls and roof. And here we came to a full stop for awhile. I thought it possible that the Commissariat stores might afford us some help in the way of disused tents. This, however, was out of the question, on inquiry, until, at the last moment, two Sepoy *pals*, or native tents, were found, which were not in immediate use, and were handed over to us for a time at any rate. Admirably they met the case. Their very style was Gothic when pitched; and this being done our church was complete. Rome was not built in a day, but our sanctuary at Jellalabad was constructed in a day, or thereabouts; and the men were heartily proud of having thus put up the first and only Protestant Church in all Afghanistan. Months after, when coming down from the front, I found on the deserted plain the remains of the structure, roof and walls of course gone, but excavated seats and other fittings remaining still. I wonder what the Afghans thought of it!

In the midst of this long lull the Commander-in-Chief, Sir Paul Haines, came up to the front on a tour of inspection. We learnt then definitely that Shere Ali was dead, and that his successor, Yakub Khan, had sent in certain proposals to Government. Now we were to wait for the answers, and our future movements were to be determined by the result of these negotiations.

Meanwhile, certain startling changes in the disposition of the tribes immediately around us were taking place. The Shinwaris were beginning to raid; and the Kujianis were gathering their fighting men together, evidently for some immediate purpose. General Tytler, who was commanding farther down the Pass, very effectively dealt with the former body. In a brilliant little action, where a squadron of Bengal Lancers dashed into a dense body of Shinwari rebels, who stood their ground for a few moments, but presently fled in terror before the threatening of the long bamboo lances, which these Sowars wielded with great skill, he completely took away their appetite for further raiding. A splendid officer this! A man who never unduly risked his men, but who, having carefully thought out his plan, carried it through with a wonderful dash, which seemed never to fail of success. He was a man devoted to his profession; who won his Victoria Cross for personal gallantry as a young soldier; and it was a matter of deep and universal regret when at the end of the campaign he returned to India with shattered health, and, a few months later, succumbed. The India army, with its long record of fame, bears no nobler name upon its rolls than that of John Adams Tytler.

But the gathering further up the valley was a yet more serious matter. The Kujianis were in large force, and the still more numerous Ghilzais beyond were beginning to be disquieted. It would be no easy matter to crush a big rebellion if allowed to come to a head. Sir Sam Browne determined to take decisive steps at once to put an end to it. One force, chiefly infantry, under Macpherson, were to march at once, making a detour, and crossing the river a mile or two ahead. The following day a second force was to start consisting of 300 men of the 17th Regiment, about 600 of the 27th (Punjaubis), and 45th Sikhs, together with a squadron of the 10th Hussars and some guns of Stewart's Horse Battery— these to move straight up the Pass: while a third cavalry force, consisting of a squadron of the 10th Hussars and one of the Bengal Lancers, were to cross the river by a special ford below the camp, in order if possible to secure the person of Azmatullah Khan, who was the head of the rebellion, and was in hiding in a neighbouring village. All the camp was on the *qui vive* for the carrying out of these arrangements. How they succeeded we shall see.

CHAPTER IX.

A Second Visit to the City—A Startling Adventure—The two *Ghazis*—Running, or Walking, the Gauntlet—Murder of the Kahars—Swift Vengeance descends on the Murderers—The Tale of Fanatic Ferocity—To be Shot when well enough—Closing the Gates of Paradise—Attempt to Capture Azmutullah Khan—I Volunteer with the Cavalry.

MEANWHILE, an adventure happened to me which had well nigh cost me my life. Since my early morning visit to the city of Jellalabad, when I saw things which did not invite me hither again, as well as the two or three occasions since when treacherous attacks had been made on some of our men, I had for the most part discreetly avoided the city within its gates. The gardens outside had been often visited, and the country around was free and open. And though ill-looking fellows were everywhere, still it was a vastly different thing meeting one or two in the open, when one is on the back of a good horse, from being in the midst of a villainous crowd in a cooped-up, narrow alley, and on foot. One bright afternoon, however, when everything seemed quiet, the hanging of my tent was pushed aside, and my friend, N——, putting his head inside, said, "Come, let us have a run into the city." Now N—— was proverbially a quiet man. Plenty of pluck, which showed itself when occasion required; a good man to have by you when things looked bad, for he was as cool under danger as when he sat down to breakfast. But still a quiet man who had no *shauk*—no inclination—for foolhardy running into peril, and, except when duty called him to face hazards, had a thought for the dear ones at home, and the claims they had upon him. So I did not feel that I was heedlessly running risks when N—— was the enticer. Still I ventured to remind him that a few things had happened during the last few weeks, of an uncanny nature, in the lanes and alleys of the city, and suggested that a little caution and provision against such possibilities might be wise. General orders were out that no man was to go unarmed to the city; and men were only to go in company, not singly. So we buckled on our revolvers and set out. Passing beyond our line of sentries, and a mile and a half across the sandy plain, brought us within sight of the Peshawar Gate. Just outside were some tracts of cultivated ground, a few small fields, where some country-looking fellows were doing a little to raise their scanty crops. But around the gateway itself we noticed signs of unwonted bustle and commotion. A small crowd had gathered, and in the midst of them were two hill-men, who were gesticulating in their wildest fashion. The crowd was an ordinary Afghan crowd. Some were shopkeepers, and some were field labourers apparently, but all, according to universal custom, were armed. But the two fierce gesticulators were specially noticeable. With their *cummerbunds* full of Afghan knives, one of them held in his hand a long *jezail*, or gun with curved stock, and the other a kind of antiquated horse pistol, which he flourished menacingly in the air, to the imminent peril of those around in case it might go off, as those old weapons sometimes have a way of doing "promiscuous-like." They were both wrought up to a pitch of strange excitement, and the crowd around appeared to be catching their spirit. My friend looked at them and so did I, and we mutually agreed that as wide a berth as possible should be accorded to them. But how was it to be accomplished? There was but one gate into the city, unless, indeed, we went a mile around to the other side, and the crowd was surging about near to that gate. We determined to go quietly on, taking no notice of them, and hoping that they would equally take no notice of us. But no! That was not to be. We were observed quickly enough, and at once the gesticulation became more excited, and, moreover, was directed towards us. Quietly we passed along, the eyes of the crowd upon us, until we came to the gateway, and passed within the city. I do not think that our stroll among the shops and stalls was made any more pleasant by the little scene which we had just witnessed. Moreover, we were now inside the walls; and we knew very well that in order to get outside, and to the safety of our lines, we should have to pass through the excited crowd again. With some such thoughts as these in our minds the time for our return came, and once more passing down the main bazaar of the place we approached the Peshawar Gateway, through which we should have to wend our way to the open country and our camp beyond. The sight that met our eyes as we neared the spot was not reassuring. Indeed, it was most disturbing. The crowd had swelled to double its former proportions. Scarcely any were inside; but surging around the outside pathway was a mob which by this time, under the influence of religious fanaticism, or what, we could not tell, was every moment becoming more and more excited. As soon as we were seen approaching, a wild shout went up from them; and without coming inside they began to range themselves on either side of the path beyond in two long lines. I said to N——, "We are in a pretty mess; you see what they intend; we are to run the gauntlet." "Yes," said he, "we have to go through it now, but we must have no running. Loosen your belt, and see that everything is ready; but don't shoot, and don't run. Be cool, and perhaps we shall get through all right." As far as I could see this did not appear probable. But I had no intention of running—that would be to court disaster; nor either of shooting, except in the last dire extremity. As we neared the gate we distinguished our two fanatic friends, who with wild words had been exciting the crowd before pushing forward prominently in front of one of the side lines. One had drawn from his *cummerbund* his largest knife; while the other, as before, was flourishing his big horse pistol. Their intentions, which were far from honourable, were perfectly evident. There was nothing for it but to move quietly forward as if there were nothing extraordinary to disturb one. It was not easy to

REV. ARTHUR MALE AND FRIEND RUNNING THE GAUNTLET AT
JELLALABAD.

To face page 152.

do this. Our hands strayed nervously near our weapons; and our eyes glanced around to watch every movement of the two long lines which stretched many a yard away from the gate. Step by step we neared the gateway. There were the two fierce hill-men right in the middle of the line, eagerly bending forward, and waiting for their opportunity. The picture of those two men is for ever burnt into my memory. They were not particularly well-favoured men by nature; but now wrought up, as they were, into fanatic excitement—their faces quivering with wild passion—their eyes glaring—they presented to us a spectacle which was the reverse of reassuring. They were waiting for us; this we knew well enough. We also knew that there was no way of escape that we could seek. So we went quietly on. We reached the two lines. No hand was lifted against us. The people appeared to be waiting for the action of the two fanatics. As we drew near to them they leaned forward from the line, weapons in hand, pausing for the moment to strike. Nearer we came. Still they paused. Presently we were level with them. Even yet they paused, straining forward with quivering limbs; and yet held back, as if some strong hand were laid upon them. Our nerves were at high tension. Every moment of time seemed an hour; every foot of progress a mile. We were passing them. We could see their faces working with strange quiverings, for their opportunity was passing too; and as yet their weapons were unstained. Whether they feared, or only hesitated, I do not say. Nor do I verture to make any explanation of that which was a simple fact. I only record that thus we passed beyond the murderous fellows, and were soon beyond their reach. Then with quickened footsteps and thankful hearts we hurried on to our camp. Scarcely had we reached the shelter of our lines, however, when news of a horrible tragedy reached us. Not far behind us as we left the city were walking two *kahars*, or native camp-followers, who had been making some little purchases in the city bazaar. They were at once seen by the crowd. They were not English; they were Hindus, or possibly Mohammedans, holding a creed like their own, but still they were servants of the accursed "infidels," and at once the rage of the men who had been baulked of their intended prey was turned upon them. With savage eagerness they attacked the poor defenceless *kahars*, who had no weapons with them, and none to succour them; and in a few seconds the bloody work was accomplished. So swiftly and with so little uproar was the murder committed that we, who could scarcely have been more than a couple of hundred yards from the spot, heard nothing and saw nothing till we reached our own lines.

But swift vengeance was already hanging over the heads of the murderers, even as they did the deed. Near the gates of the city were standing, all unnoticed, two *sowars*, or native cavalrymen, belonging to our "Guides" corps. They, too, had been buying among the *chucklers* of the bazaar, and had passed out not far behind the ill-fated *kahars*. Unobserved they were, because they had doffed their uniform, as it is the custom of our native soldiers to do when off duty, and were now attired very much after the fashion of the native population around; indeed many of our "Guides" corps especially were recruited from the country on the very borderland of Afghanistan, and some were said to be Afghans themselves. Undress or not, however, these cavalrymen had their good swords with them. As they emerged from the city gate they paused to see what the tumult was about. At this moment the murderous attack was made on the native camp followers. They did not hesitate a single instant. The turbulent crowd was surging around, with threatening gestures; but they heeded them not. There were two poor fellows, servants of the same people, whose salt, too, they had eaten, slain before their eyes. Drawing their weapons, they burst through the crowd, who fell back before their flashing swords, and in a few moments the two fanatics were writhing on the ground, cut and slashed almost to death. No man in that big crowd dared to interfere. Swift and righteous vengeance had followed the deed of blood. Hastily word was sent to our camp, and presently an armed party was despatched with stretchers to bring the bodies into our lines. And then the whole truth was evolved. The two *sowars* gave the story of what they saw and what they did. And right well did they merit the words of praise which were bestowed on them; for it needed some pluck to face an angry crowd and visit the murderers with punishment, especially when they themselves might easily have passed along unnoticed. The poor kahars were dead, and beyond testimony. But the hill-men, though slashed and wounded in a manner too horrible to describe, with wonderful vitality were tenaciously clinging on to life. And from their lips we learnt the following extraordinary facts. They were, as we supposed, tribesmen belonging to a village in the neighbouring hills. They had learnt that foreign soldiers professing an alien religion had invaded their country. To them these foreign soldiers were all *giaours*—infidels, who were worthy of immediate death, and who would hereafter burn in the great fire for ever. And under an impulse of Mohammedan fanaticism, induced probably by the fiery preaching of some *Moollah*, they determined to become *Ghazis*, that is, in a word, to devote themselves to death, if only they might slay an "infidel." By this they believed that they would gain sure passport to Paradise. A cruel faith makes cruel hearts, and brings about cruel deeds. With this thought in their heart they had come down to the city; and to the little crowd outside the gate had told the story of their faith and intention. It was just at this point that we were seen passing along into the city. Surely Allah had approved their purpose, and already supplied the appointed victims. All was arranged for the attack to be made on us when we returned. The crowd, though very much excited under the influence of the *Ghazis'* words, were scarcely brought to the point of readiness to join in the attack themselves; neither did the fanatics desire this, for theirs must be the merit of the deed, and theirs the Paradise, should they fall. The crowd would simply be there to witness the scene and shield the murderers as much as possible. As we emerged from the city gates everything seemed in trim for the successful accomplishment of their purpose; and they were utterly unable to account for the hesitancy which allowed us to pass by scatheless, and which presently put us beyond their reach. Their rage and disappointment found vent in the slaughter of the two defenceless *kahars*.

One of the fanatics gave up the ghost that night. No surgical skill could possibly avail either of them. The other clung on to life for nearly three weeks. At last, when we were about to move forward to Gundamuk, Sir Sam Browne gave orders that the man, if perchance he recovered, was to receive the punishment which was meted out to all who made attacks upon our men in the city, viz., death. The very night this order was promulgated the man died. Very much more stringent regulations were now put in force with regard to visiting the city. Our authorities had no desire to irritate or incite the people to these deeds of violence. And for a long time men were kept within their lines, or only allowed in the open country on the other side of our camp. Previously there had been two or three similar attacks, and on these occasions the *Ghazis* had been shot near the city gate, the sentence being always confirmed by the *Cadi* or judge of the city. The bodies were then cremated instead of being given up to the friends of the executed man for burial. This was a measure which did not seem altogether necessary. According to the Mohammedan creed the body of the dead man could never enter Paradise after fire had passed upon it. And thus to condemn a poor wretch after death, as well as before, seemed like an intrusion into a sphere where finite mortals had no real jurisdiction. At any rate it was a judgment of unusual severity, and was regarded with peculiar horror by the people of the city.

Meanwhile N—— and I, thankful as we were for our escape, and he thinking of his bairns and I of my skin, agreed with one another to confine our rambles to the open country, and not visit the city again until the manners and customs of its inhabitants were a little improved.

This occurred just shortly before the threefold expedition, to which I referred a while ago, set out. There was a great deal of bustle and anticipation in the camp in prospect of some fighting. All sorts of "shaves" were abroad. Some were declaring that this was only a kind of advance guard, and that presently we were all going to push on to Cabul itself.

I sought permission to accompany the cavalry force which had to cross the river by night and make a dash to seize Asmatullah Khan. This at first seemed likely to be given, but was finally refused, and all except combatant officers attached to the corps engaged were forbidden to go. A keen disappointment it was to me, but it saved me from another terrible episode of danger and death, as we shall presently see.

CHAPTER X.

Squadron of the Tenth March out by Night—The Fatal Ford—Messengers of Death—Napier Swims for his Life—Taking out the Bodies—Nineteen Buried together—Harford's Funeral—The lonely River-side Grave—Thurlow's after Fate.

IT was Monday evening, the 31st March, 1879. All through the lines at Jellalabad the greatest bustle and excitement prevailed. A three-fold expedition had been ordered. It is scarcely known in what direction the advance was to be made, but most probably up the Lughman Valley. The forces had been detailed, and the men were to be in readiness to march, some at nine o'clock, and some not till one o'clock in the morning. Strictly speaking, it was a two-fold force rather than a three-fold. One portion was to be under the command of Brigadier Gough, the other, which was split into two parts, was to be commanded by Brigadier-

General Macpherson. It was a cavalry force, consisting of a squadron of the 10th Royal Hussars and a squadron of the 11th Bengal Lancers, which were separated from the main body of Macpherson's infantry, and were ordered to cross the river in another spot below the camp, and advance along the left bank, afterwards rejoining Macpherson higher up the valley. As we have already noted, there was an idea that Asmatullah Khan, a very prominent rebel, was now in hiding in a village across the river not far off. And it was possible that by a sudden night attack, or a *coup de main*, this gentleman might be captured; which would be a very great gain to us, and a step towards the pacification of the country. To this end, the little cavalry force was detailed to march at nine o'clock.

There is always, I suppose, a natural desire on the part of those who have been a long time cooped up in camp to take part in anything of a more stirring character which may happen to turn up. Thus there were many who volunteered, especially to accompany the cavalry. Two of us chaplains were among them. We thought from what we heard that there would certainly be opportunities for making ourselves useful in more capacities, perhaps, than one. Personally I have long felt that a chaplain's post is not always in the rear and in hospital. Where men fight and fall he has a post and work to do. And, in my opinion, he gains far more influence with the men when he is willing to stand by their side in their peril, and, though fighting be no part of his duty, face the same dangers as they, than when he tarries behind in a safe place and waits for them to be brought to him.

Our wish, however, on this occasion, was not to be gratified. Neither we, the parsons, nor some others, medical officers, and special service men, who had asked to accompany the force, were permitted to go. It was a secret expedition, and was to be conducted as rapidly and with the least encumbrance possible.

Soon after eight o'clock the cavalry lines of

the "10th" were all alive. The two favoured troops which had been selected were getting themselves ready, the objects of envy on the part of their comrades who were to be left behind. Here were some who were giving the last finishing touches to the grooming of their horses before putting on the saddle. Yonder were two or three whose horses were ready, and were having a cheery word with a group of comrades. One had slipped away into his tent, and there kneeling down as well as his tight overalls would let him, he was trying to scrawl a few lines, which would go out by the *dâk* next day. It was difficult enough half-stretched on the ground to produce anything more than crooked writing and with many a blot. But how precious was that letter to be in the eyes of the dear ones who received it—his last! And how the cramped characters would be read and re-read with many a tear in the cottage home in England.

In the lines of the Bengal Lancers similar preparations were being made, but with a good deal more noise. The natives are a cheery race, and as these *sowars*, fierce-looking fellows many of them, with huge moustaches and whiskers curled upwards in true fighting fashion, buckled on their harness, many a merry shout and laugh echoed along the lines.

Not far from our headquarter camp Villiers, of the *Graphic*, and I (he a disappointed volunteer like myself) stood and watched the squadron of the Tenth ride out. There was not much jingling of accoutrements, for all our cavalry had their sword scabbards covered with brown leather. This prevented any clattering, or flashing of the sun on the bright steel. I noticed that the men were in heavy marching order, even to the jack-boots, instead of the lighter and convenient "putties."

The night was hazy, but the moon, about a quarter old, gave quite sufficient light to help them on their way. And so, with a "Farewell, and good luck to you!" the two troops passed out of the camp under the command of Captain Spotteswood, preceded by the squadron of Lancers, the whole force being commanded by Major Wood, of the 10th Hussars.

Now, what were they to do? It seems that about a mile or so below the camp, on the Peshawar side, there existed a much-used but for all that not very safe ford across the Cabul river, which was called among the people the Kaleh-i-Izack, or Ford of Isaac. Not long before a temporary bridge had been thrown across the stream at this point; but now, most unfortunately, the bridge had been removed. Through the water, therefore, the men had to cross by the line of this ford. It was a curious place. The river just here parts into two branches—the first only some thirty feet across, and then, after a kind of island covered with sand and big boulders, another stretch of water about one hundred and fifty feet in width. Generally speaking, the former portion was quite shallow, only about a couple of feet deep. The other part, however, was deeper. Still it was not too deep to be used constantly by the natives with their camels, horses, and bullocks. I myself

THE BATTLE SMOKE.

saw some of them crossing, though with a little difficulty, on foot. The special danger of the ford consisted in two facts. First, it was a zig-zag. After leaving the centre island (for of course the former part of the stream, where it was shallow, would be negotiated with ease) the line of passage lay down the stream, at a sharp angle, and then turned upwards again at the point of a tiny islet, until the opposite bank was reached. The other fact was that the winter snows had begun to melt, and from the Afghan mountains the streams were flowing down, adding already to the volume of water in the Cabul river, and causing the current to dash along at a fearful rate. It was afterwards estimated at nine miles an hour. It was a ticklish job to cross such a ford at any time; but with a body of cavalry and baggage mules it was an operation that required the utmost carefulness in carrying out.

The men were clear of the camp probably about ten o'clock. We who had watched them out had turned in, and were dropping off into our first sleep, about an hour later. A great stillness reigned over the camp. Suddenly some of us were startled by the galloping of horses from afar. I remember turning over, and wondering what was the cause of the hot haste. Had some of the Hussar horses stampeded? No! for the sound was on the wrong side of the camp. Perhaps some more native cavalry were being despatched to join their comrades! These sowars delighted in putting their horses at top speed. Yet that could scarcely be, for the galloping was from afar, and the clatter neared the camp more and more. These and other conjectures passed through my mind till I turned around again, after listening awhile, and tumbled off to sleep.

In the morning, when I turned out, I was scarcely thinking of the disturbance of the night, when outside my tent little Brown, a quaint and curious correspondent, who had travelled in all sorts of out-of-the-way places, met me with a doleful countenance.

"Do you know what has happened?" said he.

"No," I said; "I only know that there was a big row near the camp last night; some horses stampeding, or something."

"It wasn't that," said Brown. "The 10th, who went out, have all been swept away in the river, and they say most of them are drowned."

As he unfolded to me the tale of horror, with what details he had been able to gather, my very blood seemed to curdle. It was horrible. A whole squadron, or nearly so, slain—not in honest fight face to face with the foe, but by the cruel water; or kicked to death by their terrified, plunging chargers. With sad hearts we turned our steps in the direction where many were now going. The search for the bodies had already begun. We had not gone a mile in the direction of the fatal spot when we met a sad procession. Two or three *doolies* (hospital stretchers) were being carried along by native *kahars*. We knew what were being borne within. Reverently I lifted the curtain of the first. There lay the stiffened form of a gallant fellow, Mackay, of the 10th, whom I recognised at once. A few short hours before he had been standing close by my right hand at the Sunday morning parade service, devoutly heeding the worship in which we were engaged. That was a last word of warning to poor Mackay. And so the sorrowful procession, one *doolie* after another, passed us, as we hurried on to the river bank. When we arrived we learnt the correct details of the fatality. The squadron of the Hussars numbered about seventy men. Five regimental officers accompanied them, Captains Spotteswood and the Hon. James Napier (son of Lord Napier of Magdala), and Lieutenants Greenwood, Grenfell, and Harford. Dr. Cornish, too, who was afterwards most barbarously shot by the Boers while tending the wounded at Majuba Hill, was with this squadron.

Some native guides, who were thoroughly conversant with the double ford, led the way. After them came the Bengal Lancers. Then some baggage mules, followed closely by the men of the 10th. The orders were not to lose the line of direction, but to keep near to those ahead. The first portion of the stream, where the water was but shallow, was, of course, crossed easily. Then, after traversing the centre island, there came the second far longer and oblique ford. In plunged the native Lancers, and quietly and with comparative ease they seemed to get across. At least so it appeared to those who were eagerly watching from the bank. But the light from the moon was but faint, and the haze hanging over the river gave a deceptive appearance to everything that could be seen at all. Following closely on the heels of the *sowars'* horses were the baggage mules. Whether they were really on the ford or whether they were swimming in deep water could never be ascertained. Enough to say that the Hussars coming after them in half sections plunged, one after the other, into fifteen feet of water. They had missed the ford entirely. Two by two the horses leaped in; the men behind, on account of the misty light, failing to see exactly what was happening, and thus following their comrades to almost certain death. The fact was, in crossing any stream, rapid or not, there must always be a tendency to edge lower and lower down, and though the men were ordered to head their horses carefully upstream, doubtless each successive section of the Lancers was a few inches lower down than its predecessor, till the last couple was perhaps on the very edge. If this were so, the mules behind would be off the ford altogether, and swimming. And the Hussars would follow into deep water also. Some asserted that while on the ford at first there was subsequent swerving. Others, that by a sudden rush of water they were swept bodily off the ford. But from many statements which I received from the lips of some who were in the water, but escaped, I believe the above to be a solution of the mystery which led to this terrible catastrophe. The Court of Inquiry which subsequently met did not elicit many new facts. But it did elicit the fact that certain army regulations with regard to crossing dangerous and rapid streams, such as staking out the direction, and making the men pass over in single file, with a horse's length of a gap between every two, so as not to oppose an unbroken bulk to the force of the current, were never carried out. Probably with a ford which people were seen crossing with impunity, this did not appear needful. But even a pile of stones to mark the entrance would have given a true direction to begin with.

Into the water plunged the ill-fated men. They were in heavy marching order; and the horses were only able with difficulty to make headway. Lower and lower they were swept, still swimming, until they reached some rapids farther down. And here, horses and men, helpless, were dashed along. Men were thrown, and horses, terrified and whirled over, kicked in their frantic efforts the riders who were clinging to them. Below the rapids there lay a deep, calm pool, and here a few managed to disengage themselves, and to scramble or swim to the bank. Spotteswood, mounted on a powerful horse which had just come out from England, was carried safely to the opposite shore, but far down the river. Napier, getting free from his frantic beast, which had become restive, at last succeeded in swimming to shallow water, though he had given up the effort as hopeless just as his feet touched bottom. Grenfell's horse having gone part way, happily got his head around and carried his rider to the bank he had just left. Greenwood escaped, too, and Cornish. But young Harford and no fewer than forty-six out of the squadron of about seventy failed to answer when the roll was called afterwards The galloping horses we had heard in the night were the "messengers of death;" for hieing back to their lines, riderless and dripping, they dumbly told that some fatality had occurred.

One by one the bodies were found and lifted out till they numbered nineteen, the elephants of Wilson's Battery rendering help in bringing them across. One was found far down, where he had succeeded in climbing

into a native boat, but had perished from cold
and exhaustion afterwards. It fell to my lot
to read the funeral service over those first
nineteen that were found. Strangely solemn
was the scene. All the troops in camp were
present, with Sir Samuel Browne and his
staff. Several military bands accompanied
the long procession, and as the sad strains of
the "Dead March in Saul" sounded over the
camp, followed by another "march" in minor
tones, falling on our ears like the wail of
mourners, many hearts were heavy; and the
natives, servants, and camp followers were
loud in their grief. In our little cemetery a
trench had been dug, some forty-five feet in
length, almost filling one side from end to
end. And in this great grave the nineteen
bodies, each wrapped in a blanket, were laid
side by side to rest.

Lieutenant Harford's body was found a
few days afterwards, and buried at night.
This, too, was a weird funeral. The afternoon had been stormy, with thunder and
lightning and rain. As the procession moved

along vivid flashes set the dark sky ablaze every moment, and the figures of the officers who followed as mourners, wrapped up in big cloaks, looked strangely sombre.

Some of the bodies were swept far away down the country, and probably into the Indus itself. Some, however, were found within a few miles; and as a reward was offered for information concerning such, the villagers came in and told us, and they were buried there. One such case I well remember. Just towards evening the men of a village about five miles away came to say that a body had been found, drifted to the river bank. A party of the 51st, under Lieutenant Thurlow, were despatched to bury it. Nearly an hour later I was warned for duty, to go and read the service. As fast as I could go I made off on horseback to catch up the party. But I had no certain knowledge of the country or where the spot was. And it was with great difficulty, and after much wandering through villages, where I was welcomed with many a scowl, that I hit upon the place where the men had already arrived, and were digging the grave on the river bank. I was struck with the tender way in which the body of poor Cappa, a trooper of the 10th, was lifted in; and how, ere the grave was filled in, his comrades carefully covered his head with flat stones, that the earth might not fall roughly upon it. In that wild spot—the dark river, which had slain him, rolling silently by, and no Afghan village or sign of life within sight—we read the words of our beautiful burial service by the flickering light of a lantern, and left the dead man in his lonely grave.

It was late at night before we reached camp again. The long, quiet talk with Thurlow as we walked along will not soon be forgotten. Poor fellow! ere another year had passed he had fallen a victim to a murderous band who lay in ambush behind some boulders, and shot him dead as he rode along, his companion only escaping as by a miracle.

CHAPTER XI.

The Seventeenth Mess — Wiseman's Prejudice — Expedition against the Kujianis—Gallant Battye—Five Thousand Kujianis well Posted—Stewart's Stratagem with the Guns—The Kujianis are "Drawn"— Advance of the Leicester Men—Wiseman Attacks the big Afghan Standard Bearer, and is struck down—Corporal Clarke's gallant effort—Manners-Wood nearly Killed—Battye Shot—Mahommed Khan Defends his Body; but is Killed—Vengeance of the Guides—Night Scene—A Solemn Vow—The Warrior at Rest.

AT the extreme north-west of our camp, looking towards Piper's Hill, were the lines of the gallant First Seventeenth, the Leicestershire Regiment. Some little business, connected with the church rolls of the battalion, called me in that direction one morning. I was sitting in their mess tent, talking on the question with Wiseman, who was acting just then as adjutant of the regiment, and about to accept his hospitable invitation to stay tiffin, when one of the others came rushing in with the news that an expedition was afoot, and some of them were to go. Tiffin, I trow, that day was a merry meal, and none was merrier than poor Wiseman. A whole wing of the battalion was detailed for the march, and more than half the officers; those who had to stay in camp swallowing their disgust with their lunch as well as they could. I remember Wiseman had a strange antipathy to a revolver. He had some sort of an idea that it was an unsoldierly weapon; or at any rate that a sword, and a sword only, was an officer's weapon; and he would not carry a revolver at any price. Now Wiseman was a particularly small man, and some men in the regiment tried hard to persuade him to depart from his usual rule on this occasion, reminding him that the Afghans were mostly big hulking fellows, and that the regulation "Wilkinson" would have no chance against the heavy, keen, sword-like knives which they carried, and with which they could slash to dire purpose. But no! he would listen to no such persuasion. He would do his best with his good sword, and he could handle that with deft skill; and when it failed him he would go under. That was his resolve, from which he would not budge. Plucky he was, through and through. Yet better had it been for him had he for once yielded to wise counsels.

At one o'clock in the morning the force, under General Gough, marched out, consisting of four hundred of the Seventeenth (Leicestershire), six hundred of the Twenty-seventh and Forty-fifth Native Regiments, four guns of Stewart's Horse Battery, and some of the 10th Hussars and Guides' Cavalry.

Reaching a point some ten or twelve miles from Jellalabad, a temporary camp was formed, and a small reconnoitring party was detached, and sent out in the direction of Gundamuk. This consisted of some of the 10th Hussars and Guides' Cavalry, under Major Wigram Battye, a most distinguished Indian officer, who, sixteen years before, had been dangerously wounded when serving with the Guides' Infantry. He was also with the German forces during the Franco-German war, and was present at the siege of Paris. This gallant officer came of a race of Indian soldiers. One of his brothers, before he had served very long, fell at the head of the Guides before Delhi in the Mutiny days of 1857. He was but a lad; and as he fell in the fight, it is recorded that he shouted with his dying breath, "*Dulce et decorum est pro patriâ mori.*" Another of Wigram Battye's brothers was now commanding the Second Ghoorkas, and a third, a younger one, was attached to the Guides' Infantry.

General Gough had been apprised by native spies that a gathering of the Kujianis was taking place not far from the town of Futtehabad, or "place of victory," so named, probably, from some battle which had been fought in old time, when Imperial arms were triumphant. Without a doubt Yakub Khan, while pretending to negotiate peace with Cavagnari and our "politicals," was secretly stirring up the tribes down the Pass against

us. In a letter which was afterwards found, and supposed to bear his seal, they were incited to "cut the throats of all these Kaffirs and infidels, and send their souls to Jehannam." In this way a *Jehad*, or religious war, was proclaimed; and the *moollahs*, or priests, were the emissaries who moved from tribe to tribe exciting them with fiery words to deeds of blood.

These Kujianis were a very restless, fighting tribe, who apparently had responded with considerable alacrity to the summons. And as any successful movement on their part might spread to the Ghilzais—a yet larger and more powerful tribe beyond—it was felt necessary to lay a strong hand on these people at once, and stop for ever their troublesome movements.

Battye led his little force across the open plain towards Gundamuk, carefully reconnoitring the ground as he went along. At a place called Kaja he saw the Kujianis to the number of nearly five thousand busily engaged in throwing up a stone fortification, or *sun-*

gah, in a position which was naturally strong. Sending back word of this to General Gough, he himself, avoiding any conflict, pressed on for some eight miles farther. At this point the character of the country changed. Instead of being in an open plain, he found himself in a narrow defile; and on the precipitous hill sides, among the boulders and rocks, suddenly wild Afghan marksmen began to show themselves and open fire upon the little band. Battye, dismounting some of the Hussars, returned the fire with good effect, and then gradually and skilfully drew off his men to return to the main body, arriving once more at the place where he had seen the Kujianis before he found that now they were gathered in greater numbers, and were drawn up behind the strong defence of the long stone *sungah*, which stretched for some distance across the plain. It was an admirable position for defence, and one from which none but a very strong force would be able to dislodge them, unless, indeed, they were enticed to venture out themselves. The ground gradually sloped upward to the centre of their defences, while their right and left were protected by rugged ravines, the sides of which could only be climbed with difficulty.

When Battye and his handful of men reached this position they found General Gough with the remainder of the cavalry, and Stewart's four guns, already drawn up in full view of the enemy, at a distance of about 1,400 yards. They had hurried out to support the little reconnoitring party, Gough ordering three hundred of the Leicestershire Regiment and three hundred of the Native Infantry to follow as quickly as possible. Three miles of broken ground had to be covered, and it was certain that they could not reach the field for more than another half-hour.

The General saw at once that nothing effective could be done against the enemy so long as they held their strong and strongly-fortified position. Neither could he with his little force of cavalry and guns dislodge them. But a *ruse* might succeed, and this he attempted. He ordered Major Stewart to open fire with his guns at a distance of 1,400 yards or so, and then gradually advance a couple of hundred yards, halting at intervals, and pitching a few shells among the masses of Kujianis who were gathered behind the breastworks. Then Stewart was to limber up and rapidly retire a little, repeating the movement from time to time. The stratagem succeeded perfectly. Although warned to the contrary by one of their own men, who had once served in our native army, and was now standing by the Khan of his village, being regarded as a great military authority, they looked upon this movement as a precipitate retreat, and encouraged thereby they began to stream from their defences, shouting defiantly as they came on. While skirmishers scattered themselves over the plain in front, the main body advanced in Zulu fashion, wings outstretched and thrown forward, in order to overlap our men. This they were able to do by scrambling down into the ravines and advancing rapidly under the protection of the high rugged banks. Our men could see the standards held high and rapidly carried along by men who themselves were invisible.

Gough waited anxiously for his infantry. He had succeeded admirably in drawing out the enemy; but they were now swarming around him, and things looked critical. Some of them were within two hundred and fifty yards of the guns, and a few saddles had already been emptied.

But at this moment our infantry, both European and native, came upon the scene. The Leicestershire men had doubled most of the way across the rough plain; and being for a while in a dip in the ground they reached the plateau unseen by the enemy, and at once opened fire upon them when they were less than a hundred yards distant. But poor Wiseman was anxious to get to closer quarters, and shouting to the men of his company to fix bayonets and follow him, he dashed on to lead them in a charge; but fully twenty yards ahead, straight towards a gigantic Afghan who carried one of the standards, he ran, and reaching him, he gave him "first point" through the head, seizing the standard as he fell. All was accomplished in a moment. But during that moment Wiseman was alone. The wild Kujianis gathered around him, and struck him down with heavy knives and stones ere his men could succour him. At this moment Corporal Clarke reached him, and shooting a man whom he saw about to attack Wiseman as he lay on the ground, he took up his wounded officer bodily and tried to carry him off across his shoulder. But again the tribesmen gathered about him, and he, too, was struck to the ground with great rocks, which they hurled upon him and his burden; and it was while lying thus on the ground that he shot with his rifle (which he had fortunately reloaded) another man who ran up flourishing his knife. But the splendid effort of the gallant Clarke was of no avail. Some mistake arose as to a bugle call. The "retire" had been sounded, say some, but being unheard, in the din of the fight, by those who were far ahead, they were left thus to struggle against fearful odds for some moments at any rate. When the company advanced again they found poor Clarke badly wounded, and the brave-spirited Wiseman, whom the man had so gallantly tried to save, lying on the ground dead—mangled, indeed, almost beyond recognition.

Sadly I looked upon the poor gashed remains, and thought of the talk over the mess table, when they tried to persuade him to carry some other weapon than a sword. Who can tell whether it would have availed him—single almost as he was—amid that crowd of foes! Thus fell a brave-spirited young officer in the moment of victory; for his men, returning to the charge, carried out the movement which he had so pluckily led and swept the Afghans before them, rolling back the flanking party along the ravine and beating some of them into the open plain above.

But how fared it with the cavalry and guns? Gough's stratagem of firing and retreating had perfectly succeeded in drawing the Kujianis altogether from their cover; and although shell after shell was sent into the dense masses which were now covering the plain by the Horse Artillery, which had moved around to the right of our line, they were not disheartened, but pushed on with defiant shouts. Gough was watching for his opportunity. And it came. The flanking movement on our left had been shaken, and the party shattered by our infantry. That which was being attempted on our right was checked by the fire of the guns. The main body was scattered over the open plain in front of us, now dashing forward, now halting and hesitating for a brief instant. At that well-chosen moment Gough sent his cavalry at them. The Tenth Hussars went straight up the plain—some of them dismounting and skirmishing over the ground first—the Guides led by Battye bore off to the right over very broken ground to complete what our gun fire had partially done.

The Afghans fought with desperate valour.

Hand-to-hand combats were the order of the day. Whether a revolver would have been effective in putting *hors de combat* the standard-bearer whom Wiseman attacked is a question after all. For while the Hussars were fighting their way towards the *sungah*, one of their officers, who had been a travelling companion of mine part of the way through the Khyber Pass, and had then shown me with some satisfaction his brand-new weapon, with all the very latest improvements, had a hand-to-hand encounter with one of the Kujianis, who attacked him with his heavy sword-like knife. Twice did Manners-Wood shoot him, but the bullets seemed to have no effect on the vitality of the man. He then hurled his revolver at him, and though the man staggered from the blow for a moment, he succeeded in striking Manners-Wood to the earth with a down cut from his heavy knife, which penetrated his helmet, but fortunately only stunned the hussar. Still the Afghan would undoubtedly have killed him had not one of the troopers, named Hackett, at that moment come up and shot him with his carbine.

The fight all over the field was a fierce one, but nowhere more so than on our right, where the gallant Battye was leading his Guides. The Kujianis had gathered there in a dense crowd. The ground sloped down into a broken ravine. And here among the rocks and boulders the cavalry could not work, but the enemy could find perfect cover. For a few moments ere they reached this spot the keen curved blades of the Guides could be seen flashing in the sunlight as they wrought deadly havoc among the fugitives who had not gained the shelter of the rocks. Now the plain in that vicinity was cleared, but the broken ground was swarming. Battye determined to drive them out of their shelter, and to this end, followed by a few of his followers, he began to pick his way carefully among the boulders. Most fiercely was the fighting renewed, the Afghans on foot having manifest advantage over the mounted Guides, whose horses many of them they hamstrung as they

DEATH OF BATTYE.

To face page 199.

passed. And now blood was seen streaming down Battye's leg and over his saddle. In the charge just made two bullets had pierced his thigh; but he had uttered no sound, neither would he pause even to have his wound bound up. The keen soldier was intent on his work. He *would* drive these Kujianis out of their rock shelter at whatever cost.

Suddenly he came upon a group of them, desperate and at bay, behind a natural rampart of stones. They fired—several of them together—and Battye's horse, with a ball in its head and another in its body, fell prostrate, bringing its rider to the ground with it. As he fell, however, another fatal bullet, piercing his arm and chest, penetrated to his lungs, and killed him. Intent on mutilation, perhaps, the fierce Kujianis rushed forward. But old Mahommed Khan, one of the senior native officers of the regiment, whose beard had grown white in the service, stood over the body and held them all at bay for a while. He was a magnificent swordsman, and his keen blade flashed above his head as he stood there like some hero of Paladin times to fight to the death. And it was to the death. Far outnumbered, and inextricably entangled among the boulders, the little band were overpowered, and the grand old fellow fell over the body of his chief.

But assistance came. Not that it could avail to save the lives of those who had fallen, but it could avenge them. Led by the tall, long-armed young subaltern, Hamilton, the other Guides who had been charging on the plain rushed up to find their leader dead. And terrible was the cry of vengeance that burst from their lips. "*Major Sahib mardale hain! Maro! Maro!*" "The Major is killed! Strike! Strike!" they shouted. A few moments sufficed to drive out or slay those who were holding the rocks, and then, spurring across the plain in their fury, they smote and gave no quarter.

From this point the enemy made no stand. Four hundred lay killed on the field, and many hundreds more were wounded. Our casualties numbered about forty, the Guides suffering most. In wild confusion the Kujianis fled back to their villages. And next day, after General Gough had blown up some of their towers, the chiefs gave in their submission and promised to behave peaceably for the future. And so they did. In a few weeks some who had fought in this very battle formed part of an escort and bodyguard for me and some others who were passing through their country.

This action was looked upon as rather a brilliant one. Our forces numbered only about a thousand men all told, while there were fully five thousand Kujianis opposed to us.

One scene at night after the battle was very touching. The body of poor Battye lay on a *charpoy* in front of his little tent. Around in a great circle stood his faithful Guides, who had followed him many a time in the wild conflict of the battle charge. The leader whom they loved was dead, and many of them wept like children. Presently one and another stepped forward from the line, and, laying one hand gently and reverently on the body, raised the other toward heaven and uttered vows of vengeance on those who had slain the man whom thus they worshipped. It was a scene weird and solemn as well as touching, the moonbeams glinting on the cold still form and on the swarthy faces around, fierce with the spirit of vengeance. But he, the gallant Battye, after his life of conflict and wild excitement, lay as a soldier taking his rest. He slept in peace.

CHAPTER XII.

Forward! towards the Jugdullak Pass — Strange Wounds—Night Packing—Reveille at Half-past Twelve—The Lost Subaltern—Night March to Rozabad—Fort Battye—Neemlabagh—Arrival at Safed Sang—My Quarters on the High Ridge—Yakub Khan Prepares to Come in—The Meeting—General Daud Shah—Yakub's Afghan Highlanders, Kilts and all—He Rides Through Three Miles of Troops — Queen's Birthday Celebration — Treaty Signed May 26th.

"REVEILLE will sound at 12.30 a.m., and we march at two o'clock."

So said a Staff man, who was passing my tent on the evening of April 24th, 1879. Glad enough we were to hear the orders. For nearly five long months we had been encamped on this sandy plain outside Jellalabad. Life, even with the little variations of frost and snow and rain and wind, and after that, long dry heat, together with outrages by the natives, and now and again a fight down the Pass, or forward towards the

Jugdulluk, had been weary and monotonous in the extreme. Anywhere out of this would be an agreeable change, whether forward to Kabul or back to India. The former course was at present out of the question. Shere Ali was dead; but Yakub Khan, who was following his father on the throne, was following him also in obstinately refusing terms. So we were to go forward. Indeed, Sir Sam Browne with a portion of the force had already gone on. Now the main body were to follow; leaving, however, a fairly strong garrison for the earth fort, which had been constructed on the site of our old camp. The tribes around Jellalabad were far too restless and dangerous to be left alone to work their sweet will.

In the evening I went down to hospital to look at the sick men for the last time before starting. We had been having better weather for a few weeks, and our sick list was happily diminished very considerably. One case, however, was a sad and curious one. A gunner of "I" Battery, "C" Brigade, R.H.A., had been badly wounded at Futtehabad three weeks before. He had been struck in the temple by a bullet, which was buried in his brain. Nothing could be done in the way of extracting it of course. But the poor fellow had lingered on, strange to tell, all these three weeks, unconscious but living. To-night he died; and one could not but feel that it was a happy release to the suffering lad.

Another case ended more happily. A man of the Seventeenth had been shot in the thigh at the same fight. The bullet, a round one, had circulated, and finally lodged in an obscure place, where it seemed likely to form a *sac* for itself. The doctors had probed, as I had myself witnessed, and tried to get at it, but failed. On the night of our departure, or the morning after, a new surgeon in the hospital, coming on the ground for the first time, set to work and triumphantly extracte the missile, to the man's immediate relief and his ultimate complete recovery.

As soon as I got back from hospital I set about packing. Not that any one of us had much to pack. But time was taken up, and one's ingenuity taxed to the utmost in getting things together into the smallest possible space, having a regard to the burden-bearing capabilities of the commissariat camels which were to carry one's baggage. The actual loading also required time and thought, for the idiosyncracies of the camel are many, as I well remembered.

Two young officers of the Sappers who were among those detailed to remain behind came in for a chat pretty late, and when they departed to their quarters it seemed scarcely worth while to turn in at all; so the work of striking tent and packing up proceeded at once. Other men were at it too. The night was pitch dark; no moon, and as yet no stars. All over the old camp lanterns were twinkling, and the grumbling of the camels was a familiar sound, reminding one of past experiences.

At half-past twelve reveille sounded, and thence for an hour and a half nothing was heard but the knocking out of tent-pegs and the shouts of the noisy native servants as they packed up and loaded the baggage animals.

When the start was made at two o'clock it was most difficult to find the route at all. In the broken sand the hoof-falls and the tramp of the men made scarcely any sound, while the black darkness only revealed the shadowy forms which were nearest to you. One man, a subaltern of a regiment which I know had marched ahead long before, pitifully shouted to me as I passed to tell him where the 51st was. He had become inextricably mixed up with some trenches in the rear of the camp, and had lost his whereabouts altogether.

I soon gave up the attempt to give my horse the direction. His instinct, and perhaps his sight, were better than my eyes, and I left him to follow his own way, pretty well knowing that he would keep in the track of others. We were only marching, of course, slowly, and thrusting my feet well home in the stirrups, I went to sleep, and had as comfortable a snooze, with scarce a moment of wakefulness, as I could wish, until the early dawn broke, and I found myself plodding on in the line of the 51st.

Fresh and cool blew the morning air as we halted for half-an-hour in order to "gather up the fragments," for there had been some straggling, and our line was stretching away a mile or more.

About eight o'clock we reached a place called Rozabad, where we found a very respectable fort, with a residence, and even gardens attached. The Ameer was accustomed to hold this spot with a small detachment of troops. Here we halted for the day.

The next morning, marching at four o'clock, we reached Neemli or Neemlabagh, our resting-place, in five hours. On the way we passed a military post where our men had put together a little defence, chiefly composed of stone *sungahs*, which they named Fort Battye, after the gallant fellow who had fallen on the field in front of this spot some three weeks before. In the cool of the evening before mess Colonel Acton and I rode over to look at the ground where the conflict had been. There on the extreme left was the dip in the ravine where Wiseman, of the 17th, met his death, the spot marked by a huge boulder. Indeed, big stones lay all around, some of which had been hurled with crushing force on the half-a-dozen of our men who had advanced to close quarters, and were engaged in a hand-to-hand fight. On the opposite side of the field was the rough broken ground, where, picking his way among the rocks which were sheltering the Afghans, Battye was struck down. Of course long ago all bodies had been removed or buried out of sight; and there were no signs to tell of the fierce struggle which had so lately raged over the ground, except in one spot, where lay a single dead horse, belonging to one of our hussars. The bullet which killed it had passed through the fleshy part of the rider's leg too. He was a mere lad, but his wound had not so far incapacitated him as to prevent him from killing his assailant. Strangely solitary looked now the great wilderness of stones! And it was difficult to imagine amid the quiet stillness of that evening hour, as the shadows gathered about us, that only a little while before thousands of men had been engaged in fierce struggle; and that the plain had been swept again and again by the charging horsemen both of the Hussars and Native Cavalry.

One more short march brought us to the end of our journey. The brigades of the First Division were now assembled under Sir Sam Browne at Gundamuk, or, to speak more correctly, at a spot called Safed Sang, or the place of the "white stone," not far from the village of Gundamuk. The legend is that as a bridal party of Kujianis were proceeding on their way with rejoicings they were suddenly surprised by a band of their Ghilzais foes, who attempted to seize and carry off the young bride. In her helpless terror she cried to Heaven, and Allah heard her, and transformed her into a white stone, which is to-day pointed out just by the ford of the stream.

The Headquarter Camp, where I was

located, was placed upon a lofty ridge, overlooking on the one side the rapidly descending ground, where the rest of the division were encamped, and on the other the whole expanse of country, stretching away to the still snow-clad slopes and peaks of the Safed Koh, or white mountain range.

In front of my tent the ridge precipitously broke down to a litttle valley, along which a mountain stream was breaking and babbling in endless pools and eddies among the rocks. On the other side a stretch of fair country, green and cultivated, met the eye; and a refreshing sight it was amid the stony barrenness which one could see far around on every side. Very pleasant, indeed, was the sound of that mountain brook after one had turned in at night, and the camp was still. Later on, when the snows had melted, and were pouring their torrents into the valleys, that stream rushed along almost with the voice of the loud-sounding sea; and when our imagination and our thoughts of home were keen, we seemed for a while to hear the thundering of the waves on the shores of our own dear land.

At last Yakub Khan, having exhausted every means of gaining his own ends, and driving us out; having raised the tribes against us, and seen them handsomely thrashed on several occasions, was prepared to throw up the sponge. Definitely he was coming in, to make terms and to sign a treaty of peace. How much of peace was in his heart, and how much of treachery (or was it only pusillanimous weakness?) time and subsequent events showed; but now as reigning Ameer of the country he was to be received with becoming ceremony and state. Day by day his progress from Kabul was notified, until at last he and his retinue had halted some ten miles off at this extremity of the Jugdulluk Pass. To-morrow he would enter the camp.

At early dawn the camp was astir. Troops of all arms were marching out towards the Jugdulluk to line the path along which His Highness would pass. Major Cavagnari, with two hundred cavalry, and accompanied by Mr. Jenkyns, the assistant political officer, had gone on some miles ahead. They first met the Ameer, and together they came on towards the camp. I had ridden out some eight miles with our Surgeon-General and others, who were not on duty, and presently we saw the august group approaching. Behind the Ameer, who was riding by the side of Cavagnari, were some of his chosen officers and friends, and towering high above the rest General Daud Shah, a gigantic man, not altogether prepossessing in appearance, though I believe in the subsequent troubles which ensued at Kabul he showed himself loyal and faithful to the interests of those with whom he had made treaty. It is difficult to describe the retinue of chosen troops which Yakub Khan had brought with him. In any case they would on this occasion have suffered through comparison with our smart fellows as they rode along. There were our two hundred cavalry, consisting about equally of men of the 10th Royal

Hussars and of one of our best native Lancer regiments; while the Ameer's cavalry were decidedly a ragged lot. Very irregular cavalry, indeed! No manner of order or dressing was kept; and their horses, whether from design or accident, were curvetting and prancing all along the path. Behind them came a body of infantry. And here the sight was positively ludicrous, for some of them had adopted a kind of Highland costume, kilt and all. Whence the idea originated no one knew. But these men marched along at their own pace—the shabby imitation kilts about their knees, their legs otherwise bare, and a strangely-shaped felt helmet on their heads—they presented a comical sight, and exercised the risible faculties of the men very considerably.

Presently Sir Sam Browne, surrounded by his own personal staff, was seen riding forward to meet the Ameer, and offer salutations. Then they moved on until together they entered the double line of our troops. For three miles they rode towards the camp, our men, cavalry, artillery, and infantry, reaching the whole way. As their destination was approached the 40-pounders of the Elephant Battery thundered out a twenty-one gun salute. No flash of admiration or wonderment at this military display passed across the impassive countenance of Yakub Khan. What he thought we could not tell. He looked depressed, but proud, and not without dignity. His followers made no secret of their amaze, especially when the big guns gave voice from the ridge above.

The Ameer's camp was pitched in the green valley below our line of tents. There, amid the tall cypress trees, the Oriental encampments add a new and effective feature to the landscape.

As soon as he was fairly "housed" the General paid him an official visit, which visit was returned next day. This ceremony took place, not in Sir Sam's quarters, but in Cavagnari's tent, which happened to be next to mine, so I had a very good view of what went on. A hundred men of the 51st, with the regimental band, formed a guard of honour, and a detachment of Bengal Lancers were sent to escort his highness; while the guns of "I. C." fired a salute from the top of the ridge.

Many were the visits which Cavagnari and his assistant made to the Ameer's camp, and long and weary the discussions which took place over the terms of peace. General Dand Shah took but little part in these. He was a true soldier, and had no taste for the quibblings of political arrangements. But the *Wuzeer* who had accompanied Yakub Khan was at home in these matters, and he contested every point. Cavagnari, however, was as keen as he, and perhaps a point or two keener.

While these negotiations were being carried on, every effort was made to impress the Ameer with a suitable idea of our military strength. On one occasion he was very ceremoniously introduced to some of our Gatling guns, of which one or two had been sent up. But when the moment of firing came, when impressions were to culminate, unfortunately the machinery jammed, and the affair ended in a fiasco. Alas! we have had occasions since then when our guns have jammed, and when results have been far sadder and more fatal.

The Queen's Birthday celebration just now came round, and the military demonstration in connection with this really did appear to impress the Afghans. The grand review of all the troops in the early morning, the salute of the thirty-one guns, the hearty cheers of the men, and the march-past, altogether formed a spectacle which was a good deal beyond what they were accustomed to.

At last, at four o'clock in the afternoon of the 26th of May, the treaty was signed in the tent of audience adjoining the Ameer's, the pen with which this was effected being afterwards secured by my friend Villiers, of the *Graphic*.

One of the main objects of this treaty was to place the foreign affairs of Afghanistan practically under our control. Also to guarantee that country against foreign—which really meant Russian—aggression, by the aid, if necessary, of British money and troops. The treaty further provided for the support of a British Resident, and a fitting suite and personal escort, at the Ameer's capital. Moreover, three valleys—the Kurram, the Pishin, and the Sibi—were to be transferred to our Indian Empire, while our British military authorities were to have complete command over the Khyber and Mechin Passes.

All surplus revenue of the annexed territory was to be handed over to the Ameer, after the expenses of administration had been deducted. He was also to receive an annual subsidy of six lakhs of rupees (nominally £60,000) as long as he adhered faithfully to his engagements.

This treaty was by no means unfavourable to Yakub Khan. It may be said he lost territory. But it was territory which had always been little more than a burden to him and his predecessors. He had never found it possible to hold in hand the wild Afreedis and other dwellers in the Passes, or to coerce them into the proper payment of rightful tribute. The possession, however, of these mountain gateways into the country, and that beyond it, constituted a vast security to us, and was of incalculable value in the carrying out of our foreign policy in that particular corner of the world.

How long this treaty stood, and how faithfully its terms were respected, the events of after-time tell us. They opened up the dark and treacherous page of our history in Afghanistan. Many of the black annals of 1842 were to be repeated in 1879. But this, of course, could not be foreseen.

Meanwhile preparations were commenced for the return of our troops to India, at any rate from Jellalabad and its neighbourhood. It was thought that their presence might remind the tribesmen of the locality—at no time very amenable to discipline—that their Ameer was under British influence, and might render them restless if not rebellious.

Yakub Khan and his people returned alone to Kabul, and our Resident was to follow later on.

The return down the valley and through the Khyber was one which promised much risk, especially as rumours of cholera on the route had reached us. It was now the season of intense summer heat, and it was debated much as to whether a few months' sojourn on the cool hill slopes adjoining might not be more beneficial, and less fraught with danger. But home counsels finally prevailed, and preparations were proceeded with.

Ere we returned, however, some of us were destined to see a little more of the country forward, and to meet with a strange adventure.

CHAPTER XIII.

A Dark Page in our History—Slaughter of 16,000—The Remnant at Bay—A Solitary Survivor—Burnes's Cantonments—Relics of a Lost Army Discovered—The Burial of the Bones—A Villainous Escort—Strange Stone Bridge—Ghilzai Man-Stalking—A Narrow Escape—A Mother's Plea for Mercy.

WHILE we lay at Gundamuk it was but natural that our thoughts often went back to the sad episodes of the former Afghan campaign of 1841 and 1842. Not very far from our camp—perhaps four or five miles—the people of the country still pointed out the remains of "Burnes Sahib's" camp, a few mud walls standing to mark the spot where our force, when going up to Kabul, were *cantoned* for awhile. Among them were Sir Alexander Burnes, Macnaughten, Elphinstone, and others. Then, after a period of garrison in Kabul, there came the sudden and fierce rising of November 2nd, 1841, when Macnaughten was treacherously slain while holding a parley with Akbar Khan in view of the British garrison who were on the walls of the city. After this came the episode of retreat. The force, diminished in number and weakened by sickness, were promised safe conduct through the passes if they would give up the city they had defended so long, and retire to India. They did so, or essayed to do so. And then the arch-traitor, Akbar Khan, who knew no honour, lined the cliffs *en route* with his fierce followers in overwhelming numbers. They hung upon the flanks of the retreating army, harrying them, and cutting off the stragglers day after day. Some 16,000 souls, of whom perhaps 4,500 were fighting men, the rest servants and camp followers, left Kabul. On they struggled with desperate valour, almost at the outset having to abandon their baggage. It was winter time, and the snow lay thickly on the road. Thus while multitudes dropped under the fire which ever poured upon them from the high rocks which lined the Pass, many, very many, perished from the cold, lying down at night in their bed of snow, and rising not again at morning dawn. At last, when bullet, sword, and cold had ended the struggles of almost all the native soldiers and camp followers, the miserable remnant of the force, consisting mainly of men of the 44th, a few Artillery men, and a score or so of officers, and numbering, all told, barely a hundred fighting men, with two or three hundred camp followers, reached the vicinity of Gundamuk, or at least a spot some eight miles from our present camp. The day before they had crossed the stream called the Surkh Ab, or "Red Water," fighting hand-to-hand with their foe for the passage. And now what more could they do? Strength was gone, and hope was almost dead. Six officers were chosen and sent to ride as hard as their miserable ponies would carry them to Jellalabad, some thirty-five miles off, where Sale and Havelock were gallantly holding out, to seek help. It was a forlorn hope, for the journey was fraught with fearful peril. How could six worn-out men ever anticipate a safe ride through a wild country swarming with fierce tribesmen. But they started. Meanwhile the handful of fighting men who remained gathered on the summit of a round-topped hill. And there, a desperate band, they resolved to fight, and, if no help came, to die, selling their lives as dearly as possible. And they did it. Standing shoulder to shoulder in old heroic British fashion, surrounded by a perfect sea of Ghilzai tribesmen, and the fierce warriors of Akbar, they held their foe at bay till all their ammunition was gone. Then the waves of the sea closed in and swept on and over them, for every man had fallen in his tracks.

And what about the forlorn hope? For a while fortune seemed to favour them. Half the distance had been accomplished without molestation. But at the village of Futtehabad (nigh unto the spot of our fight with the Kujianis a few weeks since) they turned aside —fatal mistake—and sought milk and refreshment from some of the villagers. It was given. But while partaking of it, all unsuspicious of treachery, the false villagers attacked them; and though they defended themselves with desperate courage, five were slain. One only, Dr. Brydon, an army surgeon, escaped. Fighting his way through the traitors, he gained the open path, and though pursued for many a mile, with his broken sword he managed to beat off his assailants and then distance them.

About mid-day on January 13th, 1842, a sentry pacing the walls of Jellalabad called aloud that he saw a mounted man slowly wending his way across the barren plain towards the city. Many glasses were levelled, and they could just discern a European supporting himself on a miserable country pony, faint with travel, and perhaps wounded too. Who could he be? they asked one another, as a thrill passed over them; for the very sight of the solitary stranger seemed to bring them forebodings of disaster. Slowly they led him through the city gate, faint, bleeding, covered with wounds, grasping still the fragment of sword which had been shattered in the conflict for life. It was Brydon, the sole survivor of the force which had left Kabul to return to India, and, with the exception of the hostages who were in captivity, the only living remnant of Elphinstone's army. Riding over the very same pathway as poor Brydon, when I was going back to India, how vividly did I recall Miss Thompson's marvellous picture, where with such strange fidelity she depicts the weary, wounded man clinging to his worn-out, gasping pony. It is the same path to-day, as you look out from the Kabul gate of Peshawar, with the selfsame solitary tree standing at the corner where it bends away to the left.

With the various remembrances of this old dark page in our history all around us, it was not strange that some of us desired to see a little more closely the very spots where some of these events had taken place.

One morning accordingly two of us rode out beyond our lines, and towards the Jugdulluk Pass, accompanied by an old Kujiani who knew the country around, and every spot of interest. The old fellow professed to remember well the time of the last campaign from 1839 to 1842. The names of our leaders then were familiar to him; Pollock and Sale, Elphinstone, Burnes, and Macnaghten. For six miles he led us across the stony plain, and by tortuous hill paths, until we came out upon a board stretch of country which led away, we could see, to the entrance of one of the Passes. And here on the flat ground, the hills away in the distance, and no cover or protection near, we found the remains of the old mud walls, and even the remnants of huts, which had once formed part of the cantonments of Burnes. He was our envoy to the Court of Kabul, and a most distinguished Oriental scholar and traveller. But for some time before proceeding to the capital he had been permanently "cantoned" in this spot. With sad interest we moved among the broken walls, and tried to imagine the scene of thirty-nine years ago, when in this spot the little European force were located and lived, surrounded by tribes who were at any rate hostile in heart, aliens in a strange land.

But there was more than this to see, and so we turned to our old guide, one of whose accomplishments, very important to us, was that he could understand a little Hindustani.

"*Larai ki jagah kahan hai, buddha?*" "Where is the place of fight, old man?" said we.

And the old man said not a word, but pointing with his finger forward, silently led us on. Away to our right, perhaps two miles off, we could see a conical hill rising out of the plain, round topped and solitary. The hill ranges were around it, but distant. It stood alone, a monument itself! We did not say much as we neared it. Both my companion and myself were thinking of the old tragedy and its consummation on that hill top. We thought of the devoted band who had struggled down the passes from Kabul, fighting every inch of the way; men, women, camp followers, and soldiers dropping in their tracks under murderous fire or savage attack;

or perchance lying down at night, weary of life, to rise no more. We thought of them—a diminished band indeed—sixteen thousand souls reduced to about five hundred; four thousand five hundred soldiers to a bare hundred—reaching the river four miles ahead and finding the ford and bridge barred by an overwhelming host of savage foes. But they cut their way through, and came on—thus far. And here they paused awhile, and then climbed the hill yonder to die. We could see it all again after a lapse of thirty-seven years. The little band toiling with painful effort up the hillside, and forming up on the top shoulder to shoulder—at bay. The fierce tribesmen gathering around, closing in more and more, the band of heroes lessening moment by moment; and then the great wave of the human sea around surging over them and burying them away out of sight—unshaken in discipline, undaunted in spirit, faithful unto death!

We reached the bottom of the hill. My companion, who had brought his photographic apparatus with him, and was anxious to get a view first from the base, waited to do it, the Kujiani with him. I slowly ascended, my horse, which belonged to a hill breed, climbing like a cat among the big rocks that covered the side. Soon I reached the summit, and prepared to look upon the very spot where our gallant fellows had made their death-stand. There it must be, I thought, towards the centre. And I made my way towards it. The summit of the hill was of fairly large extent; but as I came nearer the middle, I saw that there the surface seemed strangely white. What could it be? I hurried forward; and to my horror there I saw gathered together in a great heap the skeleton bones of that heroic band. There, where the men had fallen, their remains had been lying for thirty-seven long years, bleached by the sun, and swept by every tempest which had broken on that hill-top. It was a ghastly sight. But it was not the ghastliness so much as the sadness of it that struck me most of all. Alien feet had trodden around that hill summit; the wild shepherds who tended their mountain sheep and goats, Kujiani and Ghilzai tribesmen, all had looked upon that open sepulchre; but never before had foot of brother Englishman been there, nor had friendly eye lighted on the unburied remains. Here were truly the "relics of a lost army."

I shouted to my companion, who was still at the bottom of the hill manipulating his camera, and waiting for a peep of brighter light to get a good view.

The day had been gloomy, in consonance, I seemed to feel, with the sad sight on which I had been gazing. I understood now why our Kujiani friend had been quite content to stay below, while I went up alone. He knew what I should find; but he had told us nothing to prepare us for the sight. In response to my shout, Burke, leaving his camera, came hastily up, and looked with horror and amazement on what again revealed itself as we together came to the centre of the hill. They were truly the remains of our poor fellows. Probably when Pollock's avenging force, after relieving the "Illustrious Garrison" at Jellalabad, had marched on up the Passes towards Kabul, they had found the bodies here and had buried them out of sight by covering them with a great stone cairn. This, no doubt, had been subsequently rudely cast down by the Afghans belonging to the tribes around, and the bodies left shamefully exposed; the Mussulman creed allowing them to desecrate the place of sepulture, but not the dead bodies themselves. This was the general opinion. And, indeed, in connection with our own campaign we had cases where graves in which we had laid some of our men to rest were rudely broken open—outrage enough indeed—but the remains within not otherwise disturbed.

Burke brought up his camera, and from the top of a neighbouring height took a picture of the "Hill of Bones," as afterward came to be called. It was a gloomy, weird picture enough! All around the mountain spurs reaching down to the barren plain, the furthermost peaks still capped with snow. Yonder away the dark entrance to the Jugdulluk Pass. And here in the middle the one solitary round-topped hill—monument and grave at once. Two human forms could be discerned, myself and the old Kujiani, who had now been induced to come up too; we two looking down sadly on the gathered bones of the brave men, as they lay resting on God's earth, and looking up into the face of God's heaven.

When we returned to camp we unfolded the tale of what we had found, and arrangements were made soon after for the reverent burial of the bones. A detachment was sent out, and over the great grave they raised a tall obelisk, which no doubt still marks the spot.

Before this was done, however, a party of three or four of us desired to visit the place again, and indeed to penetrate farther towards the Jugdulluk Pass.

We found that for political reasons.

Cavagnari being just now in the midst of negotiations with the tribes around, there was an objection to our going alone. Still more so to our being accompanied by an escort of British soldiers. The presence of "Tommy Atkins" moving hither and thither at his own sweet will among the paths and passes of these tribes was not calculated to reassure them. It touched their pride too. Our "political," however, solved the difficulty by securing the kind attentions of the Khan of Gundamuk, who promised us sufficient escort and safe conduct as far as his territory was concerned.

Early in the morning we left our camp. About a mile beyond the lines we were to meet the Khan and his men. And sure enough, galloping around a bend in the path, we came suddenly upon them. Had we been out simply for a morning ride, and encountered them without any previous knowledge of what we were to expect, I think we should have drawn our weapons, and gone right at them, or else turned tail and galloped back to camp;

for a more murderous looking crew I never set eyes on. There were a round dozen of them, wild fellows of the Kujiani tribe; probably some of the very men who had taken part against us in the fight at Futtehabad a few weeks ago. Clothed in the coarse blue blouse, or perhaps white tunic which these people wear, rather I should have said, once white—long, long ago—with *cummerbund* presenting the usual array of cutlery, not Sheffield, and long *jezail* in hand, they appeared a veritable band of brigands, as they lay reclining by the wayside, waiting for our coming. The old man, the Khan, however, who was riding a little sure-footed pony—the rider as big as his steed—came forward, and through the medium of our interpreter, a native post office official, who had polyglot powers, reassured us somewhat. He would escort us as far as the Surkh Pul or " Red Bridge," and guarantee our safety thus far. The stream there appeared to be the limit of his kingdom; and over the men of the Ghilzai tribe who lived beyond he had no control;

indeed there appeared to be a feud between the two tribes, especially as now the Kujianis were supposed to be friendly towards the English. This Surkh Pul, crossing the Surkh Ab, was a full ten or twelve miles ahead, some distance beyond the Forty-fourth Hill, where the unburied bones lay; so we had a fair stretch before us.

When we started we found our escort split up into three parts. Two men at once made the pace ahead: the bulk remained in the centre, and a couple or three lagged behind. Despite the assurances of our Khan, we did not feel very comfortable, and we thought it wise, while his men escorted us, to keep an eye on them. I was detailed to go ahead with our advance guard, one remained in the rear, while the others stayed with the main body. Thus we progressed mile after mile, my men in the front making an astonishing pace. In some places the path took a strangely tortuous direction among the hills, twisting and turning in the oddest way; and it was necessary to ride at a trot to keep up with the two swift-footed Kujianis, for I was not willing to lose sight of them for a single instant.

When we reached the fatal hill we climbed to look once more on the remains which as yet lay exposed. A few days later they were reverently interred, and the Burial Service read over them.

Then we pressed forward, maintaining the same order of march, towards the Surkh Ab. About here the scenery was grander than anything we had yet seen. The path we were traversing was a Pass in miniature itself. The mountain range had closed in on either hand, and the sharp spurs, no longer barren and stony, but well wooded or grass covered, reached almost to our feet.

Presently we came in sight of the river, not a mountain brook, but a fine broad-flowing stream, coming round a bend in the hill on the right, and pursuing its course till one lost sight of it in a magnificent gorge on the left. For a moment or two I had ridden ahead, lost in admiration of the beauties which were opening out before me, strange enough in a land of barren hills and stony plains.

As I approached the river, the *pul*, or bridge, was before me, a little to the left. And here again was cause for wonderment. It was no light bridge thrown across the stream in rude, barbarous fashion; but a strong, well-built, stone structure spanning the river from bank to bank in one wide arch. Surely an engineer's hand of no mean skill had been at work here.

I rode forward and paused in the middle of the bridge, examining a big rent in the parapet where some of the stonework had been thrown down. It was well I did pause. At this moment a shout from behind, "Sahib! Sahib!" put an end to my observations, and up came clattering at a gallop two of our own native followers, one the post office interpreter, who entreated me not to advance a step, meanwhile gesticulating and pointing up the hillside on my left, and just across the stream. I saw nothing, but they did. While I had been curiously examining the construc-

INCIDENT AT SURKH PUL.

To face page 238.

tion of the bridge, the keen eyes of these men had detected on the side of the slope up the gorge a Ghilzai tribesman, *jezail* in hand, on the watch. What is more, he had detected me. Whether he was placed there as a kind of sentinel to watch the borderland of his tribe, and regarded me as a trespasser or not, I cannot say, but assuredly he marked me down, and was proceeding to action. A wise man he, too, at his own game! He was not going to risk a shot from a distance, though he could not have been more than eighty or a hundred paces away. Crossing the bridge, as I should presently do, the pathway bending round to the left would bring me close to the slope on which he was doing "sentry go." And when he was detected by our sharp-eyed people he was stealthily moving from rock to rock, stalking me with considerable skill. Presently he would have had a fair shot point blank from behind some big stone.

I paused, if I did not turn back; and sent the two natives on foot up the hillsides after the fellow. Helter skelter they went, climbing from point to point, until at last they ran their quarry to earth, captured him, and brought him down to us.

Great was the glee of our Kujiani escort. It was a Ghilzai sure enough, a tribal foe of theirs, and therefore to be incontinently slain. His *jezail* was carefully loaded, and ready for immediate work. The fellow had not much to say. He knew the manners and customs of his neighbours, and I do not suppose he thought his chance a rosy one.

But, presently, springing from the heaven above, or from the earth beneath, for there was no sign of human habitation anywhere near, his old mother, led by another son, appeared on the scene. With a mother's eloquence, and many tears, the old woman pleaded for the life of her son. No word was uttered to our Kujianis. What would be the use? But Englishmen were different; and she passed round our little circle, as we sat by the brink of the stream, timidly touching each man's beard, or failing it, the place where the beard ought to be. It was a strange act, and yet in itself eloquent. By it she claimed our mercy on behalf of her boy.

Of course, we had no intention of either killing him ourselves or allowing him to be killed by our wild escort. Feudal foe or not, he was henceforth under our protection, and his life at least was safe.

But we did not trust him out of our sight while we remained there. And when on our departure we sent him off with his grateful old mother, we took the precaution of removing the flint from the lock of his *jezail;* and keeping some of his ammunition also. One of his bullets is now lying before me, and a villainous missile it is, a jagged stone rudely wrapped in lead; for the latter is a scarce commodity in those regions. Acting as an explosive, it would have made a pretty big trouble in my body, or anybody else's whom it might have struck.

Our Kujianis murmured loudly at our clemency in letting the man go with a safe skin. Besides he was their tribal enemy, and having caught him, they dreamt of no other course than to chop him up with their accustomed barbarity. Even when we had started on our homeward journey we had to turn back and drive on some two or three who were lagging behind, with the manifest purpose of trying to conclude the adventure in a way more satisfactory to themselves, by recapturing the Ghilzai, and finishing him off at once.

The mystery of the strong stone bridge spanning the Surkh Ab remains such still. When was it constructed, and who built it?

CHAPTER XIV.

Return to India in Intense Heat—Cholera Wave Sweeping up the Pass—An Unfortunate Start—"Budmash" Mules—The First Stage Down—An Al Fresco Bath—Jellalabad once more—Thirty Miles a Day—The Cholera Touches us—God's Acre—A Strange Thirst-Quencher—The Cholera Camp—A Sad Spectacle—We Shift our Camp in the Night—The Grip of the Sickness on me—A Hard Ride to Save my Life—The March of Death Begins.

WITH the signing of the Treaty our campaign in Afghanistan, for the present at any rate, came to an end. But what was the next move to be? Here we were comfortably settled on the ridge of Safed Sang—well, not exactly comfortably; for the heat in our tent was something to be remembered, the thermometer registering sometimes 12 degrees, the temperature falling at night as much as 50 degrees. This was intensely trying, even to the strong men. As to our sick, they fared badly indeed. One contrivance which was adopted very largely in the headquarter camp, was the "hutting in" process. A light framework of bamboo was fixed over the tent, and then it was filled in with a species of brushwood which was found in abundance thereabouts. Thus one's dwelling-place was completely concealed by this thatching, which being a foot or two apart from the tent all over, allowed the air to pass freely, and at the same time acted as a good protection from the intense glare of the sun. The Madras Sappers were very clever in these constructions. And presently the spectacle of the headquarter men dwelling in "leafy bowers," added to the picturesqueness of the scene; certainly it added to our comfort vastly.

But while the men suffered from the heat severely, and would fain have been back in India, there were serious points to be considered. It was quite certain that a march through the Khyber just now would be a perilous thing. The open slopes where we were encamped would certainly be at least cooler than the shut-in Pass. And besides, the rumours of cholera which had reached us awhile before, now became more than rumours. Steadily and with fatal certainty, the wave of dire disease having smitten the pilgrims to some of the sacred spots in North India, had been sweeping up the country and then across the frontier; and was insidiously creeping along the Pass. Already some two or three had fallen victims. Were our authorities prepared to march the force right down into the very jaws of death, or would they form a camp upon the cool slopes yonder, and stay here outside the zone of the sickness until the cooler months came round?

Long and anxiously was the question considered. The doctors were in favour of tarrying. Cholera outbreaks in India, where men had fallen by scores, and even hundreds, before the fatal blast, had taught them lessons of prudence. But for all that the desire to get home was strong; and finally it prevailed. On the 29th of May orders came out that the force was to be retired; the first detachment marching at daybreak on the 1st of June.

Accordingly on that morning the gallant 10th Royal Hussars and "I. C." Battery left on their journey back to India. Already the cavalry regiment had been sadly reduced in numbers, what with their fatal river accident, and other casualties with which they had met during the campaign. But it would almost seem as if a yet darker experience was before them.

The next day the merry little Ghoorkas marched away, to be followed by their staunch comrades of the 4th Battalion of the Rifles, who were always brigaded with them. Between these two regiments a very keen feeling of *camaraderie* existed, which no difference in colour seemed to affect.

In this way the force was detailed day by day; until on the 9th of June it was anticipated that the backs of the last detachment would be seen, when our Guides cavalry, with their faces towards India, would march from their camping ground.

On the 5th or 6th it was probable that nearly all the European portion of our force would have got away; so I made arrangements to move then. Colonel Hunt, of the Commissariat, was going down at the same time, and we determined to join forces and make the first stage, a distance of perhaps ten miles, starting in the afternoon. It was none too safe even now in the wild country between Gundamuk and Rozabad. Only a short while before we had two or three cases of native camp followers being cut up by the fellows from the hills, who infested the road, chiefly for purposes of pillage, especially in the evening and night time. Still we thought, though not marching with the troops in the morning, that we should be sufficiently strong, with our combined forces, to face any possibilities of that sort; Hunt would be sure to have a few European commissariat men with him, besides our armed native servants.

My "indent" on the Commissariat Department for transport was attended to, and three strong-looking mules were sent to me to carry my baggage. My previous experience of baggage animals had always had to do with camels; and while their grumbling propensities, their stupidity in always getting up when the load was half on, and their slow rate of progress, were sufficiently trying, I now found that I had to do with beasts who were positively diabolical in their wickedness—some of them.

We succeeded in loading up two of the creatures. The burdens were not heavy, as we wished to push along. Then we began to tackle the third. He was the meekest looking mule one could pick out in all the commissariat lines. All the time we had been engaged with his companions he had stood with nose to the ground, apparently pondering sadly over his lot. But I fancy a close observer might have detected a wicked leer in the corner of his eye, as now and again he looked around to see how his companions were faring. This mule had a character to maintain, though I did not know it then; and this character he would not allow to suffer even on the present occasion when carrying the parson's goods and chattels. We proceeded with him. The remnant of baggage was safely placed—and almost secured.

Now was the moment of supreme opportunity for which that diabolical mule had been waiting. I was adjusting a cord or strap on one side, and standing fortunately near the head of the animal; a 17th man who had come to give my servants a help, was holding on to the other side, when suddenly I beheld a vision of heels in the air, higher than I ever believed it possible for mules' heels to reach, and I was dimly conscious of my baggage, in portions, raining down from the sky, towards which they had rudely been propelled. Oh, that meek-looking mule! How we all loved him! Again the process of loading up was carried through—partially, but again with the same result—until at last I sent him back as an incorrigible "budmash" to his own lines, and asked for another mule in his place. I found that his return was quite expected, for his repute had long ago been established.

When his substitute had been obtained, and the baggage safely placed and secured, it was getting late in the afternoon. Colonel Hunt, sympathising with my misfortunes, but weary of waiting, had gone on. I resolved to make a start, hoping to catch up him and his men a mile or two outside the lines; and our strong party combined would ensure our safety the rest of the distance. But though I pressed on rapidly, and the mules made a good pace, no sign of the party was to be seen. I was now four miles out, and the shades of evening were beginning to descend. Discretion told me that I ought to "right about face" and return to camp. And this I very reluctantly did, getting back to my old quarters, where now only the thatchwork remained, for the tent had been struck about seven o'clock. The General and Colonel Macgregor, our smart chief of the staff, took compassion on me, and gave me some dinner. And I turned in under my leafy shelter betimes, so that I might make an early start in the morning.

About five o'clock we were off. But early as we were, the Fifty-first had been gone a full hour. The morning was singularly bright, and the keen air freshened one up in body and in spirits too. Just before getting into Rozabad we came up with the Fifty-first, who had evidently marched at a good pace. They were resting here for the day, and going on another march on the morrow. Their mess tent was soon pitched, and in a little while we were trying, with fair success, to get rid of a hunger which our ten miles' ride in the early morning had aroused.

My mules, which I found to be a capital trio, able to step along at a good pace, were unloaded, and we camped beside a little stream which ran near us, making a little oasis in the dry waste. Here, after breakfast, I had a very refreshing bath, and having rested a few hours we prepared to push on to Jellalabad, which was some seventeen or eighteen miles farther. My own horse I had sent on quietly two days ago, and I knew he would be awaiting me at this next stopping-place. A friend's horse which had to come down to Rozabad had served me thus far from Gundamuk, but the second part of the journey I had to be content with a Dâk (Post) horse, which was a very different beast altogether.

On account of the long distance to be covered, we were compelled to start again in the very heat of the day; and soon we had left behind us Rozabad, with its little stream and pretty garden—a green spot in the great desert. On we went, mile after mile, until just as the sun was setting we discerned the walls of Jellalabad in the far distance. It was not a pleasant journey in any sense; the heat was intense, and the necessity for keeping a watchful eye all around for any wandering Afghans who might covet my mules and baggage added the zest of anxiety. Fortunately we were not traversing hill paths or gloomy passes, where these fellows so often used to lie in wait. It was for the most part open desert where concealment was not possible. One band of armed men I fell in with, none of whom would get a good character, if looks went for anything. I took the bull by the horns here by riding up to them and attempting to engage them in conversation until my baggage had passed on a long way ahead, when I followed, after mutual salutations, at a gallop.

We were pretty well done up as we passed through the old gate of the city and out again at the other side to reach our camp beyond. We had done a big march of nearly thirty miles in one day; and with baggage mules this was very good indeed.

I found the camp, which was pitched now within the limits of the earth fort, was crowded with detachments and others coming down from the front. Mightily surprised was Colonel Hunt, who was to have been my companion from Gundamuk, to see me, when we met at the Rest-house mess table. He thought he had been pretty brisk in getting down in two marches; but the thirty miles in one day was a little beyond him. He told me that he was going to negotiate the next dozen miles or so by means of a large raft on the river. This mode of conveyance had been utilised for the transport commissariat and other stores, and it was a much cooler and pleasanter way of travelling than on horseback.

We had bad news here in Jellalabad concerning the cholera. It was quite true that we were marching into the very jaws of it. Indeed the fatal wave had already touched Jellalabad; and many cases had occurred farther down. I took the opportunity of visiting our little cemetery. It lay now nearly a mile and a half outside the fort, and as far as I could see nothing as yet had been disturbed. There was the long trench-grave of the poor fellows of the 10th Hussars. There, the spot that marked Battye's resting-place; and by his side Wiseman's, and others. The remains of my old dug-out church also could be seen, looking oddly out of place in the desert without its tent, roof, and walls.

The march next day was a long one—eighteen miles—to a post called Barikab; and a more trying and dreary journey I never had. The heat was very intense, and our thirst was excessive. In my holster I had a bottle of lime juice which I was carrying to a man farther down. Not a drop of water was to be got; and at last in desperation I sucked a little of this lime juice with some sugar that I happened to have with me. It was a foolish thing to do, for naturally it only increased tenfold my thirst. I soon found this and desisted.

At three o'clock in the afternoon we reached Barikab; and at the entrance to the little camp found some native stalls, where buffalo milk, amongst other things, was to be bought. I think I must have swallowed a round quart. This proceeding, too, was not the wisest after my dose of lime juice.

At Barikab I found a small detachment of Sikhs under a European officer encamped just outside a little native fort. A refreshing "tub," which was attained by squatting on a chair in a hut and letting the water-carrier teem water over me, seemed to set me all right for dinner in the evening, which Yeilding, who was in command of the Sikhs, hospitably provided.

He gave me a bad account of the place. Cholera had already smitten it with fatal severity. His own men had been dying rapidly. The "Rifles," coming down from the front, had marched right into it, and were encamped a mile or so away on the plain with a great many cases. In the evening I went over to see them. I saw the little group of tents at the end of the camping ground, with the red cross flag flying. And these I found crowded with the sick men, mostly cholera cases. The doctors were working among them with their invariable devotedness. But alas! so little seems to be possible in successfully coping with the fell power of this very demon of disease. Here were men just stricken, and in the first agonies of the sickness. There others with the terrible cramps. And yonder one or two with the unmistakable signs of collapse: the clammy perspiration, the sunken eyes, the dulled brain, and fading consciousness. Oh! it was sad to see, and to feel that one could do so little to help!

I went back to our dinner; but it was little that one could eat. The Sikhs had been falling victims too rapidly, as the natives always seem to do when the epidemic breaks out.

I turned in, feeling very poorly indeed. About one o'clock in the morning Yeilding looked into the hut where I was lying on a native *charpoy*, and told me to turn out, for he had to shift his camp, so many of his men had died.

This was a regulation. After a certain number of fatal cases it was hoped, by moving from the spot, that the fatal influence might be averted. I turned out and began to put my things together, but I knew that the fatal sickness had laid its grip upon me, for all the indications had come. Chlorodyne I had with me, and a little brandy I was able to get, and with these I endeavoured to check the symptoms.

I was not a bit surprised at the attack. What with the lime juice and the milk, but especially the fatigue induced by the long marches and the hot sun, I was a perfectly fit subject for the epidemic. I do not believe in any contagious or infectious influence in the case of cholera; and I never had the slightest fear of going freely among the men in the hospital, and helping with them as far as I could render any help. The influence, subtle and noxious, is in the air, as it seems to me, perhaps in germ form, and comes upon all alike in a given locality, gripping, however, those only who are in a receptive state, by reason of weakness or fatigue.

We changed our camp, going some two hundred yards off, and finding shelter within the mud walls of the native fort itself. I told my syce to load the mules with the baggage, and go on with the "Rifles," who were marching from the spot about three o'clock in the morning. Utterly exhausted, I lay down again and tried in vain to sleep off the choleraic symptoms.

At five o'clock I got up. I felt that something must be done. To die here like a rat in a hole would be wretched. Medical help there was none at hand, for the "Rifles" had gone on, and only a native apothecary was with the Sikhs. Twenty-five miles farther down I knew the 4th Ghoorkas were, and their skilful doctor had helped me before. Could I reach them? There was my good horse tethered near me. I knew that he would carry me staunchly, light weight that I was, if I could only sit on his back in my weak state. But then the Pass was not safe. Indeed it was the most dangerous bit of the whole march, said to be infested by the hill men, and I should be alone. What was to be done?

A few native cavalry were attached to every outpost, as occasions often arose when messages had to be swiftly sent; and Yeilding, who commanded here, said I might have a couple of *sowars* of the 10th Bengal Lancers if I cared to ride with so small an escort. I jumped at it. Something must be risked, and

I did not feel inclined to give up the struggle while a chance remained. When a man's pluck fails, and he gives up, in cholera, he dies.

Painfully and with difficulty I climbed upon my horse, and with the two native Lancers, with their fluttering pennons behind me, rode forth. Truly a "March of Death" had already begun. But much of sadness and of horror were to be witnessed before it came to an end.

CHAPTER XV.

The "March of Death" continued—My Gay Escort—Tracks of Death—Fallen by the Way—The Lonely Grave—A Gallop for Life—The Perils of the Pass—Good Escort Work—A Halt at Basawul—The "Rifles" En Route—The Dead Colonel Borne Along—My Escort Done Up; Get Fresh Men—Dakka Fort—Shadow of Sickness and Death—The End of my Twenty-five Miles' Gallop—Rest at Last, and Life—A Staunch Horse, and his end—Men to be Buried—"Dandy" Transport—The Nemesis of Laziness—Lundi Kotal Hospital and its "Padres"—Last Stages—Farewell to the Ghoorkas—A Tough Old Veteran—Home Again—The Later Dark Page—Russia and Afghanistan—England's True Responsibility in connection with India.

CLINGING with difficulty and pain to my saddle, I rode forth from the gates of that old fort at Barikab. Behind me were two staunch *sowars* of the 10th Bengal Lancers, their picturesque costume seeming strangely suited to the wild country through which we were passing. As we galloped along the gay fringes of their *puggaris* streamed out on the morning breeze, the red pointed cap peeping up from the centre. This was their head gear. Their tunic of *khaki* was held in by a bright-coloured cummerbund, and the pennon of their lances fluttered like a streak of scarlet with every movement of the horses. Away we went, all three of us experiencing, no doubt, a sense of relief at leaving behind, as we thought, *the* spot of death.

The keen morning air had an exhilarating effect upon us all. The horses galloped freely, and presently it became less of an effort to me to ride.

But death was before us, as well as behind. The "Rifles" had marched some hours before; and hitherto we had seen no one but some of the men of the country passing along with loads on their backs. Suddenly in the distance we descried a group, evidently of our own men—the *khaki* colour told us that—standing together around a spot some little distance to the left of the bridle path along which we had to ride. Who were they? What were they doing?

BURIAL OF QUILLEN, RIFLEMAN.

To face page 265.

We drew rein as we approached, and slowly rode along. As they saw us coming near I was recognised, and one of the group came forward. Alas! we were riding in the very tracks of death. It was a poor fellow of the Rifle Brigade, who had fallen by the way, carried forth from the camp sick unto death; or, perhaps, stricken on the very road—for the smiting of the cholera fiend is awfully sudden—strength and life had failed; and even as the breath went from him, his comrades paused on the march to lay him to rest. Poor Quillen! his grave is a lonely one indeed. Would I stay, they asked, and read over him, or repeat the words of Christian prayer which are enshrined in our Burial Service? I turned aside, and, joining the little group, dismounted. The scene was one which will ever be engraven on my memory. The early morning hour! No busy life to disturb the stillness of nature! The great hills in the distance bright with the early risen sun! And here the one solitary group of men standing about the grave of their comrade—the lonely grave—where presently they were to leave him in his sleep. Behind the group, the three horses held now by the native *sowars*, who had quietly dismounted too, and whose bright uniform gave a little gay colouring to the otherwise sombre spectacle. As I stood in front of them, no garb of church, except a white collar, to mark my calling and office, and repeated the words of Christian prayer and comfort and hope, they seemed to fall with strange, soothing effect upon our hearts. All the surroundings lent themselves to the peculiar solemnness of the scene. I saw one or two rough warriors rubbing the back of their hand significantly over their eyes. Hardened in body, perhaps, but tender still in heart. There were two officers present, Captain Fitzherbert, who had first approached me on the path, and young Lieutenant Lord Ossulston. How well I recollect the appearance and bearing of the latter. A great awe seemed to have fallen on him. Silently he gazed into the grave, which had been hastily dug, as if he could not look away from it. Had he then a premonition of what was even at that time hanging over him? Who can tell! But sure it is that within a week or so the sickness had stricken him also, and he had fallen. The cholera is no respecter of persons. Humble "Tommy Atkins," and his lordly officer alike, are touched by its fatal hand; and in death and the lonely grave the comradeship is maintained.

The little service over, sadly we turned aside, leaving the group still tarrying there, while some of the men were filling in the grave. Presently we were pressing along at a hand-gallop again, the horses nothing loth to go ahead.

Passing out of the comparatively open country, with its little road across the plain, we were now entering again the gloomy Khyber Pass. Oftentimes the towering cliffs seemed almost to close in upon and bar our onward march, until a sudden bend in the bridle-way brought us into the open again. But the path twisted strangely enough around the rocks hither and thither; and we began to meet more frequently, and sometimes with startling suddenness, the usual armed Afridis with which some of the more lonely spots seems to be peopled. My *sowars* were a splendid escort, understanding fully the genius of the country and its people. Possibly they had been recruited from the frontier. As long as the path was open and all could be seen ahead they rode abreast behind me; but as soon as the path began to twist, when a sudden bend might bring us face to face with some hidden foe, one of the two invariably rode ahead, the other remaining behind, with me in the middle. As soon as the path opened out again and was straight away my leading man fell back to his comrade's side.

In this way mile after mile was negotiated. The fresh morning breeze had so exhilarated me at first that I felt able for anything; but presently this temporary fillip wore off, and I began to feel weak and ill again. More than half the distance remained to be accomplished, and it was a grave question with me whether I could stick on my horse's back long enough to do it. So we galloped on, the horse not flinching a moment from his work. But it was different somewhat with the *sowars*. They were big men. And though their horses were tough and well-seasoned they were scarcely up to a twelve mile gallop off-hand.

At Basawul, the half distance, we pulled up. Here we found a temporary camp and a small detachment of the Ghoorkas; but the rest of the regiment were still a good thirteen miles ahead; and that is where I had to be as quickly as possible, for the doctor was there. This was being increasingly borne in upon me.

The Rifles, too, had marched thus far, and sad accounts I had from some of them. Death had been in their tracks all along. One officer, Colonel ———, not of their regiment, had been brought along in a *doolie*. The sickness had attacked him some days before, but with marvellous pluck he had resolutely fought against it. He would not give in; and the doctors thought he would at last pull through. Still the cholera kept its grip upon its victim, and the symptoms scarcely abated. On this morning he was being borne along, the curtains of the *doolie* closed around of course. But when they came to the end of the march, and the native bearers lifted the curtain to carry out the sick man, they found him dead. Weary nature could fight no longer, and without a word, or a groan, he had breathed his last. Probably for many miles they had been carrying only the dead body. There were specially sad circumstances connected with his death. His wife had come from India to the borders of the frontier, and indeed over it, as near to her husband as she was permitted. She had learnt of his sickness, and wanted to nurse him back to health; but her task of love was destined not to be fulfilled, and she never saw her husband again.

Bolton, who was commanding the Ghoorkas at Basawul, got some breakfast for me, of a rough sort; but I could not take it. A little more medicine and a piece of bread were all that passed my lips: then I prepared to press on again. I was fortunately able to change my escort, and get a couple of fresh *sowars*. Those who had come with me thus far were beginning to wonder who the mad rider was whom they were escorting, who galloped on and on, and scarce ever slackened rein. They did not quite understand that he was riding for his life.

We passed the "Rifles" on the way. They were continuing their march also towards Dakka, and terribly weary and low-spirited the poor fellows looked as they trudged along, often pausing to sit down by the wayside, as if they could scarcely drag themselves on. I stopped now and again, and tried to cheer some of them up with a few words of greeting and encouragement; but I fancy they came only from the lips and not from the heart, for I felt despondent enough myself.

At last we came in sight of the old mud fort of Dakka. As I have already noted this is an extensive and fairly strong place. Within the walls are rows of huts, where the Ameer's troops used to be quartered. Now it was one of the main halting places of our men as they marched down. And here I found gathered a curious assemblage of men from all regiments. Some detachments had just come in, and were remaining only for the night. Others seemed to be in permanent quarters. Just inside the gate I found some of the enterprising natives had set up a few stalls and were selling "Europe" and other goods at exorbitant prices.

I dismissed my escort with a good *bakshish*, for which, though soldiers, they seemed as gateful as any other natives, and then turned into one of the mud rooms and sat down to rest on an old box, which seemed the sole piece of furniture there. I was thoroughly exhausted, and felt that scarce a pinch of vitality was left in me. But I must find the Ghoorkas, for that meant medical help. Alas! an inquiry elicited the fact that they were three miles away across the plain.

Rightly enough, their Colonel had thought that Dakka Fort, with its mixed multitude from all regiments, and its gathering of cholera patients, daily increasing, was no healthy place for his little men. So he had taken them out, and led them away over the plain these three miles, and there they were now encamped.

It was weary work climbing up on my horse again, both for him and for me; and slowly enough we set out once more. Each mile seemed then as long as three. But at last we came near the white tents which we had seen long before afar off. Reaching the mess tent I felt no longer able either to cling on to my saddle or to get off in any orthodox way. Chesney, the doctor, ran out, with one or two more. The poor horse with heaving flanks told its own tale; while I, almost dropping from its back, seemed in a worse plight. They lifted me off and laid me down on a rough mattress inside the tent. The doctor would not let me be touched or moved from the spot till evening. He told me afterwards that he thought I was in a state of collapse, and on a fair way to "knock out," as they termed it. The strange part of it was that the choleraic symptoms, which were so marked at the outset, had left me entirely, and nothing now remained but the weakness, almost unto death. If I could only recuperate, and get over that, I should pull through.

Presently, thank God, I fell into a slumber and slept there for a clear two hours. When I awoke I looked through the tent door as I lay on the ground, and there right in front was the dear old horse, and the *syce*, who had meanwhile come in with the baggage, giving him a good groom down. Now that the saddle was off, I could see how "tucked up" he was. The staunch, true beast! He had not failed me at the pinch. A full twenty-five miles had he carried in an incredibly short time; and I felt I could love him like a human being, for I believe he had saved my life. I never parted with him. He went back to India with me; but he did not thrive in the plains—the mountain land was his home. And in the end, since I returned to England, he contracted a sickness peculiar to the wet season in India, and had to be destroyed. He fell before a trooper's carbine, and in that particular it was a fitting close of life to the gallant old war-horse.

Dakka Fort was full of cholera patients. And there also were lying the bodies of many poor fellows who had died that very day. I had been seen riding in through the gates, and as I was supposed to be "available for duty," orderlies came after me to the Ghoorka camp in the evening to summon me to read the Burial Service. Of course I was unable; indeed, I knew nothing of it till afterwards, the medical officer sending back to report me sick. Skilfully I was tended and nursed, and when the regiment marched next day and on several succeeding days, I was carried in a "dandy," a comfortable kind of hammock slung on a pole. I had no strength to ride. Nor was I sorry; for through this I felt that the old horse would have easy marches, without a load to carry—a rest and luxury which was most thoroughly deserved. What, however, was my disgust, at the end of one day's march, to see him come toiling into camp carrying one of the native servants—a big, strong, hulking fellow, who could well have carried me on his back. He had noticed the unburdened beast, and knowing that I was ahead in the "dandy" and should not probably see his little game, he had seized the luxury of a ride. I felt justified in "going for" that rascal. The Colonel wanted to sling him up, and give him an honest dozen; but I tumbled out of my "dandy," and seizing a handy leather strap I laid on to his lazy bare legs with all my little strength, but with right good will.

All along the Pass we were in the line of the Death March. At Lundi Khana we came up with the 10th Hussars. They, too, were dropping their men by the way, and the mortality had already been very heavy among them. On the top of the Kotal the hospital was established. It became for a time at least a sort of permanent one, since this point marked the limit of the territory over which we had control under the treaty just made at Gundamuk. I climbed the hill, and managed to visit the men. I found another chaplain, Mr. Spens, at work here. He was a most devoted fellow, and seemed almost to live in a hospital; and many a poor fellow owes him a debt of gratitude. The Roman Catholic padre, too, Father Julius, was, as usual, to the fore with his quiet, kind manner.

Mr. Simpson, the genial correspondent of the *Illustrated London News*, became my *compagnon de voyage* here; and together we marched from day to day India-wards and homewards. He was a tough old fellow, sure enough! An old Crimean veteran, and having served amid many stirring scenes since, he had been with us throughout this campaign, no hardship of march or climate appearing to affect him. The country, with its old Buddhist topes and strange remains, was specially interesting to him, for he is an antiquarian of no mean standing, and since this campaign he has been thither again with the " Boundary Commission."

From Lundi Khana to Kata Khushta, where we were within a stone's throw of Fort Ali Musjid, and from thence to Shagai, where an Afridi was shot and toppled over the cliffs near to us by some of his own people, were short marches. The next morning Simpson and I marched with our friends to the Indian end of the Pass, and there parted from them, the gallant little Ghoorkas cheering us lustily as we said our farewells and galloped away. We felt, certainly I especially, that we owed much to the officers of the regiment who had welcomed us as comrades, and looked after us so kindly and hospitably. As for Chesney, the doctor, he will always have a warm corner in my heart.

The burning heat of Peshawar and Rawul Pindi, scarce less than the 126 degrees in our tents in the Pass, made as short a stay as possible desirable in those northern stations of our Indian Empire. Everyone was hurrying down through Jhelum, and on to Lahore;

and then south, by *Dâk Ghari* and rail, men were making their way as rapidly as the service could push them forward. And thus finally, after many strange vicissitudes and some few perils I came in sight of the white buildings of Lucknow, and the faces of home friends greeted me once again on the morning of June 23rd. So the first phase of our Afghan campaign came to an end; alas! to be renewed in a darker page of our history ere three months had passed over our heads. Even now the leaven of treachery had begun to work in the city of Cabul. And when presently our envoy, with his retinue, marched into the capital, though received with a show of hospitality and welcome, the spirit of fierce hostility was only slumbering in the hearts of the populace. Presently, as we know, it blazed out, and a weak and, perhaps, traitorous Ameer was powerless or unwilling to check it, or to prevent the deed of blood which stains the annals of those few fatal days. Gallant lives were sacrificed, men who were "faithful unto death." But with swift foot and sure hand inexorable Nemesis followed, and the day of retribution came.

It is not needful to enter upon a discussion as to what was gained by our action in Afghanistan. It would be more than possible to speculate on what was *prevented*. What new departures were being stealthily initiated, as the thin end of a wedge driven in, were known specially to those most conversant with Afghan and Russian affairs. One thing appears tolerably evident. The "Bear" turns not back. He only pauses and bides his time. Will that time, and its opportunity, now patiently being waited for, come ere long? The future only can disclose. Meanwhile let England be vigilant—always; and doubly vigorous in smiting when the moment of dire necessity arrives, for most surely Afghanistan is not the final goal of that military Power which has been marching on with steady foot over the wide expanse of the Steppes, crossing the dark Caspian, traversing the great deserts of Tartary and Bokhara, and which pauses to-day, as for a moment of breathing-time, on the banks of the Oxus. India is the fairest jewel in the diadem of our Queen. We hold her, and with her a burden of vast responsibility from the King of Kings, the Ruler of Earth's Nations. It is for us to see that we make the jewel brighter with the light of Christianity; the fair land fairer still with the "beauty of holiness." Do we accept the charge? Shall we flinch from the duty?

CHAPTER XVI.

Clarions of War in the East—Causes of Egyptian War—Mohammed Tewfik Viceroy, and Ahmed Arabi Pasha—An Alien Government—England's Interests in the Nile Valley—The Suez Canal—Naval Demonstration—Massacre of 11th June—The Egyptians will Fight—Bombardment of the Forts—Charlie Beresford and his little "Condor"—Incendiarism in the Town—Deeds of Blood all through the Country—Beresford's Police—Military Expedition from England—My Summons—Sir John Adye—Getting my Kit—"Tommy White's—Little Tailoring Mistake's—My Friend's Dilemma—Detailed to Sail with the Head-Quarter Staff.

THE clarions of war were sounding once again, this time from another corner of the globe. Egypt was now to be the scene of one of our little campaigns Up to the middle of the year 1882, people in England had heard nothing of any disturbance in that interesting little country of the Mediterranean. But it seemed that for some time previously what might be termed family squabbles had disturbed the peaceful serenity of the land of the Nile. The father of the family was not able to exert all the strong authority which ought to belong to that paternal personage, and the children, headed by a certain naughty boy called Arabi, were carrying on, to use a mild expression, in a very masterful fashion, and fairly ruling in the household.

Soberly stated, the facts, which were confirmed by subsequent developments, were these. Ahmed Arabi, a reckless and ambitious colonel of infantry in the Egyptain army, taking advantage of the widespread feeling of national discontent on account of the grinding oppression to which the people, and especially the lower classes, were subjected, by a system of taxation which crushed out the very heart of the *fellaheen*, and at the same time seizing upon and fomenting the soreness which the senior military officers were feeling as a result of the Khedive's late army reforms, headed a rebellion against Mohammed Tewfik, the Viceroy of Egypt, and

ARABI PASHA.

he, weak ruler as he then was, was powerless. There is no doubt that Arabi had not only the army but the people at his back. In fact it was a national protest against a government with a weak ruler at its head, and men alien to the country as its ministers; for it was notorious that all sorts of foreign adventurers were occupying the highest posts of government, even Cabinet offices; Turks, Armenians, Italians, Circassians, almost everyone but native Egyptains; and that under the oppressive tyranny of such a Ministry the whole land was groaning. Little wonder that the people were ready to follow with enthusiasm any man, especially one of themselves, who would rise up to deliver them out of their bondage. But Arabi, strong as he was, was not able to hold in perfect check the restless powers which he had aroused. Perhaps he was not over-anxious to do so. Certain it is that anarchy began to reign throughout the country, and an intense hostility to foreigners began to be manifested.

THE KHEDIVE.

England had vital interests in the Valley of the Nile which, it was felt, must be safeguarded. So, indeed, had France. Our £4,000,000 in the Suez Canal could not be hastily thrown away. Nor, indeed, the safety of our highway to the East heedlessly left in peril. The Khedive, who had honourably fulfilled all his engagements to us, must be supported. So it came to pass that an agreement was come to between England and France that a joint naval expedition should be despatched to Alexandria, first to demonstrate, and if necessity arose, to act. Our French allies fulfilled the first part of the agreement, but, strangely unlike them, when the time came for the second, stood aside.

About this time the Khedive, with strange vacillation, or perhaps impelled by the weakness of his situation, had appointed Arabi Minister of War. This was directly contrary to one of the terms of England's *ultimatum*, which demanded his exile as the only step towards the restoration of quietness.

The combined fleet had meanwhile sailed, and were lying off Alexandria, when the riot of the 11th of June took place, in connection with which some three hundred persons were killed and wounded, the British Consul, among them, being savagely beaten. When one speaks of the rabble of Alexandria one cannot get much lower down in the social scale, for this Levantine city seems to be the very cesspool where the scum of all the Mediterranean nations has gathered. And on this occasion this vile *residuum* of the population, aided by the thieving Arabs who swarmed in from outside, had the city for hours under mob law, while they belaboured with bludgeons or savagely slew with knives all the respectable Europeans whom they could lay hands on. The police looked placidly on; but at length order was restored by the Egyptian troops.

All this time Toulba Pasha, who commanded the city, was employing the troops in strengthening the harbour defences and mounting heavy guns wherever possible.

Against this the British Admiral protested. Toulba denied that any such work was going on, and certainly by day it seemed as if all were quiet. But when suddenly in the night the electric lights of the fleet began to flash across the forts and harbour, and revealed hundreds of Egyptians busy at work, denial or concealment was no longer possible. Admiral Seymour's *ultimatum* was now sent, that if by a certain hour the extra works were not dismantled he would certainly bombard. No response to this *ultimatum* was received, although a pseudo negotiation was attempted by a party of Turkish officials after the hour had elapsed, and which effected nothing.

At half-past six o'clock on the morning of the 11th of July the order to load passed round the fleet, and at seven o'clock the first shot was fired from the Alexandra. Eight ironclads and five gunboats took part in the bombardment. For twelve hours the boom of the 80-ton guns, the roar of the lesser one, and the rattle of Nordenfeldts and Gatlings from the tops of the vessels was continuous;

while a dense curtain of sulphurous vapour began to hang between the combatants. The Egyptian gunners stood to their guns right pluckily, and worked them with some effect. But the Armstrong guns, 12-ton and 18-ton, with which the forts were armed, were no match for the heavy ordinance of the British fleet. Besides, the Egyptians seemed to have but few shells, and used for the most part round and conical solid shot.

Lord Charles Beresford, commanding the little *Condor* gunboat, did a plucky thing. The guns of Fort Marabout, worked under good cover, were doing execution on some of our ships. Amid a perfect storm of shot which fell around and swept over the little vessel, fortunately, he dashed in; and standing close in shore, pounded away until he succeeded in silencing the troublesome guns.

Finally the batteries were shattered, guns dismounted, and outworks dismantled completely. Our casualties were only five killed and twenty-seven wounded; but the

Egyptians had lost in killed and wounded over a thousand.

Very amusing were some of the statements published in the Arabic newspaper by the native war correspondent. According to him most of the British ships were sunk outright; the total number engaged reaching twenty-eight.

After the bombardment the city became a prey to incendiarism and rascality. The blood-thirsty mob were plundering and slaying on every hand. It was necessary to put a body of marines and blue-jackets ashore; and these under Lord Charles Beresford acted as a very efficient police. Clearing the streets of the murdering gangs that were swarming there, with the aid of their Gatlings, and shooting at once those who were taken red-handed, they succeeded at length in putting an end to the horrors which for days had haunted the city.

Arabi and his forces had retired precipitately towards Kafr Dawar and Ramleh. All up the country at Tantah, Zazazig, and other places, massacres the most brutal had taken place; and it was evident that a strong hand would be required to effectually end the anarchy of the country.

In England these events, which were reported in the newspapers in outline, caused considerable excitement. The bondholders no doubt thought of their imperilled bonds. Others remembered that the Suez Canal, our highway to the East, was practically in the hands of the rebels, and might be destroyed or blocked at any moment. Others, again, spoke of the brutal massacres of English and other Europeans. A military expedition was inevitable, and the country accepted the dire necessity.

I was at this time home on short leave from India. For six months, coveted and long-anticipated, I was expecting to enjoy the happy companionship of friends, who for years past had only lived in my thoughts. I confess I had much thought about Egyptian eventualities, since I had only lately sailed out of the harbour of Alexandria on my way home. I therefore read the account of the bombardment with enkindled interest, and was able to imagine the scene in some small degree.

One day an official letter came which in brief amounted to this, "We shall probably want some chaplains; will you go?" I thought of my curtailed leave, and a few other plans which would have to be given up, and then sent my answer, "Yes." It did not take me long to make up my mind.

A few day passed, and the big official envelope announcing my appointment came from the War Office. I was just now busy enough with other matters, that there seemed neither time for bidding farewell to friends or making the necessary preparations. Thus, when a telegram was handed to me one Sunday evening in a certain northern town, curtly informing me that I was to sail on the following Tuesday at noon, from Queenstown, in the *Iberia*, with the Coldstream Guards, I felt myself in a bit of a fix. Not an article of my outfit had yet been obtained. My Afghan campaigning kit, even if at all suitable, was packed up in India, awaiting my return. What was to be done? To write and ask for any change of arrangements would scarcely be a prudent step. The Departments in the bustle of sudden emergencies cannot stop to consult the convenience of any single individual. It might end in the appointment falling through altogether. But I thought something might possibly be accomplished by going *in propriâ personâ*, and seeing the Deputy Quartermaster-General at the War Office. Hastily packing my bag, I set off to London, first telegraphing to a saddlery firm to meet me with a case of saddle equipment, such as I specified, ready packed at the station. Arriving there, I found it awaiting me. Off I went as hard as a hansom could carry me to Pall Mall; and there at the War Office saw Colonel K——, who in the kindest manner met my difficulty; putting in another man, a surgeon, to take my berth in the *Iberia*, and telling me that passage should be found for me in one of the transports sailing later in the week. I found the War

Office fairly besieged with officers making inquiries and seeking instructions, and everyone, from the highest officials to the under clerks, were hard at work getting through the press of work which had suddenly come upon them.

One act of kindness I shall never forget. Sir John Adye, an old and distinguished officer, who had passed through a long term of soldiering, and had seen active service in various parts of the world, was to be our Chief of the Staff. I found him in his office, like all the rest, pitching in to get the work through. When he heard I was going out as one of the chaplains he came to me most kindly with words of encouragement. "If ever you want any comfort," said the fine old soldier, "when you are out in Egypt, just come to me." He did not know at the time, of course, that I had already had a stern taste of soldiering in the wild Passes of Afghanistan. To him I was the young fellow just entering, with, perhaps, many misgivings, on an untried and rough field of labour; hence the considerate thoughtfulness which prompted the kindly encouragement. We often afterwards met during the progress of the campaign, sometimes in the midst of the thick of duty, and many a word of cheer did I receive from our Chief of the Staff. Nor indeed did his kindness fail afterwards in the reports of service which he made at the end of the campaign, and which stand in the War Office records.

But an outfit must be got, and everything must be ready in two or three days at most. I concluded my best course would be to go straight down to Tommy White's, of Aldershot fame. They, if anyone in the kingdom, would know exactly what other men were getting, and would be most likely to have all necessary things in stock, What a scene it was, to be sure! Like other places which were touched by the war preparations, this big emporium of the thousand and one things which a soldier needs in peace or war had caught the contagion, and all hands were working at full pressure. Here were men buying camp equipages of all kinds, portable beds, warranted to weigh a few pounds, and not to break down under eighteen stone; canteens with all appliances for the table, plates, knives and forks, cups, kettle, &c., packed within the limits of the big cooking pot. Alas! mine was looted just after Tel-el-Kebir. Some were laying in some stores of provisions; how they were to carry them no one knew. And others, in the tailoring department, were getting measured for parts of their uniform. By-the-bye, the special regulations with regard to this were tolerably strict; and some who wished to follow their own ideas as to what would be suitable in shape and looseness for the rough knock-about of a desert campaign had to put their ideas in their pocket, and confirm strictly to regulation. Scarlet blouses of a Norfolk jacket cut were *de rigueur* for the Head-quarter Staff, together with brown leather gauntlets, and many other little specialities. Each department and arm of the force had its own particular colour in the *puggarees* which were twisted around the sun helmets; these latter now white, but later on to be stained a light brown to accord with the sand of the desert. Some of the little special addenda which belonged to a man's kit in this Egyptian campaign were calculated to provoke a smile here in England; but many a man found the utility of these things later on.

One of our gallant troopers of the Life Guards, for instance, whom we are accustomed to behold in all the gorgeousness of bright cuirass and flowing plume, with smart breeches and jack-boots, presented almost a comical appearance in his looser and more serviceable costume now. *Puttees*, or cloth bindings, around the legs, in place of boots; a roomier tunic of blue, and no heavy steel cuirass; the white helmet, plumeless, but adorned with a blue veil, which can be let down at will, surmounted by a pair of grotesque goggle spectacles, to be dropped at pleasure over the eyes. A trooper at the charge, and thus in full fig, would suggest something diabolical, I can imagine, to the terrified Egyptians.

It can easily be understood that the difficulties of the tailoring department were especially multiplied just now. Everyone wanted his uniform ready in a day or two; and as was inevitable, in the hurry articles got sadly mixed, Captain Smith, who stood six feet and had no calves to speak of, receiving, in the place of his own overalls, those of his friend, Captain Brown, who was about five feet nothing high, and had a leg all the way down like an elephant's. These little mistakes would usually be discovered just as a man was hastily jumping into his uniform, preparatory to marching to the station *en route*.

Indeed, one of my friends, a chaplain too, had an episode of this character in his own experience, which afterwards caused both him and others many a laugh. He was to leave Aldershot at five o'clock in the morning. But his uniform, or at any rate the "overall" part of it, did not reach his quarters until pretty late the night before. He was busy packing, so he did not begin to get into his campaigning clothes till nearly 2 a.m. To his horror, the trousers, which slipped on easily enough, reached some little distance below his knee. He looked at them. Yes, they were a chaplain's overalls sure enough, the braiding all correct. But they were not his most certainly. In his dilemma a good-natured comrade ran down to the tailor's, knocked him up with difficulty, and after much search returned with the trousers in triumph. Those of the Roman Catholic chaplain, a little man, had been sent by mistake. It was nearly five o'clock, and hastily my friend donned his recovered trousers with a sigh of relief. But alas! all was not right yet. I know not what was really wrong, whether it was a misfit, or still a second time some other man's nether garments had been sent, but the fact remains that my friend had to pop into the waiting-room at the station, and with some friendly pieces of string arrange matters approximately to his satisfaction. There seemed to be a good deal too much room in this second edition of tailoring. We often have a hearty laugh over the start he made in that early morning.

I had put all my things in train for readiness, and expected them to hand in a day or two, when I received another summons from the War Office. I was detailed to sail next day from Liverpool in the steam transport *Capella*, with the Headquarter Staff. This was luck indeed! I knew it was a picked boat, and instead of a big crowd, as on the other transports, there would only be the members of the Staff, special service men, clerks, servants, &c.

Another run down to Aldershot sufficed to get my traps together, everything as ready as could be expected under the circumstances, and I reported myself on board by twelve o'clock on Saturday, August 5th.

CHAPTER XVII.

Embarking for the War—The Headquarter Staff Boat—The "Wolseley Ring"—Selection by Merit—Some Distinguished Names—Convict and Brigand Style—Board Ship Lecturing—"Gib," and First News of Bloodshed—Final Preparations—First Sight of Alexandria — Near Inspection — Dark Horrors—The Guards in Service Kit—Horse Dealing under difficulties: I Score a Point, however—Wolseley's Ruse—A Feint on Aboukir Bay—Seizure of the Suez Canal—We Steam towards Ismailia.

A DISMAL, wet Saturday afternoon! The steam transport *Capella*, No. 41, lying moored at one of the Liverpool docks! A great heap of boxes and cases of all sizes waiting to be put aboard! Men hurrying to and fro on the decks, and up and down the ladders! And yet no great confusion; for something of military precision was noticeable amid all the pressure and haste. Such was the scene which greeted me as I went on board, *en route* for Egypt. When I had reported myself to the officer in command, I had little else to do but watch the ever-changing scene. Stores for the front were being rapidly lowered into the hold. The multifarious paraphernalia of Headquarter Staff offices—chests of books and records—were being brought up under care of the Staff office military clerks; while here and there a little pile of personal effects, such as my own, for instance, were being packed away in some corner, until the berths were allotted. Two or three, like myself, were leaning over the side watching it all, and wishing we were off. But on the other side in a quiet corner, away from the rush, and apparently oblivious of all the noise, I noticed one man, a very distinguished officer, who was having a last half-hour's chat with the young wife whom he had so lately made his own. After adding to his laurels in Egypt, he came home, only soon to face the heaviest bereavement which can befall a man. It was a loss from which he never seemed to rally, and not a great while afterwards he himself sickened and died. Husband and wife both gone!

At last we had everything and everybody aboard that ought to be, and about four o'clock in the afternoon the vessel, loosing from her moorings, began to move slowly down the river. Our good ship, the *Capella*, belonged to the Star Navigation Line, and was practically a new boat, only having made one trip before, and that to Calcutta. Everything was spick and span, and looked almost brand new. It was evidently a picked ship, both for comfort and speed; and we anticipated a quick voyage, and a pleasant one. Wolseley was not with us. He had been laid up a little while previously, and it was thought advisable for him to go in another vessel, the *Calabria*, with the doctor who was looking after him, that he might rest, and be nursed, and get all the good he could out of the voyage. And, indeed, when he reached Alexandria, while looking a bit shaken after his illness, he was pretty well ready and fit to face the hardships of campaigning once again. But we had with us his own personal Staff and the Headquarter Staff, in fact, what the enemies of "our only General" will persist in calling "the Wolseley gang or ring;" and I must confess I was a little curious to see the material of which the famous "ring" was composed. Very few distinguished Generals have been subjected to so much criticism, hostile, and otherwise, as Wolseley has been. He has had very much to do with carving out his own fortune; and when a man, by energy of character as well as inborn genius, does that, he usually makes some enemies for himself. The Service is not free from the envyings and jealousies which afflict civilian circles, as Wolseley has found in his distinguished military career. But his star has been usually in the ascendant; and success has most often followed his banner. I feel sure, however, that he would be the first to acknowledge that much of this success is due to the splendid human instruments whom he has picked out here and there, from this quarter and from that, for the carrying out of his plans of work. "Always the same men," say the critics; "just the ring."

Exactly so ; and naturally so ! Wolseley has always shown a rare faculty of discernment, a quickness to perceive genius, and a capacity for hard work, which is often another name for genius. And when he has found such cases, one from this arm of the Service, and one from that, he grapples them to himself, brings them into his "ring," and leads them on to distinction. These and other special service men were to be my temporary parishioners, and I began to look around to see who they were. General Goodenough, the genial gentleman and the scientific soldier, was senior officer, and therefore commanded on board. Then we had Grenfell and Grove, indefatigable Staff men, the former of whom is now Sirdar of the Egyptian army. The late Sir Owen Lanyon, too, was with us, modest hero of many a West and South African exploit. And the Duke of Teck, by no means the play-soldier that some people imagined him to be ; for he served in his first campaign, as he told me, when he was but twelve years old. Among the special service men there was Watson of the Engineers, faithful henchman of General Gordon in the time of his first Soudan Governor-Generalship ; and Conder, of Palestine exploration fame ; and Lawrence, one of the grand old Indian family, and a "chip of the old block," too, for he won his spurs in this Egyptian campaign, and for distinguished service gained his promotion, becoming at the age of twenty-five the youngest major in the British Army. And again there was Macgregor, "Rob Roy's" brother, who feared God, but never man. These, and other such, were the men who kept the great war engine in trim, wheels within wheels, working together in perfect harmony, so that Wolseley's plans were brought to a speedy and triumphant issue. No wonder he chose them again and again. They were tried men, and never failed him ; staunch and true soldiers every man of them.

The second day of our voyage a dismal fog set in. Everyone, of course, was eager to get on ; but this fog effectually checked us.

Half-speed, instead of the thirteen knots we had been doing, was the order of the day; and the hoarse tones of the steam whistle sounding at constant intervals gave a weirdness to the scene as we slowly ploughed along through the impenetrable curtain of fog which enwrapped us.

Two or three days sufficed to work strange changes in the appearance of my fellow-passengers. I found that it was a custom largely practised when starting on a campaign, to have the hair cut as closely to the head as scissors would do it, but to allow nature to have her own sweet way in every part of the face. The spectacle, therefore, of these erstwhile smart soldiers, the very dandies of Pall Mall, some of them, daily growing more and more like a cross between a convict and a brigand was somewhat tickling. Appearances, however, went for very little now. None of the fair sex were present to admire or reprobate; and what was serviceable and saved trouble was the thing aimed at.

After a couple of days of dense fog the weather cleared, and we made rapid progress, for the ship had a good turn of speed. Almost every afternoon one of the men, specially qualified, gave a lecture on the quarter-deck, dealing with some subject of present interest or utility. In this way Conder told us of his life in Syria, and gave us hints for Eastern travel. Watson unfolded the strange wonders of Upper Egypt and the Nile Basin, indenting on his experiences with General Gordon. An artillery officer lectured on modern guns, tactics, &c. ; one of the senior surgeons on the sanitation of Egypt ; and the General himself on equipment regulations. And then in the evening the indefatigable Barrington Foote led the way in some musical arrangements, to the huge delight of the men who were then allowed to come forward, as well as ourselves.

In five days we sighted the grand old rock of Gibraltar. There she stands at the head of the Mediterranean, jealously guarding the narrow channel, with an eye across the broad Atlantic, too, as if to watch and ward the interests of Old England across the range of the two wide seas. Of course we had had no news for five days. Much might have happened in that time, and a good deal of eagerness was manifested to know how events had been progressing. One of the naval officers of the port was soon aboard, and was rapidly plied with questions. What had become of Arabi? Had he collapsed? Had there been any fighting? He told us, to begin with, that the reconnaissance in force of the 5th of August had taken place, and young Howard Vyse, of the Rifle Brigade, and two or three men had fallen.

Three days more brought us to Malta, where we remained for a few hours; and then pushed on again towards Alexandria. During the last few days of the voyage preparations to the extremest detail were being made for the anticipated work ahead. A sort of brown liquid composition was served out, and all helmets, both of officers and men, were darkened from white to *Khaki*. Saddlery and accoutrements were being furbished up, and kits were being cut down and re-arranged, so as to be able to leave everything not absolutely necessary at the base of operations, and march in the very lightest possible order. Arabi was supposed to be a few miles from Alexandria, and many thought that in a few days at most we should attack him in force, and there would be a big fight. Of course this was only speculation, and never came off. Wolseley had his own plans, and he did not yet make them public.

On Thursday, August 17th, about noon, after some eleven days' sail we came into the harbour of Alexandria, and lay off a mile and a half. At once every glass was levelled on the batteries and the city. Scarce a month had elapsed since the bombardment, and our minds were full of harrowing newspaper accounts, and we could only picture to ourselves a scene of ruin and desolation. But as we looked through telescopes and field-glasses the long line of low-lying forts were scarcely visible, certainly not prominent above the water level; and thus they failed to reveal to us the really shattered condition to which they had been reduced by the fire of our guns; while, as for the city itself, it appeared to me, from our vessel, very much as it was when I had sailed out of its harbour some four months before on my way home from India. Landing, however, as we were able to do, for a few hours, a nearer inspection revealed to us very much more than could be seen from the ship. We first visited some of the forts, and the sight that met our eyes there I shall never forget. The fire of our ironclads must have been effective beyond all accounts published. The way in which those batteries had been battered, granite blocks shivered, embrasures knocked out of shape, and huge Armstrong guns fairly struck and toppled over like ninepins, with some of the poor Egyptian gunners buried beneath the ruins, gave one a keen idea of the terrible effectiveness of modern heavy artillery. Afterwards we wandered through the desolate streets. The track of a shell was scarcely to be seen, but the horrible results of incendiarism and rascality were visible everywhere. It was not difficult to imagine the scenes of fire and blood which had been enacted there when the wretches from the slums of the city, as well as plunderers from outside, were working their horrid will ere our Marines could land and prevent them. Streets in ruins; grand squares and public gardens which had lost all beauty and shape; great buildings half-shattered, or charred with fire. It was not a pleasant sight to behold this ancient city, once the seat of the world's civilization and literature, brought down thus to desolation. Along the waterside we found the black chargers of the Life Guards picketed in a long line, looking sadly pulled down after the tumble and tossing of the sea to which they had been subjected. The troopers, too, were not the smart-looking fellows the gorgeous appearance of whom is so dear to the London nurserymaids. Ah! but the men were the same. Smart enough they! though they had laid aside their gay trappings for a time. And honest, good work they did through the campaign.

It had just been decided that chaplains going to the front were to be mounted—an absolute necessity, indeed, if work was to be done with a force that might be on the march every day, and whose posts would be over an extended line of country. One of my missions ashore then, at this present, was to procure an animal which would serve me. More easily said than done, a good deal! Others among the Staff were looking around too, hoping to add to their chargers. But everything decent had been seized long ago, and a turn around the various stables brought to light only a few old " crocks," such as even a parson would not care to ride. It was one o'clock now, and we were to be abroad by five o'clock at latest, for some unusual movement was going to take place. I was determined, if possible, not to fail in my mission ; so getting hold of an ancient-looking *dragoman* I promised him unlimited *bakshish*, and showed him a silver gleam, if he would bring me to something decent. Straightway that old man led me forth through the city gate into the country beyond. And there, away in the desert, I found a Syrian family encamped, dwelling in tents and surrounded by flocks and herds. There were sheep and goats in abundance ; a few camels, too ; some asses, and some wiry-looking horses. The look of the last named I did not particularly like. Nothing to be got here, I thought. But after a little talk the old patriarch of this nomad family led out from a kind of inner stall a beautiful bright bay—a real child of the desert, and a high-caste Arab, too, as I could see from his points. I did not say how much I liked him. But dealing with the old man as with Eastern traders generally, and perhaps Hindus in particular, I concluded that the price he asked was just double what he was prepared to take. But it was not. He bated not one piastre from his first-named sum, and in hard gold (no other coin or money would he accept) I had to pay to the full. Neither had I any reason for dissatisfaction. When I got the beautiful creature on board a couple of hours later I was the object of congratulation, not to say envy, on the part of many who had tried and failed to add to their string.

But what was the movement which was about to take place? Lots of "shaves" were about. Some battalions which had been quartered in Alexandria were now being hurried on board. The general impression among the Staff men was that we were to bombard the strong forts in Aboukir Bay next day, land under fire, and storm the entrenchments. And, as if to carry out this idea, we steamed away from Alexandria, some eighteen transports in all, convoyed by ironclads and accompanied by the *Salamis*, with Wolseley himself aboard. When Aboukir Bay was reached we lay off, and line of battle was at once assumed. We could see plainly the batteries ashore crowded with men; and as our warships struck their topmasts, as if in preparation for a fight, the Egyptian gunners could be seen standing to their guns, evidently determined if possible to repel the anticipated attack. Thus we lay from three o'clock in the afternoon till evening. No lights were to be shown by our ships, so that when the evening shadows fell we were completely hidden from the sight of the men ashore. Then, just as the the cresent moon was beginning to peep out from a bank of clouds, suddenly signals flashed in quick succession from the *Salamis*, and in obedience to the signals we silently moved away, stealing off under cover of the darkness in single line, led by the " old fighting *Temeraire*," or rather by her descendant and namesake. In the morning when the dawn broke the amazement of the vigilant Egyptians could be imagined as they swept the sea and found no hostile warship in sight. This was Wolseley's ruse— a feint on the batteries in Aboukir Bay—a real and rapid advance northward to seize the Suez Canal. And this was successfully carried out, Port-Said, Kantara, and Ismailia falling into our hands with scarce a struggle at all. And Ismailia henceforward was to be the base of our active operations. Doubtless Wolseley had worked out this little plan in his mind from the first; but any premature revealing of it might have brought about the very catastrophe which it was intended to avert, viz., the complete blocking of the Canal waterway, a step which it would have been at any time earlier perfectly easy for Arabi to take. Now by this one sudden stroke all danger was removed. Of course it was impossible for the great ironclads to enter the Canal on account of the depth of water they required. It was difficult enough for some of the large transports; but while torpedo boats were patrolling up and down, the big liners one by one began slowly to make the passage towards Ismailia.

CHAPTER XVIII.

Ismailia—Landing of Troops — Difficulty with the Horses—Merry Jack Tars — I take one for an Arab—" Baines's "—Bivouacing—The Palace Hospital — My Quarters — Greek Looters and Swift Justice—Highlanders Fighting at Chalouffe—Lang Swims the Canal—Plan of Campaign—Arabi Cuts off our Water Supply—The Fight of the 24th of August—British Tenacity—Long Odds against us —Hickman's Two Guns against Arabi's Twelve— Gunner Knowles's Pluck—Reinforcements—Night Bivouac.

THE little French colony of Ismailia, on the Suez Canal, just where it broadens out into Lake Timseh, was busy, if not gay enough, on the morning of August 21st, and onwards. Along the canal a string of transports and troopships had been advancing slowly, and were now, most of them, gathered on the bosom of the lake, just off the town. Usually only two or three comparatively small boats are to be seen here. Now, however, the blue expanse of water was crowded with large vessels, some of the biggest liners on the seas, drawn up with almost military regularity side by side, and all discharging as rapidly as possible their living freight of men and horses. Boats of all kinds and sizes were alongside, and as soon as they were filled they made for the little landing-stage where their cargo, living or otherwise, was deposited, and they returned for load after load. I landed pretty early, but not before I had come nigh having an awkward accident with my horse. It had been lowered over the side and placed in a kind of barge like transport boat, with some horses belonging to the Duke of Teck. This barge was curiously constructed with ends which were capable of being closed up, boat-shape, or let down, raftwise. By some accident, when the horses were in, the end subsided and the water rushing in; the whole business, horses and all, began to subside too. With great promptitude the men aboard let down the crane chains and undergirded the boat, holding it up until things could be made ship-shape.

When I got ashore I found the quay and the adjoining ground covered thickly with packages and stores. Major Macgregor, who was the Staff officer superintending, was working in the heat of the sun, here and there and everywhere, striving to get things cleared off. The sailors of the ships, too, were doing really splendid service rolling barrels and carrying cases, or pushing trucks along the railway which had been hastily laid down from the shore up to the town. There was a number of native Arabs and mongrels who were supposed to be working under a contractor, but they affected to feel the heat far more than the jolly Jack-tars, who whistled, shouted, and sang merrily at their work. Grimy enough they were too, scarcely to be distinguished from the dark-faced natives. I blundered myself over one of them, much to his indignation and my amusement. Wanting a coolie to carry some of my private baggage, I possessed myself of a few necessary words of Arabic from Conder, who was ashore, and picked out one who I thought would answer my purpose. He was lying down on the ground, either very lazy or very tired. *Enti hamar* ("come, coolie-bearer"), I shouted, and pointed to some of my baggage. The man looked up from under his head-gear and stared at me.

Enti! Enti! I shouted, with a decision which was meant to be commanding. Presently his grimy face expanded into a broad grin as he called out to a messmate not far off:

"Why, he takes me for a coolie!" with some addenda, characterised by that forcefulness which is peculiar to the sailor. I suppose he thought it was no compliment to him. I roared, and turned away to seek my coolie elsewhere.

Near the water's edge was a decent hotel, the Hotel des Bains, so called because an arrangement for sea-water bathing was adjacent. It soon came to be known among the men as plain "Baines's." Probably Tommy Atkins had something to do with the new designation. He always has his own pronunciation for foreign names, and sticks to it in the most conservative fashion. I found this hostel crowded inside and outside literally with men of the departments, who were seeking temporary quarters, some being accommodated in the verandah. At the other end of the town there was another inn, which was just as full. Indeed, every place was crowded, the very ground outside in some parts being covered with men bivouacing. Around a shaded fountain in the centre of the place, where I suppose the French colonists were accustomed to congregate in the evening, two regiments had taken up their quarters, and the double camp was in full swing. Along the lime-tree avenue to the right, from end to end, regiments and batteries had fixed themselves just where a cool shelter could be obtained from the trees, and a refreshing breeze blew off the lake. Dr. Hanbury, the Surgeon-General, who came out on board our ship, told me that the Khedive's Palace was going to be requisitioned and prepared as a base hospital; and that I might perhaps find an empty corner

there, where I could shake down for awhile.
So I made my way past the line of encampment till I presently came upon the magnificent stone building beautifully embowered amid the trees of a rich garden. Outside, the sentries were pacing up and down before the big gates with that imperturbable demeanour which always seems to characterise the British soldier when he is doing "sentry go." Within the gates, in the garden itself, I found a row of outhouses in which a sort of kitchen establishment had been hastily extemporised. I passed up the flight of stone steps, and just inside the doors in the lobby I found a huge pile of stretchers belonging to the Bearer Companies—the men who follow their fighting comrades into the field, to pick up and bring in their comrades who fall under fire; and very tenderly and skilfully they do their work, as I have many a time witnessed. Soon there would be ominous stains upon those stretchers. The most magnificent reception halls were to the right and left. Polished mirrors reached almost from floor

to ceiling. Gilded chandeliers hung all around. Decorations and carvings everywhere. What gay court scenes those splendid rooms must often have witnessed! Now they were empty, the beautiful furniture removed. Yet not empty, alas! for even thus early a great crowd of sick men had gathered here, and were lying, in the present unfinished state of arrangements, in long rows on the floor, looked after as carefully as possible by the doctors who had landed, and the hospital orderlies. Reaching the upper storey by a great sweep of stone staircase, I found most of the rooms there utilised much in the same way. An officers' ward had been prepared; and a ward for serious cases, amputations, and such like; and a fever ward, as far off as possible. All were not thus occupied, however. I came upon one door jealously locked and barricaded, and labelled " Duke of Connaught's baggage." I was fortunate enough to discover a tiny room, probably a kind of dressing-room, which was too small for hospital purposes, and which, therefore, the Surgeon-General was good enough to assign to me as quarters for the present. It was a bit of kindness on his part, and of good luck on mine ; for the other chaplains, and the department men, were entirely unprovided for, and were most of them unable to get any roof shelter, having to camp as best they could under the trees. It was a great boon to be within four walls, for the heat during the day was excessive.

For the most part, when we landed, the houses and shops of the colony were shut up, and the Arab part of the population had almost entirely fled. But there were plenty of rascally Greeks and Levantines hanging about, whose object was plunder, and, if need be, murder. Nineteen of these were caught by our military police red-handed. During the confusion of our landing they were engaged in the congenial task of breaking into the houses and looting. Ten of them were at once shot in the square. And this prompt justice effectually checked any further developments in this direction, much to our comfort, for some of the shopkeepers began cautiously to open their stores ; and finding that all goods sold were paid for at once, and that they could with impunity demand exorbitant prices, they began to do a roaring trade.

The Indian contingent with the 72nd Highlanders, who had started from India to join us, had by this time reached the Suez Canal, and moving up from the Red Sea end had already come in contact with Arabi's forces at a place called Chalouffe, where they were apparently engaged in preparations to cut off the supply of water by damming that end of the Sweet Water Canal. Some four hundred of the Highlanders were hastily landed, and found Arabi's men entrenched behind a strong embankment some distance on the other side of this Sweet Water Canal. There seemed no way of getting at them, until Lang, a young officer of the regiment, pluckily swam across under a sharp fire from the enemy, and captured and brought over a boat from the other side. In this our men were conveyed over, and at once dashed at the enemy's position, capturing it at the point of the bayonet, and putting nearly a hundred of them *hors de combat*, including their commander, who was killed.

This damming of the Sweet Water Canal, and consequent cutting off of our drinking supply, was a serious menace to us in Ismailia. The level of the little lake where it was gathered for the use of the French town was perceptibly and rapidly lowering, indicating that Arabi already had been operating to this end farther up in the desert.

Wolseley determined on action at once; for if our water failed, with an ever-increasing force gathering daily at the base of operations, things would be very serious, and it would mean a decided check.

Even as we landed some of Arabi's forces were discovered, within three or four miles of Ismailia, at a place called Nefiche. These were scattered without difficulty, however; a splendid long shot from one of the gunboats in the Suez Canal fairly striking and literally cutting in two a train in which the Egyptians were hastily making off.

It may here be remarked that, presupposing Ismailia to be the base of our active operations, it did not, I think, require any transcendent military skill to mark out the general plan of the campaign. Stretching before us, as it were, on the road to Cairo, we found first of all a great expanse of dry burning desert, for some thirty miles or so. This was intersected by the Sweet Water Canal and a line of railway, the two running close to and parallel with one another. The canal originally had been constructed for the purpose of supplying the many thousands of workmen, who had been engaged in the cutting of the Suez Canal, with drinking water; and it was still the only source of supply to the dwellers in Ismailia and around. Hence its importance. Arabi, of course, held command of it higher up the country, and also of the railway line and all the rolling stock. The canal he used for himself, cutting off the water *below* him ; and the railway was excellent for throwing forward his troops rapidly, and also for purposes of retreat, which were frequent. It was certain that the Egyptian leader would leave to us the task of marching across the sea of burning sand, harassing us perhaps on the way, but allowing the chief difficulties to be provided by the nature of the country, and the season, for it was now the time of intensest summer heat. These thirty miles of dry desert ended, however, the cultivated Delta of the Nile commenced, a country comparatively rich in resources. This must be held by him at all costs. Moreover, this spot marked the village of Tel-el-Kebir, where it was well known that he had been erecting strong defences, and where a large force was occupying an entrenched position. All the preliminary fighting was to take place along the lines of the railway and the Sweet Water Canal.

On the morning of Thursday, August the 24th, Wolseley moved out with a comparatively small force, numbering about fifteen hundred men, and comprising some of the Household Cavalry and the newly-formed Mounted Infantry, two guns of the Royal Horse Artillery, and the Marines and York and Lancaster Regiment. Grimy and bearded looked the men as they formed up and marched about 4 a.m. But they were ready enough for their work, though the horses of the Guards were at present in a soft condition, and suffering from their recent sea tossing.

For some few miles the march was eventless. As one swept the horizon with glass no sign of human being or habitation could be seen. But clouds of sharp-cutting sand swept over one's eyes and face, making both goggles and veil eminently acceptable.

At last, reaching a spot some nine miles away, between El Magfar and Tel-el-Mahuta, it was found that Arabi had here constructed his first dam, and a few of his troops were holding possession of it. Two squadrons of our Life Guards were sent at them, and in a few minutes had cleared out the Egyptian

Light Cavalry who had opposed them and scattered the infantry.

And now it was seen that a mile and a half or more ahead from the canal, and stretching away to the right, the enemy had constructed a strong position, and were occupying it in considerable force. A very big dam had been thrown across the water there, and was continued by an embankment which crossed the railway; and shelter trenches and other smaller defences were numerous. It was quite evident the Egyptians were going to stand and fight here, especially as trains could be perceived puffing up from the Tel-el-Kebir side, and discharging reinforcements of troops continually. Wolseley estimated their strength at about 10,000. He was not far wrong, for afterwards it was ascertained that Arabi had nine battalions of infantry and one of cavalry numbering 7,000 men, together with some of the wild fighting Bedouins, with him, and also twelve guns which were admirably served, and began to open fire at once.

To this force Wolseley could oppose only some 1,500 men, who occupied no strong position like the foe. But, as he said, "it would not be in consonance with the traditions of Her Majesty's army that we should retire, even temporarily, before Egyptian troops, no matter what their numbers might be." He therefore decided to hold his ground till evening, when he knew that reinforcements would reach him from Ismailia.

Accordingly shelter trenches were hastily constructed and our infantry lay down within them, our left resting on the captured dam, and the right being covered by the cavalry and mounted infantry.

Plump! Plump! came the Egyptian shells well among our cavalry. But they were common shell, with percussion fuses, and the dry, yielding sand which was such a cruel test in marching to our men and horses, served us a good turn here, for the shells plunged deeply into it, and bursting there, seemed to throw up few splinters. And the black chargers of the Guards, if they were not in a condition to do much heavy work yet, stood there as quietly with their big riders, amid the bursting missiles, as if they were in the gateway of Whitehall. Only Drury Lowe's horse, the gallant little ex-commander of the 17th Lancers, proved timid and restive, and gave his rider a lot of trouble.

Wolseley did not at first permit his solitary two guns to return the fire of Arabi's artillery. But presently, as the shells were more and more frequent, and the Egyptian infantry were pushing forward with the aid of their shelter trenches, and seriously menacing our centre and right, he ordered the guns, which had with infinite difficulty come up through the soft sand and taken position near the railway, to open fire. And right gallantly and well did they do their work under the command of Lieutenant Hickman. Two guns against twelve were no small odds. But, nothing daunted, the men, one and all, stuck to their work like true Britons and made excellent practice. One of the gunners, named Knowles, was struck in the face by a shell fragment quite early in the fight, and a nasty wound was inflicted. They wanted him to go to the rear and be attended to, but he would have none of it. Hastily and roughly binding it up, he went back to his gun, and pluckily served it throughout the day. I am glad to say that afterwards he was rewarded with the medal for "distinguished conduct in the field," and right well did he deserve it. For many an hour did the gallant fellows of these two guns work and fight away, exposed to the concentrated fire of the Arabi's twelve, and to the intense heat and glare of the sun; but they only lost a couple of men.

On our right the Cavalry and Mounted Infantry were manœuvring under Drury Lowe, and checking as much as possible the constant but cautious advance of the enemy. It was during these operations that Captain Hallam Parr, of the Somerset Regiment, who was now commanding the Mounted Infantry, received a very serious wound. Lord Melgund, too, who was serving as a volunteer with the same corps, was slightly wounded.

The day was beginning to close in when reinforcements arrived. First the Cornish Light Infantry, the old 46th, came up from Nelfiche. The Duke of Connaught had hurried along with the brigade of Guards from Ismailia; and some of the Naval Brigade brought up a couple of Gatling guns. Welcome indeed was the help to our wearied men. Some of the Marine Artillery went to the aid of our exhausted gunners; while the Gatlings, under King Harman of the *Orion*, got to work most effectively. At once the advance of the Egyptians was checked. And when presently Baker Russell came up with some squadrons of the 4th and 7th Dragoon Guards, they retired to the shelter of their defences.

The shades of evening fell around; and the men, utterly worn out, and suffering from hunger, too—for it had been found impossible to get the stores forward—lay down upon the field they had so tenaciously and pluckily held during the day. To-morrow the fight was to be renewed, though not at all upon the lines that Wolseley had pre-arranged.

CHAPTER XIX.

The Fight to be continued—Captain Hallam Parr and Lord Melgund Wounded—An All-Night Journey through the Desert—Cruel Marching—Schreiber's Guns—We Lose our Way—Halt!—A Soft Bed—Morning Dawn—The Egyptians Bolt—Cavalry Fight at Mahsameh—Guns in Action—Major Bibby Shot—Charge by Squadrons—Enemy's Fire Effective—A Ghastly Group—Effects of a Shell Explosion—Waiting for a Surgeon—A Scare—All's Well that Ends Well—Commissionaire Sheppard and his New Leg.

IT was Thursday evening, August 24th—a perfect tropical evening too. Scarce a movement in the air as I galloped in from Nefiche across the desert. Wolseley had sent down to Ismailia for the " 3-60th " Rifles Schreiber's guns, and other detachments, to reinforce those at the front. They were to march through the night, so as to be in position for the big fight which was anticipated at dawn on the morrow. I purposed to go with them, and hurried off to hospital to make my arrangements accordingly. Later in the evening Hallam Parr and Lord Melgund were brought in. The former was in a bad way ; the latter not so seriously wounded. It is wonderful, though, how our fellows manage not only to pull through, but to get up and back again to duty after a comparatively short spell of hospital care. It is not only a testimony to the skill of the doctors, but to their own fitness of form, as well as to their keen anxiety to be at work at the front again. I did not anticipate that the task would be a big one to-morrow, and quite thought that I should get back to quarters by noon. So contenting myself for the most part with wrapping up and stowing away on my saddle a feed of corn for the horse, I concluded that his master would do very well till the time of the next square meal came.

About 10 p.m. we started. It was a pitch dark night—one of those still, motionless nights that you get often in Eastern lands, not necessary portending a coming storm, but hot and weird, no breeze or movement in the air. A night, too, which often changes about midway with dangerous suddenness, the closeness giving place to unexpected cold which chills you to the bones. Thus it was with us. When I joined the force, not far from the drawbridge of the canal on the outskirts of the desert, everything was black. The "Rifles," in their dark uniform, popularly known as the "Sweeps," were drawn up like a line of dark shadows; and the artillery on the flank were not much better.

It was not possible to maintain anything like a line of regularity, and the men marched at ease. What a satire we found in that expression, "Marching at ease." It was the most cruel bit of marching I ever witnessed or experienced—for men and horses alike. On the one flank lumbered along with deadened sound the heavy guns, wheels sinking sometimes a good foot into the yielding sand, and making it almost impossible for the poor, willing beasts who tugged at the traces to extricate them; for they themselves sank in up to the fetlocks, and above, at every step.

All the night through I witnessed, however, a grand triumph of kindness. Schreiber, a splendid man for such a bit of work, rode alongside all the time, constantly saying to his men, "Encourage your horses, men! Encourage your horses!" And the men did encourage them, not with spur and whip so much as with kind hand and word. And thus—though with infinite toil and strain—those guns went on through the heavy sand, and sometimes over the banks and ditches which now and again intervened. There was a fifteen-mile march to be compassed, for we were making a wide detour for strategical purposes, and neither men nor horses flinched for a moment or dreamt of not accomplishing it. It was almost as bad for the men of the Rifles as for the horses of the Battery.

It was soon quite evident that other difficulties besides a heavy line of march were before us. A straight-away route could be easily followed, for the double line of railway and canal would be a constant guide. But it was a part of Wolseley's plan for us to move around by the enemy's left flank, keeping far out in the desert, and circling around, till the morning dawn would find us fairly in rear of his entrenched position and able to cut of his retreat, when the main body, consisting of those whom the General had already with him, struck their decisive blow in a front attack.

A young Staff officer who was supposed to know the circuitous line of route was detailed to guide us. But, alas! and no wonder, he was as much at sea as the rest of us. Scarce a twinkling star was seen to give any aid. The black waste of darkness completely enshrouding us, we plodded on through the heavy sea of sand, on whose bosom was no beaten line of way.

For six hours thus we marched until at last the Staff man, mistaking me riding by the "Rifles" for Ashburnham, who commanded the force, groped his way up to my side, and said with almost piteous hopelessness, "I am sure I don't know where we are." I directed him to the Colonel, whom I could dimly perceive through the shadows not far off, and presently Ashburnham called a halt. It was no use going on aimlessly. We might arrive at anything but the right spot. We were to rest for an hour. Perhaps by that time a gleam of coming day would help us on our march.

The way in which that black mass of 3-60th Rifles in a moment subsided into the sand was a sight to behold, so far as it could be seen at all. And in a minute or two not a sound broke the stillness as each poor worn-out fellow was resting his weary legs in the sandy bed. As for me, I tumbled off my horse, who had been mechanically plodding on half asleep, as I was myself in the saddle, and wrapping my cloak around me, and twisting the bridle around my arm, lay down with infinite content under his nose. The night had changed; the thick murky closeness had passed away, and now sharply blew the night breeze, chilling one to the bone. But I never had an hour of more delicious rest than this. What more luxurious bed can a man desire. If he be stout and well padded it is not so much a matter of concern to him how hard may be the ground upon which he rests his *corpus*. But if he be otherwise, with a form largely consisting of framework, with sharp points and angles, it is a matter of grave moment whether the ground be soft or not. Oh! that delicious, yielding sand! How kindly it seemed at once to provide a convenient orifice for each hard, sharp point of my body. And absolutely at peace, I and those around me rested for one brief hour.

At the end of that time we were aroused. The black shadows of night were just beginning to give way to the faint gleam of dawning day. It would be possible in a few minutes, perhaps, to see where we were, and how to reach the spot where we were to take up position.

Great was the satisfaction when it was presently discovered that we had not wandered much after all. Perhaps we had made a wider sweep than was necessary, thus extending a twelve miles march into a fifteen but we were fairly in the line now. Another short hour would bring us into position in rear of the entrenched Egyptians.

Meanwhile could we be seen by them? That was the question. With the aid of their field-glasses our leaders could make out far back and on our left flank as we marched the lines of their position. Very cautiously, still keeping away, we pressed on. But, alas! they were as keen-eyed as we. They saw the line of their retreat threatened. They were Eastern troops who could not brook that. And very soon we, and no doubt the bigger force which lay immediately in front of them, waiting to strike, saw with huge disgust that the enemy were making off as hard as they could from their entrenched position, in the trains which were kept handy on the adjacent railway. To the great disappointment of the Guards and all the others, who were keenly set on the coming fight, the puffing smoke of the locomotives clearly indicated a retreat to their standing camp, some four miles back, at Mahsameh.

And how did this change of position affect us? Why, it simply meant that we by our further march were brought almost into a front position for an attack on that camp, if only they would stand.

And they did stand. The stores gathered there were far too valuable to be yielded up lightly to such a handful of men as ours—only one infantry battalion and a single battery. In half-an-hour's time, however, the cavalry came clattering up, Life Guards and squadrons of the 4th and 7th Dragoon Guards, together with the Mounted Infantry. Wolseley was extremely anxious, if possible, to get possession of some railway plant—locomotives and waggons; they would be of immense value in transporting our stores from the base to the front.

The "Rifles" were halted then a little to the right front of the enemy's camp, and Schreiber's guns took up position on a bit of rising ground within range and opened fire on the position, which lay across the railway, and reached to the bank of the Sweet Water Canal.

THE BATTLE SMOKE.

The cavalry dashed on half a mile ahead with some guns of the Horse Artillery. These guns, rapidly unlimbering, set to work and sent shell after shell into the enemy's camp, while the cavalry, though their horses were in no condition for heavy work, prepared to make a dash when opportunity should present. Thus, for a while, it was an artillery duel, for the Krupp guns of the Egyptians were served with accuracy and good effect.

At first I was with the "Rifles," waiting for the development of events. But it seemed to me that the work of the day would altogether lie with the cavalry ahead, so I prepared to push on to the field of conflict, where I knew that presently there would be duty for me.

To prepare for emergencies I first unbridled my horse, and gave him his feed and a hasty rub down. I had scarcely done this when a man came galloping up for the surgeons and the hospital stretchers—already some of our poor fellows were down.

I hastily mounted and rode off to see if I

could be of any use. Schreiber's guns now on my left, and those of the Horse Battery, which had taken up a position on the right, were thundering away, and I could see bodies of our cavalry charging again and again to break the Egyptian front.

One of these charges had just been vigorously delivered by a squadron of the 7th Dragoon Guards. The mass of Egyptians against whom they dashed made no stand at all. Wavering for a moment, and then turning, they were scattered like chaff before the wind, almost ere our men touched them. But as the squadron wheeled about to return some of them rallied, and joining with others who were lying half concealed poured a volley, sharp and effective, into our retiring Dragoons. Several were hit, both men and horses, and among them Major Bibby, who was struck in the back, the bullet, as it was then supposed, passing clean through his lungs and out in front. As I rode up and dismounted by his side he lay on the ground, certainly in a very bad way, and the doctors did not think much of his chances. Carefully and tenderly he was lifted up and carried out of the fight, and later in the day I went down with him to the Base Hospital at Ismailia. But strange are the chances of war, and stranger still the devious course taken by some bullets. The surgeons were happily mistaken in this particular case. Either the bullet had circulated and pierced no organs at all, or it had sped through, perhaps just grazing the lungs, but with little or no laceration. Certain it is that Bibby was sitting up in a week, and soon afterwards was invalided home, to return in a few months as strong and well as if his body had never been ventilated by an Egyptian bullet.

But meanwhile how went the fight? I saw Schreiber still pounding away in the distance, and the other guns near to me now very hard at work too. The cavalry was a very movable body indeed; here one moment, and away the next. I essayed to join myself to one squadron which was just resting behind the shelter of a little rising ground. But no sooner had I done so than they were ordered for more work, and were off at the trot and then the gallop. I found myself alone. Plump! came the enemy's shells, one after another, making very good practice against the Horse Artillery guns, and putting one or two of their men *hors de combat* very soon. It would have been quite consonant with one's spirits to have gone off with the cavalry and ridden with them in the charge, for I found, alas! that the wild exhilaration of the battlefield seizes parsons as well as other men; but this course, though, perhaps as safe as any, would scarcely have been within the strict lines of duty. I therefore began to make my way towards the battery, where things were getting pretty hot, but which at least was a little more stationary than the constantly charging squadrons.

I was thankful that my horse behaved well. He might have been foaled on a battlefield. Neither the booming of the guns nor the bursting of shells seemed to disturb his equine equanimity, though, strangely enough, after the campaign was over, and when he was the property of another man, he was accustomed to carry himself anything but quietly on the ordinary field days—a volley of musketry being quite enough to make him plunge and break rank so as seriously to test the horsemanship of his rider.

Quickly I rode along, getting near to the battery and watching some of our men who were away in the distance galloping toward the Egyptian lines. Suddenly I started at a little group lying in ghastly irregularity just in front of me. A tall, slim lad, a trooper of the Life Guards, lay stretched, pale as death, on the field, his leg torn and lacerated with a horrible wound; close by his side the body of a comrade, or all that remained of him, for he was frightfully shattered; and around three dead horses. Another trooper, who had been hit in the foot but not severely wounded, was near by. It was a group of horrors! I got off and bent down by the living man to see what I could do for him. It appeared that a handful of the Life Guards had been halted at this spot, indeed dismounted, and standing by their horses, when one of the enemy's shells had fallen right into the middle of them. It struck the leg of the first man and exploded, tearing it to pieces. His near comrade was swept down, his skull shattered, and he never moved again. A third man was slightly wounded, and the three horses were killed. There they all lay. What could be done for the living man in his suffering? I found that the horrible first agony had passed away; the man's sensibilities seemed numbed. The pain was not the difficulty, but there was danger of quick collapse.

Happily, a tiny flask which I had put into my saddle bag was infinitely serviceable now. A few drops of spirit aroused the flickering spark of life. But that was about all that could be done except to tightly fix the poor fellow's own waist-strap around his leg above the wound, and thus stop the bleeding. How I longed for the surgeon and the stretchers to come our way! Herein it seems to me is a grave defect of the medical system. Why should a young surgeon be compelled to toil *on foot* through a long day's fighting and work when his services are a hundredfold more valuable when rendered quickly? In this case no help came to us for nearly two long hours. The burning heat of the sun was terrible, and we still lay in the line of the enemy's fire, both of shells and bullets, which was none too pleasant. A broken sword and a tattered cavalry jacket enabled us to rig up a little shade over the man's head. And this done we waited and waited.

Suddenly, far off in the distance, I discerned a strange group, mostly white clad, approaching. Who were they? I knew that our squadrons, by repeated charges, had scattered a part at least of the enemy's force, and that they had broken away on both sides. Were these some of them, fugitives, but who, seeing the solitary group, had turned aside to do us a mischief? Earnestly I tried to make them out through my glass; and finally by their dress could only conclude that they were Egyptians, and that we were in a desperate case. I had no doubt or hesitancy as to what I ought to do. Parson or no parson, not only my own life but the life of another was in my hands. Easily enough could I have cleared off, for my swift-footed "Selim" stood by me, and no Egyptian horse could come on his heels, I knew. But the poor lad in whose body I had managed to keep life for the last hour was my charge, and I could not leave him. Very carefully, therefore, I examined my weapon, and placed it ready to my hand. I said nothing to my man; indeed I thought in his semi-conscious state he would notice nothing, but I resolved to do all I could for him and myself, and felt perfectly justified for once in assuming the militant. I mounted my horse, and through my glass watched the on-comers. Nearer and nearer they came, toiling through the sand, or else using great caution. How long the moments seemed! Not a soul of our men was near to give us a hand, for the tide of battle had rolled on far to our right front.

But now, as I strained my eyes to make out the advancing group, some of their faces seemed strangely European. I wiped the ends of my field glass and looked again. Yes, surely, they were some of our own men. Where their white clothing came from I know not. But I know that in a few moments our anxious thoughts had gone, and up came a young surgeon, almost worn out with his long march through the sand; a few men of the Bearer Company, and, best of all, a stretcher. My work now was at an end as far as this case was concerned. Carefully and tenderly they lifted the wounded lad on the stretcher, the shattered leg, or what remained of it, lying limp and ghastly. I scarcely thought to see the poor fellow alive again; but I did. Six miles through the desert they bore him, and in the evening, in a boat, transported him other twelve miles to the Base Hospital. Wonderfully successful was the amputation which relieved him of his shattered limb, but saved the knee joint, and eventually he was invalided home.

Sequel! Some years after, indeed quite lately, when passing through the doors of a large public building, a great big Commissionaire rushed, or rather limped up to me. It was my old Guardsman Sheppard, who, being on duty there, had recognised me before I did him. No wonder, either! The slim, wan lad had developed into a burly giant. With thankfulness and pride he told me how the Prince of Wales had given him a new mechanical leg, and he was now able to get about and earn his living as one of the Corps of Commissionaires. "Ah, Sir," he said, "I thought it was all up with me when I saw those fellows coming and you draw your revolver." "What! did you see, Sheppard?" said I. "Indeed I did," he answered. "I said nothing, but I was watching all the time, and thought they were Egyptians, as you did, and that we were both done."

But this is a digression. The fight was by no means over yet. What more happened I must proceed to tell.

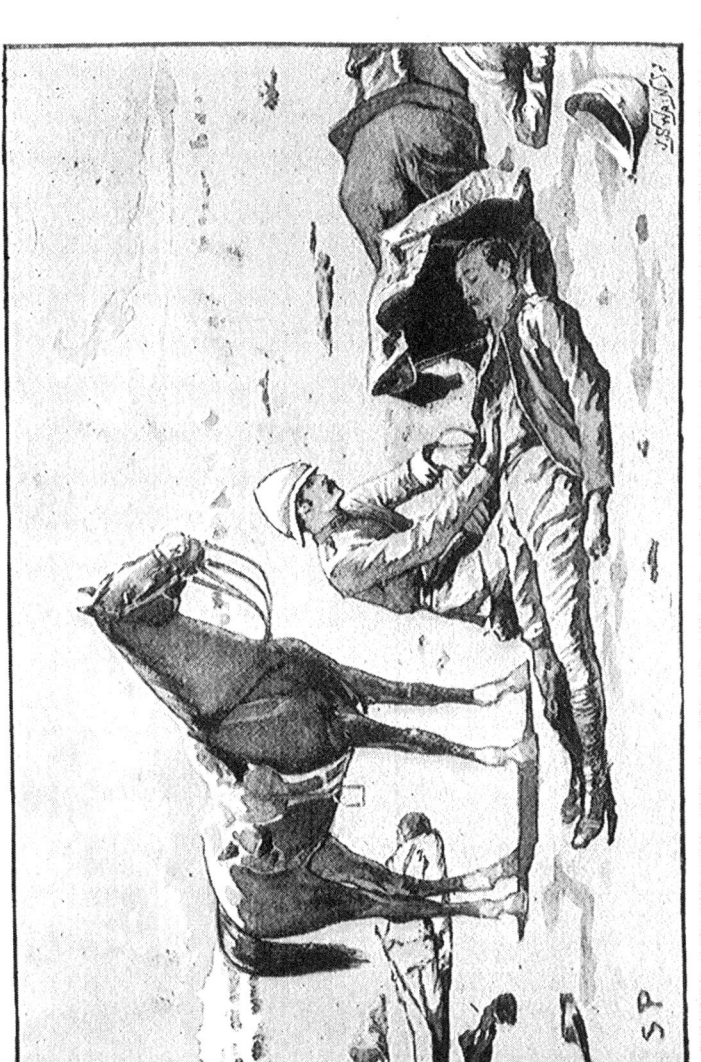

REV. A. MALE AND SHEPPARD. *To face page 356.*

CHAPTER XX.

The Fight at Mahsameh Continued—Terrible Thirst—Final Dash—Description of a Cavalry Charge—Trooper Browning Halves (?) an Egyptian—The Crafty Mahmoud taken Prisoner—Rush for Water—The Polluted Canal—I Carry Despatches—A Lonely Desert Ride—The Solitary Old Troop Horse—The Duke of Connaught's Disappointment—Wounded Transported in Boats—Sun Blisters—Naval Officers' Escapade, and its Result.

IT was now approaching noon. The sun poured down its fiercest rays upon us, and our faces were blistering and peeling as before the blast of a furnace. Not a drop of water was to be got, for the enemy was posted on the canal, and until he was broken and scattered there was no access to it. The men were suffering terribly from thirst. One tall Guardsman, his face as pale as a sheet, came riding towards me. "Oh, sir, for God's sake, give me some water!" he cried piteously. I had to tell him that I had none, and that I was almost in as bad a plight as he. "Then I can only lie down and die," said he; "and my horse is as bad as I am." We had been marching and fighting for some sixteen hours, and the little supply that the men had brought in their bottles was long ago exhausted. Something must be done, and that quickly.

About one o'clock, then, a final and combined effort was made. The guns for a while worked away hard, and poured in shot and shell, the Egyptians still replying effectively; and then, detachments from the various cavalry regiments being gathered together, the squadrons prepared to deliver a blow which it was anticipated would be finally effective. I was near by, and fairly caught the exhilaration of the moment. The wild excitement of a cavalry charge is something to experience rather than describe; and it is an experience which once felt is never forgotten. And yet I think that expression—wild excitement—perhaps scarcely describes with accuracy a charge of English cavalry, at any rate. Rather there is stern endurance, quiet pluck, high-souled courage manifested in the countenances and attitude of men who are just getting ready for this kind of work. There the squadrons were massed for a few moments, just resting their horses behind the shelter of a little rising ground. The men were dismounted and looking to their harness and weapons. Presently the sharp words of command were heard in quick succession, "Stand to your horses, men!" "Prepare to mount!" "Mount!" With smart alacrity the commands were obeyed. And a moment later, with that indescribable jingle of spurs and steel accoutrements, the whole body of men moved off at the trot, the line, two deep, opening out, and every man proving distance, that he might get clear sweep for his sword arm. Then the word was given to gallop, the horses began to stretch away, and the men settled down in their saddles, and gathered up the reins, and thrust their feet home, or perhaps took them out of the stirrups altogether, as some men wisely do under those circumstances. And now you could see clearly that strange new light, the very battle fire, flashing and gleaming from every eye. On they swept across the desert in a great cloud of sand and dust straight towards the Egyptian lines and camp, making wonderful pace with their weary horses; and in a few moments they were in the very midst of Arabi's infantry and gunners. Most, of course, broke and scattered at once, but some made a good stand. The fugitives, too, were checked by the canal, and many were cut down and others taken prisoners on the bank.

Just now an incident happened on the left of our line. A gigantic trooper of the Life Guards named Browning, seeing one of his officers in some peril from a crowd of Egyptians who had surrounded him, galloped to his assistance. Most of the crowd cleared off at once, but some of them stood, and Browning presently found himself pretty hard pressed by three who thought that the odds of three to one were good enough to secure them the victory. Browning dismounted and laid about him with Yorkshire vigour to some tune. Two of the men soon thought that discretion was the better part of valour and took to their heels. The third, however, stuck to his man, and succeeded in wounding the Englishman in the wrist with the point of his bayonet, when Browning, with a sweep of his great sword, cut him down, and almost cut him through. Indeed, he is credited with having bisected the man. I did not myself see any such result, though I was on the spot, nor did Browning mention it to me in the detailed account which he gave me when I visited him in hospital. I fancy the tale arose from a little bit of graphic word-painting in which the big swordsman afterwards indulged when giving his comrades an account of the fight. "He prodded me in the arm," said our cavalryman, "and got my monkey up." "What did you do then, Browning?" said the listeners. "Why," said he, "I up with my sword and just *halved* him." Very graphic; and quite near enough to fact! One can easily suppose that the sweep of that big sword would not find much to stop its swift course in the slim-bodied Egyptian. And indeed it came away from the sanguinary operation strangely bent and twisted.

Stores of provisions and ammunition, lots of railway waggons, and seven Krupp guns fell into the hands of our cavalry as the result of this fight. The railway waggons were a most welcome addition to our means of transport.

Suddenly, as Baker Russell and his staff were standing on the field directing some of the after operations, there came along a strange-looking individual, curiously clad, and preceded by a youth who bore a little white flag. Who he was no one at first could tell. Whether he was an Arab, or an Egyptian, or a Levantine was not very apparent either from his face or his costume. However, he began, very volubly, and with profound *salaams*, to introduce himself in very broken English, declaring that he was a Greek merchant, who had been trading in the neighbourhood; but amid the disturbance which had come with the fighting he had lost all his goods, and was now penniless. He had come from the village near by, as soon as he heard that the English were victorious, to offer his salutations and so forth, A clever tale truly, and not badly concocted and told. But somehow there was a ring of unreality about it, and Baker Russell looked a little suspiciously on the man, and finally ordered him to be kept under arrest.

Shortly after this some of the prisoners whom we had just taken were passing by under escort, and one of them, an Egyptian officer, casting a glance on the pseudo Greek merchant, said quietly to one of the English officers near him, "Do you know who that is over yonder?" "No," said he, "except that it is a Greek trader, who has just been taken prisoner." "That man," said the Egyptian, "is Mahmoud Fehmy Pasha, the chief of Arabi's staff, and the leading spirit of the rebellion, next to Arabi himself." This information was at once verified by others, and then the whole tale came out. We learnt that during the progress of the fight, while the Egyptians were making their stand

Mahmoud Fehmy, who was the skilful engineer of Arabi's forces, and was responsible mainly for the admirably-constructed lines of defence at Tel-el-Kebir, had left that post on a railway engine and had steamed up to Mahsameh to see how affairs were progressing. Arrived at a spot not far from the fighting, he had got down, and standing on the railway, was watching the preparations for the final charge. So engrossed was he in his observations that he did not perceive that the engine-driver, terrified by the oncoming rush of horsemen, though at present they were a good distance off, was seized with sudden panic, and putting on steam, made off with his engine up the line. Hence when Mahmoud Fehmy, seeing that the Egyptians were making no stand, thought it prudent to do the same, and looked up for his means of escape, he saw his locomotive making all steam back again towards Tel-el-Kebir.

But his Eastern craft did not forsake him. In a moment he had turned his undress uniform literally inside out (hence his curious costume), and rigging up a handkerchief on a stick to serve as a white flag, he sent on his son, who was accompanying him, to walk ahead as his servant, and assumed the rôle of the Greek trader with skill, and at first with comparative success. Indeed, had it not been for the treachery of his brother-officer, I suppose that Mahmoud would soon have been back at Tel-el-Kebir to give us a little more trouble. Huge was his disgust when he found himself discovered. At once he was put under strong guard ; and though he complained bitterly of the treatment he received, grumbling almost as badly as any Englishman, he was sent down to the Base, and finally to Alexandria, where he was well taken care of to the close of the campaign Later on he stood his trial with Arabi and four others on charges of treason and rebellion, and was exiled to Ceylon, where he now is.

I shall never forget the rush to the canal for water as soon as the camp was taken and the Egyptians scattered, although we found it horribly polluted with dead carcasses which had been thrown in. I was bending down, and drinking eagerly, my horse doing the same by my side, when a man said, "I think there's a dead Egyptian in the water just by you, sir." "Oh," said I, "I can't help the dead Egyptian;" and I drank away. When I had satisfied myself, I turned to the "dead Egyptian," and found that he was really a poor fellow desperately wounded, who was lying there in the water. We lifted him out, and under the care of our surgeons he ultimately made a good recovery. True it was, however, that the water was in a horrible state: and had it not been that intense thirst destroys many prejudices, we could not possibly have drunk it.

Just now up came M'Calmont, one of Baker Russell's staff, and said, "the General wants you to carry some despatches for him back to General Willis, the divisional commander." I regarded this as rather out of my line of duty, and an honour not to be sought after by any means, since it involved a long six miles' ride through the lonely desert; exposed also to any wandering party of the enemy, who had scattered all around when they were broken. However, an army chaplain has to be a many-sided man, as I had ere this learnt; so I buckled up my saddle again, and followed M'Calmont to a little Egyptian tent where the General was resting himself on the broad of his back. "The fact is," said he, "our horses are all done up, there is not one that can do another march: yours seems to be pretty fresh." Fresh, indeed! He was an Arab, certainly, and therefore acclimatised, and I was a light weight; but it was almost a cruelty to give him another six miles in the burning heat.

Presently, with a written despatch carefully secured, and a verbal one in my head, the particulars of which I well remember, but will not record, I set off about half-past two. I had just ventured to ask Baker Russell whether he thought I was likely to meet any of the Egyptians *en route*, and his answer was not particularly reassuring. I, therefore, kept my eyes well about me as I slowly rode along. Slowly, I say ; for my " fresh" horse I found had come pretty well to the end of his tether, and no gallop could be got out of him in the heavy sand.

The loneliness of an African desert is something of which we in England can have but a very faint conception, surrounded as we are by smiling fields, and bright hedge-rows, and gentle slopes, and silvery streams. But when it is sand to the right of you, sand to the left of you, sand behind you, sand in front of you ; nothing to break the monotony of this dreary expanse of dry yellow sand, far as the eye can reach, except, perhaps, here and there a dark speck, marking the presence of some ill-omened bird, raven or vulture, the desert solitude is terribly oppressive then.

As I rode along wearily I discerned far away a solitary form which I could not for a time make out. There it stood without movement. Was it a man doubled up on the sand ? Nay, it seemed too bulky for that. As I neared it, I made it out through my glass to be a horse. Presently I came up to it. It was an old troop horse, fully accoutred, but riderless; probably a fugitive from the field just won, where doubtless its rider had been killed or dismounted and the old horse had galloped away. There it was, miles from our camp, standing stock-still, with nose to the ground, a perfect picture of mournful desolation. I was glad to take it in tow, and later on restored it to some of its equine friends; and I think the old trooper quite looked the thanks he could not speak.

It took me nearly two hours to accomplish those six or seven miles. But at last I reached General Willis's camp, and gave up my missive and messages to him; for which he gave me his thanks, and a welcome cup of tea, which he had just been boiling in a big camp cooking pot.

I found that Sheppard, the Guardsman, had been brought down thus far. As I was going into the hospital, which, by-the-bye, had been established in the village Mosque, to see him, I was met by H.R.H. the Duke of

Connaught, who buttonholed me, and made me give him a full account of the engagement. He was evidently keenly disappointed that he and the Guards had been out of it. Instead of joining in a brisk fight, as they had anticipated, they had been toiling at fatigue duty, digging through and cutting the dams which Arabi had thrown across the canal; and there had not been much excitement in this.

I was now twelve miles away from my quarters in Ismailia. It was quite certain that my horse could do no more at present, so I left him here to rest for a day or two, and in the evening accompanied our wounded men who were to be conveyed by boat on the Sweet Water Canal to the Base Hospital. This was a capital arrangement. They could thus be moved without the shaking that was inseparable from stretcher transport, and which added so much to the agony of their sufferings. Large shallow lighters, with a thatching overhead, were specially prepared for this kind of work, and were usually towed by steam pinnaces down to Ismailia.

When I got there, about seven o'clock in the evening, and had seen the men safely placed in hospital, I began to count up experiences. Forty miles on horseback and in boat, six hours' cavalry fighting in the burning heat, and twenty-six hours of almost entire fast, was not a bad test. The sun had blistered my face badly, and my lips were swollen to an abnormal size, and were very painful. I went on board my old ship to get some decent food; but when it was set before me I found I was beyond eating.

Everybody was eager to hear of the day's doings. I found that one of the ship's officers, accompanied by one of the naval men, had set out on their own responsibility to see the fight. All through the night they had toiled across the desert, but had lost their way, and were brought back in a sad plight. The naval man was suffering from a kind of sun-stroke, and was presently invalided home.

I was very glad to turn in, and a good long

night's rest set me all right—except my blistered face—for another experience of the same kind, should it come in the way of duty.

CHAPTER XXI.

Our Indian Contingent under Herbert Macpherson—O'Brien and his Cooking Pot—Graham Seizes Kassassin Lock—Arabi Strikes out at our Advancing Column—First Fight at Kassassin—Bad Odds—A Struggle all Day—The Attack Pressed at Evening—Drury Lowe Brings up the Cavalry—Moonlight Charge—Baker Russell Leads—Lipscombe's Victory—Plucky Hospital Men—To the Front in a Steam Pinnace—Biscuit Bag Defence—A Big "Scare"—My Night Ride through the Desert—Animated Bushes—A Near Shave for the General—The Press Den—How the News was Flashed to England.

ABOUT this time our Indian contingent began to appear upon the scene. Two British regiments accompanied them from India, the 72nd Highlanders, and the 63rd Manchester regiment, two of the smartest battalions we had on the ground; the 72nd men hardened with their two years' campaigning in Afghanistan. The native corps were among the pick of our Indian army, proud to stand shoulder to shoulder with their English brethren in battle-line, and worthy comrades in arms. There were the 13th Bengal Lancers, with their fluttering pennons; and the 2nd and 6th Bengal Cavalry, with their picturesque costume, most of them of the proud Sikh race, with whom we had fought in the terrible campaigns of the Sutlej; they were our sworn allies now. Then there were Punjabis and Beloochis from the far north-west, men of noble bearing and commanding presence; and Rajputs, born warriors, from the provinces lower down in India. And they all worthily maintained the traditions of their race, never flinching before odds, but riding straight, and striking hard and home.

I had been obliged ere this to give up my little room in the Palace Hospital, for every available inch was now required for the accommodation of our sick and wounded. Outside in a grove of trees I pitched my tent, and made myself as comfortable as circumstances would permit. Not far from me were the lines of the red-breeched Beloochis; and now and again the strange weird music of their *tomtoms* sounded oddly enough in the evening hour. The Indian headquarters, too, were close at hand; and here Herbert Macpherson, the gallant commander, who afterwards died in Burmah—an old comrade of mine, too, in the Afghan war—kept his eye on his native *baba-log*, who loved him keenly, and would follow him anywhere. Just outside the tent was the ground peg, to which my horse was usually tethered; and, farther along, the square foot or so of ground which embraced my kitchen, and where O'Brien, my soldier servant, concocted the daily "illigant Oirish stew," as he was pleased to call it, which served both him and me for a dinner about eventide. I never had the temerity to inquire very closely as to what went into our cooking-pot, but accepted with quiet thankfulness what emerged from it, "asking no questions for conscience' sake." It was nothing very elaborate, certainly; but the Irish lad usually produced something very tasty, and many a fellow in the force was worse off. Epicurean tastes had long since been left behind.

At the front we had not anticipated any stirring work yet awhile. Saturday and Sunday, August 26th and 27th, passed—days of welcome rest to our weary fellows up there. General Graham had pushed forward from Mahsameh with the York and Lancaster Regiment, the Cornish Light Infantry, some of the Marine Artillery, and a few cavalry and the Mounted Infantry. With these he had seized and occupied the canal lock at Kassassin; while Drury Lowe, with the main body of the cavalry, and also the Marines, was still at Mahsameh.

It was no longer Arabi's intention to leave Graham unmolested in his occupation of so forward a position. He saw that the British force was slowly but surely advancing on the lines of Tel-el-Kebir. Therefore he decided at once to make a direct attack on the advancing column. Everything was favourable for such a blow. The force under Graham numbered scarce more than 1,800 men, together with two guns; and the position they had taken up was not strategically a favourable one, for they were really astride the canal, and in case of any necessary retreat would be inevitably cut into two separate forces. The Egyptian leader, by means of his railway communication, could throw forward any number of men with ease and rapidity. This he did about half-past nine o'clock in the morning, trying hard to outflank our force on the right, all the time pounding away with his twelve guns; to which our solitary two effectively replied. The firing was heard at Mahsameh. The trumpets sounded "boot and saddle," and the cavalry, consisting of the Life Guards and 4th and 7th Dragoon Guards, prepared to push forward. The heliograph signallers, however, stayed them. As yet there was no critical need. Our little detachment of cavalry and the mounted infantry were indefatigable in feeling the enemy; while the Cornishmen, with the "York and Lancaster," held their position tenaciously. The flank attack on the right failing, a second and more determined attempt was made on our left. And so at intervals the fight continued throughout the day, the enemy gathering in numbers every hour.

Towards evening affairs began to look very serious. Our men were getting exhausted; our casualties had been rather heavy; and more than this, reinforcements were perceived still coming up to swell the Egyptian host already gathered around. Worse than all, the ammunition for our two 13-pounders had given out. Fortunately, a Krupp gun which had been captured by our men on Saturday at Mahsameh from the Egyptians was able to be used, for it happened to be supplied with plenty of ammunition, and it was worked with splendid effect by the Marine Artillery against its old masters.

Already, during the day, Drury Lowe's cavalry had ridden over to within a couple of miles of the scene of fight, but as the enemy had ceased from attack for awhile, the squadrons had returned to their bivouac.

Now, however, as the shades of evening

were settling down, and Arabi was renewing and pressing the attack with vigour, a hasty message was despatched ; apprising the cavalry commander that affairs were assuming a critical appearance. The Egyptian guns thundered unceasingly. The white-coated infantry were pressing in, and a storm of bullets swept the position to which our men were clinging. The slender entrenchments and defences which had been hastily constructed afforded scarce sufficient shelter, for some of Arabi's men were intentionally firing at a high elevation, and the bullets were dropping over. Thus Surgeon-Major Shaw, while attending a wounded man behind the earthwork, was struck, mortally, by a shot which seemed to drop from above, piercing the brain.

The cavalry at Mahsameh had scarcely unsaddled, and were hastily eating their scanty rations (for transport both of ammunition and food had sadly failed again), when young Pirie came galloping in with his message for Drury Lowe. In a moment orders rang out. Smartly the horses, weary as they were, were saddled up again, and the whole body of men moved off to succour their comrades, and to accomplish that magnificent charge, which, for its dash and effectiveness, is worthy to live in the annals of English warfare.

Gliding along through the night, our horsemen kept a ridge between them and the enemy. The moon had not risen, but the stars were clear. Besides, the constant booming of the guns gave them ample direction. Eight battalions and twelve guns were pressing upon Graham, besides hordes of *Bedaween*, who swept around in clouds, anticipating the possible loot which would shortly be theirs.

Presently, as our men, working around the flank of the Egyptians, crossed the ridge, they were perceived, and Arabi's men at once opened a heavy fire upon them, sticking to their guns, and holding their ground, for they were unwilling to relinquish the victory which seemed just within their grasp.

The front line of our cavalry now opened out, and the Horse Artillery guns which had accompanied them, came into action, and splendidly enfiladed the Egyptian lines. This done effectively—Baker Russell, who commanded the brigade—a *beau sabreur* of known dash, ordered the charge. His mighty voice rang out above the battle din as he gallantly led the men. Down went his horse, shot under him; but he seized another and followed on. The English horsemen dashed forward, straight towards the dense masses in front of them, sweeping through the guns, and making terrible havoc among the infantry and gunners, the long swords of the Life Guards searching between the very wheels and under the body of the guns, where many a terrified Egyptian sought hasty shelter when the storm burst upon them. It was a grand charge, worthy of the best traditions of the British Cavalry.

One of our lads, Lipscombe by name, during the charge met with an incident having a comic side; but, alas! with a tragic ending. Away to our left he perceived an Egyptian mounted officer making off as hard as his horse could carry him. Away went Lipscombe in pursuit. The eager chase was not a long one. As he ranged alongside, however, the Egyptian, over his left shoulder, levelled his revolver point blank at him. But ere he could pull the trigger, the Englishman dashed forward, seized the weapon by the muzzle, and turned it against the enemy. The result need not be told.

This charge of the cavalry effectually broke Arabi's attack and shattered his force. Without it, who can say but that, perchance, the catastrophes of Isandhlwana and Maiwand might have been repeated here in Egypt. Our casualties, heavy enough, numbered nearly ninety men, killed and wounded.

A plucky thing on the part of some of our hospital men came to my knowledge. Some of the 1st Bearer Company of the Army Hospital Corps had the wounded under care in a certain part of the field, which presently, by the movements of the troops, became

LIPSCOMBE AT KASSASSIN.

To face page 384.

isolated. The surgeon, however, in charge would not allow any change of position lest the wounded should suffer. So the forty men, filling their haversacks with sand, made a little defence with them ; and then, with the rifles of the wounded, themselves defended the spot, until the cavalry had scattered their foe.

Of the stirring work of this day I had, unfortunately, not been an active eye-witness. I had gone down to Ismailia, after the fight of Friday, and there, busy with my hospital work, was waiting, as we all were, the orders for a general advance. I was destined, however, not to be out of it altogether. Indeed, a little more "in it" than I care to be again.

Strangely enough, not a word of the fight had reached the ears of our people down at the Base, though the sound of the guns had been heard during the day. Towards evening I found that a steam pinnace was going up the Sweet Water Canal to Tel-el-Mahuta. It was only a dozen miles or so. Why should I not take advantage of the opportunity to fetch down my horse, which had been resting here after the "bucketing" he had had in the fight at Mahsameh three days ago? Villiers, of the *Graphic*, thought of going too. But he did not turn up at the canal bridge, so we started without him. On we went in the cool of the evening, which was delightfully pleasant after the intense heat of the day. The shadows closed in upon us, and it was night. It was eleven o'clock before we drew towards Tel-el-Mahuta. As we came up we saw signs of stir and excitement. Not far from the bank was a little round hill, on the top of which General Willis's tent had been pitched on the Friday previously. Now we perceived the men from the lines around hurrying towards the spot, and piling up bags of biscuit, which the Commissariat had just sent forward for the men's rations, in order to form a kind of rampart of defence. Hart, V.C. of the engineers, was directing operations. We hastily landed, and learnt from one of the hurrying men that fierce fighting had been going on all day at the front; and that now an attack by the *Bedaween* of the desert was momentarily expected. They were going to swoop down on our solitary posts simultaneously from Front to Base, and thus cut our line of communications.

Well! This was a pleasant prospect! The main part of the First Division had gone on. A few detachments and the Hospital Corps men only were here. I first of all went in search of my horse, and found him being hurried from the line where he had been tethered to the mound where the stand was to be made.

Just at this moment the dull thud of a galloping horse struck upon our ears; far away at first, but drawing ever nearer. Then the hoarse challenge of our sentry, who was standing fifty paces out, followed in a moment by the crack of a rifle, and in upon us rushed Lagdon, of the Diplomatic Service, but who, just now, was doing correspondent work for the *Morning Post*. He had ridden down from the Front, and brought us news of the fight and the splendid charge. He had no time to reply to the sentry's challenge, and so had been fired at, fortunately without effect. He knew nothing about the expected swoop of the Arabs. At any rate, he wanted to get down to Ismailia to Wolseley as soon as possible, and if he could get a fresh horse would start at once. These correspondents are keen fellows, and like to score off one another with first news. Cameron, the gallant representative of the *Standard*, who was afterwards killed in the Soudan, was riding hard for first honours, but was a mile or so behind now, for his horse had tripped and come down.

I found that the wounded, of whom there was a large number, were being sent down without delay in thatched boats on the canal. The doctors at the Base Hospital would have to be aroused, and the bearers and stretchers sent down to the canal side to await their coming. I decided that I would go with Lagdon and do that part of the work.

The difficulty of the horse for my companion was soon met. Somebody, whom I could not discern in the darkness, lent him a big, strong, English mare; and I mounting my lighter Arab, we rode off into the gloom.

I very quickly discovered that there was no gallop to be got out of my horse. Whether he had been really resting during the previous three days I have since thought was exceedingly problematical. At any rate, he could not keep up with Lagdon's mare. So I told him to go on and I would follow at my leisure. We neither of us were very keen to part from the other, the rumours of the wandering Arabs having made us conscious that now "two were better far than one." But there was no help for it. Lagdon was supremely anxious to get his news off to England as well as to Wolseley, so he hurried forward; and once more I was alone in the great solitary desert. There was no difficulty in finding the way, the canal, by the side of which I took care to ride, giving the direction. It may be readily premised that I rode on the alert—eyes and ears open—intently watching each shadow, lest, perchance, it might turn into some animated foe. I could not altogether lose sight of the expected Arabs. Quietly now I was riding along, letting my horse pretty much take his own time, for what was the use of hurrying? I was far ahead of the boats and the wounded. Along the canal side were some scraggy, stunted bushes planted at intervals. Dreamily wondering how they could possibly live and grow in that dry sand, water though there were close at hand, I seemed to see away along the line, far as my sight could reach, what appeared to be a movement. Why, surely the bushes themselves were endowed with life and were stirring! And then presently the shadowy bushes assumed the form of shadowy men on horses. Yes, sure enough, they were men—mounted men. In the gloom at first that was all I could make out, though I drew rein in a moment, and strove with all my power of vision to pierce the darkness. Are they some of our own men or are they Arabs? As I strain my eyes and gazed, such thoughts as these flashed through my mind:—if they be our own people, they will, of course, ride boldly out, for they will easily see that I am but one; if, on the other hand, they be marauders intent on spoil or slaughter, I may expect to see them, according to their custom, dodging behind the bushes. All this passed through me in a moment or two of thought. They were coming nearer now. And sure enough, in and out, behind and around the bushes, they made their way with apparent stealth. They were in single file. I saw the leading man reach the bush nearest to me. Behind it and around he came. A second more and he would emerge by my very side. I had loosened my revolver case, and pulling "Selim" on his haunches, flashed out my weapon right in the face of the form just appearing. The tremulous moonbeam shimmered on the bright barrel, and in another instant it would have given voice and brought catastrophe to two individuals—myself and another. But somehow or other a strange calmness had seized me, and that accounted for the fortunate moment of pause. I was not *quite* sure of my man; he might be an Englishman after all. It was during this infinitesimal part of a second, while my finger forbore to press the trigger, an English voice rang out, " Why don't you loose off? " Oh! the superb coolness of the English race! He looked verily down the shining barrel; he knew not who I might be any more than I knew who he was, yet this was all the remark he made. I made some hasty reply and rode hurriedly on.

What I learnt subsequently was this— that one of our General officers, with his personal staff, was riding up to the front, taking advantage of the cool night. It was he whom I had met, and it was he whom I, by a little loss of coolness or a little trembling of the finger, might have seriously damaged.

When I reached our next post, which was held by some of the West Kent men, I found that the "scare" had affected them too. They were working hard to entrench their position a little. I was able to assure Carr, who was in command of the detachment, that no Arabs at any rate were on the way, and that he and his men might turn in again with easy minds.

About half-past two in the morning I came into Ismailia. I aroused the doctors who were quartered in the Base Hospital. The Bearer Companies, too, were warned; and presently, with their stretchers, they were gathered at the canal side awaiting the coming of our wounded.

Then I steered for the correspondents' haunt, where I knew I should find some half-dozen of them. Bursting into their rough bedroom, where the sound of loud snoring heralded the sleep of the just, I announced the fight and the victory; not forgetting a vivid picture of the moonlight charge.

Out tumbled the Press men, one from this corner, and another from that: here Le Sage of the *Daily Telegraph*, and there Burleigh of the *Central News*, and yonder Villiers of the *Graphic*. And they all listened with eager ears, grouped around me in their bare legs for a few moments ; and then hastily donning a few garments, they made a rush for the little telegraph office to flash the news to England.

The next morning, as the good people at home took up their paper from the breakfast table, and read the record of the dashing cavalry charge which had been made the night before, their hearts would kindle with pride and enthusiasm. But little would they know of the lonely desert ride, through the dark night watches, by means of which two or three solitary fellows carried the tidings.

The first gleam of breaking dawn was flashing across the Eastern sky as I turned in, and was soon in my dreams re-traversing the desert track by which I had just come from Tel-el-Mahuta.

CHAPTER XXII.

Tedious Waiting—Short Commons of Water—A Handy Sausage Machine—Arabi Aroused—Cavalry Reconnoitring—Graham's Reconnaissance—September 9th—Second Fight at Kassassin—Shells as an Early "Eye-Opener"—Pennington's Plucky Lancers—They Check the Advance—Egyptian Guns Search our Camp—Volunteers under Fire—The Enemy Four to One—Our Cavalry let loose—Wolseley Comes Up—Arabi begins to Fall Back—Marines Capture Two Guns—Stanhope's Muscular Feat—The Lines at Tel-el-Kebir—Gribble Found—The Dead Lancer—Nine Hours and no Breakfast—Shall we Rush the Entrenchments?—Wolseley Returns to Camp—Bengali Courtesy—Field Hospital Scenes—Both Legs Lost—The Dead Riflemen—A Chaplain Knocked Up.

ALL the difficulties and hardships which are associated with tedious waiting were now being experienced by us. Down at Ismailia, even, we were badly off enough. We had a steamer constantly at work condensing water for drinking purposes; but the supply from this source was very insufficient in quantity, and very poor in quality. In fact, the men were for several days on pint rations. But the water of the Sweet Water Canal! Ugh! It was horrible—poisoned with dead carcasses. Nevertheless the men would fill their water bottles with it. "Better die of poison than of thirst," they said. But they did not die, strange to say; nor was there any outbreak of cholera or enteric fever among us then; though I believe the prevalence of the latter, some months later, when we were at Cairo, may fairly be traced to the poison taken into the system by the men at this time.

At the extreme front, up at Kassassin, matters were a good deal worse. The transport had been much improved. Trucks were sent forward on the line, drawn by horses; and one or two small locomotives even were at work, but it was found, as usual, difficult to get the stores forward. Fatigue parties of the men were hard at work helping to unload the vessels, and gangs of workmen, French, Arabs, and Italians, were drawing wages at the rate of seven shillings a day, for which they did precious little. The lads at the Front had to do as well as they could on the hard, dry biscuit that was served out, with an occasional relish of " Bully Beef," as they called the Australian tinned meat. We, who could come down to Ismailia sometimes, were able to fare better ; for the Greek traders, always keen to turn an honest penny, or a dishonest one, the latter for choice, were opening their stores along a certain little back street, where one found nearly everything in the way of tinned provisions and other handy articles ; and these were sold at exorbitant prices.

The commissariat beef which was served out in the daily rations about this time none of us will ever forget, I think. Woe to the man whose grinders were few !

In a certain Artillery mess where I was lunching one day, I observed that one of the most popular men was one who had possessed himself of a small mincing machine. This was borrowed by most of the members, and after it had gone the round and each portion had been reduced to an edible condition, the work of eating commenced.

Men were now beginning to make their way to the Front. Correspondents were gathering in force. Sir Henry Havelock-Allan, one of the keenest soldiers who ever drew sword, could not remain idle at home. He must witness if he could not strike. So he was out here with us. His departure to Kassassin was comical and practical both. He had secured for the transport of his necessary stores a small cart, and for purposes of draught, a pony and a camel. His servant was in command of these animals and the cart, and drove away from Ismailia tandem, the pony being in the shafts and the camel in front, much to the amusement of the spectators who had gathered round to see the start. An animal of any kind was valuable now. Hence I met one plucky correspondent plodding towards Kassassin and leading a patient "moke" on which his goods and chattels were packed.

Arabi was by no means idle. He seemed alive to the fact that the moment of crisis was approaching. He knew well enough what was transpiring at our base and right along the line to the Front. Battalions were gathering; the Highlanders, the Irish Fusiliers, and fresh English regiments were all coming up.

Between Kassassin, our extreme front, and the enemy's lines at Tel-el-Kebir was a stretch of perhaps seven or eight miles; and across this desert expanse reconnoitring parties, both English and Egyptian, were constantly passing, keeping a sharp eye on each other, exchanging shots which were, for the most part, harmless, and getting occasional sight of one another's main positions.

Thus General Wilkinson, the Brigadier commanding the Indian Cavalry, returning from a morning reconnaissance on one side of the canal, saw, some distance off, a body of Egyptian cavalry dismounted. Neither party took much notice of the other. Presently, however, he passed close to a group of Arab peasants who were on the canal bank, but the other side. Scarcely had he passed when the innocent peasants produced their concealed rifles and fired a volley. The *Bedaween*, too, were pressing in from the desert, and on our very line of communications at Ramses, attacked 300 Commissariat mules as they made their way to the Front under escort.

Graham himself took out a force, consisting of the 46th Cornish, two squadrons of Indian Cavalry, the Mounted Infantry under Lawrence, and four guns, on a final reconnoitring expedition. He hoped to surprise a body of *Bedaween* which had gathered in the neighbourhood; but the Arabs fled at once towards Tel-el-Kebir. The Egyptians, however, turned out in force from their lines, and Graham had to fall back speedily, covered by the Indian Cavalry and Lawrence's Mounted Infantry.

The next morning Arabi made another supreme effort. It was the 9th of September, the anniversary of the original revolt of the Egyptian Colonels; and perhaps a superstitious idea that victory might follow his arms on such an auspicious day possessed him.

It was scarce more than dawn when our men in camp at Kassassin, just turning out, were startled by a heavy fire being suddenly opened upon them. Shells came thick and fast, dropping into the middle of the camp and through the tents where the men, but a few minutes before, had been sleeping.

Just then two of Pennington's Bengal Lancers came galloping in from the desert, their fringed turbans streaming out behind. They told how trains had been seen coming up from Tel-el-Kebir crowded with men. Already Arabi, under cover of night, had brought up a very large force (it was afterwards estimated at nearly 15,000 men in all), and was endeavouring to repeat his tactics of August 28th, viz., to out-flank us on our right, and, if possible, seize the camp. He had no fewer than twenty-four Krupp guns, and was shelling vigorously now.

The first discovery of the movement illustrates well the pluck of our Bengal *sowars*, and shows the splendid material of which our Indian cavalry is composed. Far out in the desert, just as the night shadows were beginning to creep away, a little outlying picket of only four *sowars* found themselves suddenly confronted by some ten or a dozen of the enemy's cavalry. The ordinary course to pursue would have been for our men to fire a volley with their carbines and then fall back on the stronger inlying picket. But this did not seem to occur to our gallant Indian horsemen. Couching their lances, and with a mighty war shout, they rode straight at the foe; and in a few moments four Egyptians were *hors de combat*.

Pennington himself was nigh at hand, for he had ridden out very early with thirty of his men to post vedettes. As he came up, the dozen or so of Egyptian cavalry had swelled to three squadrons, while a column of infantry was steadily advancing in attack formation. Afar off, through the morning haze, a stronger body of cavalry still could be seen coming across the desert: and the steam of several locomotives indicated trains of advancing troops.

Pennington sent off two of his men to gallop to camp as hard as they could, and give the alarm. And then, with infinite coolness and pluck, he dismounted the rest, and from behind a ridge of sand opened carbine fire on the Egyptians. Immensely superior in numbers, they continued to advance, until the little band of Indians was completely overlapped and practically surrounded. "Stand to your horses! Mount!" was the word. The swarthy Lancers leaped into their saddles; and in another moment with levelled lances they had crashed at charging pace through the Egyptians, and wheeling around with a whoop, were galloping home to Graham's camp.

This check, which Pennington had given the advancing Egyptians, was most timely. Our men had time to form up, and in exactly twenty-five minutes the whole force, consisting of six battalions of Infantry, the 19th Hussars, the 13th Bengal Lancers, and afterwards the Household Cavalry, together with three batteries of artillery, numbering perhaps 4,000 men, began to move out.

Not one moment too soon! Already the Egyptian guns were on the crest of the ridges overlooking the camp, and their shells were bursting in the midst of the columns forming up. Horses and cattle, terrified, were breaking away. The Volunteer force just now, in the persons of some Post Office men, came under fire for the first time. They seemed rather to like it, and were cheering vociferously, while hard at work helping to secure the frightened animals.

At first it was an artillery duel, for our guns came into action and replied to the Egyptian batteries. This fire, however, was only masking a turning movement, and presently Arabi's men were able to unite with a strong additional force which had marched across the desert from Salahieh. We were completely overlapped.

Now Graham gave the cavalry their chance, as on the 28th of August. Away went Drury Lowe with Guards, Hussars, and Mounted Infantry, menacing in turn the Egyptian left. Their cavalry then fell back, and each force riding far out into the desert tried to work around the other. Borradale's Horse Battery was with Drury Lowe, and the Egyptians also had light guns. These were every now and again hard at work.

The Egyptian infantry were a bare thousand yards from our line, and the rifle fire in volume and sound was tremendous. The artillery were still pounding away; but our guns were getting the mastery by reason of the superior accuracy of aim. Then our men began to push forward, and the foe to fall back.

At this point Wolseley himself arrived. It had been decided for Headquarters to come up from Ismailia on this day. A few trucks and one solitary railway carriage, which had seen better days, had been prepared. Wolseley and his staff, however, preferred an open waggon to the stuffy and not too odorous carriage, and accordingly arrived in a cattle truck at Kassassin, reaching the fighting ground about ten o'clock.

Very slowly Arabi's force began to fall back as our men pressed on. Their firing, mighty in volume as it was, had been contemptible in result; and I am afraid ours had not been anything to boast of.

Suddenly the Marines, in their advance, found themselves close to one of the enemy's batteries. Quickly the Egyptian guns were limbered up, and some of them succeeded in getting off. But two of them were not quick enough. The Marines came on with a rush; and though the gunners whipped up their horses they were captured. Some of the Rifles succeeded in taking another " Krupp," but were unable to bring it off. Stanhope, one of the young officers, swam the canal, and by sheer muscular strength toppled it into the water lest the Egyptians might return and carry it away.

Steadily the tide of battle rolled forward, our men advancing all along the line, and the Egyptians being beaten back step by step.

They were very unwilling to relinquish the positions they had so stealthily seized, for they outnumbered us nearly four to one. But our men would not be denied—Rifles, Marines, Cornishmen, they were lessening the distance between themselves and the lines at Tel-el-Kebir.

By this time Drury Lowe with his bold riders was far out to our right, having succeeded in completely turning the enemy's cavalry. So favourable seemed all the circumstances that he and Redvers Buller were actually taking counsel as to whether it might not be possible to make a dash on Zagazig, some dozen miles beyond Tel-el-Kebir. Wolseley's orders came just in time to stop them.

From five o'clock in the morning to two in the afternoon our men had been moving across the desert and fighting back the foe. I was on foot, and so was Chapman, another chaplain, for our horses were down at Ismailia, and we had a full taste of what the men's experience must have been, toiling hour after hour through the heavy sand.

As he and I were making our way towards the 46th, who were some distance ahead, we came across the body of the one Bengal Lancer of Pennington's gallant little band who had fallen in the morning. The barbarous Egyptians, or perhaps some of the wandering Arabs, had made an attempt at mutilation, but had apparently been disturbed and stopped in their vile work. He lay peacefully enough now. Presently some of his comrades came up, and buried him there in the sand, far from his native country.

Poor Gribble's body was found, too, on this afternoon. He had dropped in the moonlight charge of August 28th.

The line of our troops was now only some two miles from the defences at Tel-el-Kebir. There they were stretching out before us; reaching from end to end a full four miles. Strong redoubts mounting heavy guns could be seen here and there, at intervals, in the line of entrenchments. Wolseley carefully reconnoitred. The Egyptians had been driven close up and were firing at long ranges, the guns, however, dropping their shells still in our midst. For nine hours the force had been out, and as yet no breakfast had passed their lips. Very welcome was the appearance of some of the men who had been left in camp, who now came laden with big camp kettles containing a supply of coffee roughly made. Bags of hard biscuit also arrived, and these, with a mouthful of the coffee, formed a most welcome meal.

Some of the hotter spirits of the force would fain now have pushed on, and rushed the position at Tel-el-Kebir at once. But Wolseley stayed his hand, and curbed their impatience. And he was right. We should doubtless have gained the stronghold; but the Guards and Highlanders were not yet up; and with our scanty force we should not have been able to break up Arabi's army; it would still have remained a solid body to dispute our road to Cairo.

At half-past two o'clock then the orders were to turn back to Kassassin, and in the blazing sun we began our march to camp. My companion, Chapman, the other chaplain, was completely exhausted. I managed to fraternise with a small detachment of Bengal Lancers, who were glad to talk with an Englishman able to speak in their own language. One of the courteous fellows seeing me on foot, soon offered me his mount, so I put Chapman up, and got him safely to camp.

I made my way to the little Field Hospital, where our wounded were being temporarily placed and cared for. Here, at the door of one tent, lay two big Marines. They had each lost a leg; but as I talked with them one of them said, with evident feeling, "Thank God it's no worse; see, we've only lost one leg, sir; yonder's a poor fellow that's lost both." So it was. On the other side of the tent lay a Rifleman. A shell had exploded literally under him, blowing him into the air, and shattering both legs, injuring his arm as well. Poor fellow! He bore the double amputation well, and was doing splendidly a week later; when suddenly an artery gave way, and he bled to death before help could come to him. Close at hand lay Purvis, of the *Penelope*, who commanded the little naval detachment that brought up a big forty-pounder. He had been struck by a shot which shattered his foot. In another tent lay two dead Riflemen. One was said to have died from heat and exhaustion. "But I don't believe it," said Wilkins, the Quartermaster, who afterwards fell gallantly fighting on the Suakim side; "the lad was born and bred in India, and he would not give in to the sun." So we examined him, and sure enough found that a bullet had entered his side and passed right through him. It was evidently a chance shot; there was no external bleeding; he had just dropped in the ranks, and his comrades thought the sun had done it.

We had over sixty casualties, and the surgeons were hard at work with the wounded Egyptians as well, some of whom were writhing and shouting under their hurts.

As soon as the cool shades of evening had fallen the poor fellows began to be sent down in thatched boats on the canal to our Base Hospital at Ismailia.

It was pretty late at night before Chapman and I turned into our little tent in the cavalry lines. He was thoroughly done up, quite ill, indeed; and I shall never forget the kindness of our Brigade-Major, the gallant Herbert Stewart, and of Drury Lowe himself, who extended mess hospitality to the sick man and myself. The next day I took Chapman down to Ismailia, and put him aboard the Carthage, our hospital ship, which lay in harbour.

He was not strong enough for rough campaigning.

CHAPTER XXIII.

Wolseley Carefully Reconnoitres — Arabi's Strong Position — Details — His Numbers — The Odds Against Us—Quiet Sabbath in the Desert—I Take Down a Sick Chaplain to Ismailia—Railway Service —Sepoys Eager for the Fight—Hospital Arrangements Perfect—The Convent Sisters—Netley Nurses Arrive—The Hospital Ship *Carthage*—Death of the Rifleman—Everyone Keen for the Front—The Highland Brigade Veterans—No Boy Soldiers—Laying in Stores—Off to Kassassin Again—Force Gathered—Ready ! Aye Ready !

WOLSELEY was not satisfied with the peep he had had at the enemy's position on the afternoon of September the 9th. On the mornings of the 10th, 11th, and 12th he and his Staff rode far out and carefully reconnoitred. He could make out easily the long line of entrenchments stretching away from the canal, and even beyond it, across the railway, and then far out into the desert, very nearly four miles in actual length. Then from the centre of this front line there appeared to be a diagonal line, striking away at an angle to the bottom of the position; and in the space enclosed between these two lines were a great number of shelter trenches. Most of the white tents of the camp could be seen clustering down near the railway and canal lines.

At intervals along the line were strong redoubts mounting heavy guns. These were most skilfully constructed so as to deliver not only a front and flanking fire, but they circled around, and guns were mounted to sweep even the rear of the position. To complete the description with details which of course only afterwards came to our knowledge when the assault had been delivered, the front line consisted of a ditch some four and a half feet deep and five or six feet across, and beyond it a steep earthwork, with hurdle *revêtement*, rising a clear nine feet from the bottom of the ditch. Mahmoud Fehmy Pasha, whom he had captured at the cavalry fight of Mahsameh, was no mean engineer, and the position owed its strength to his excellent skill.

Thousands of *fellaheen* had been toiling at the works for many weeks past; and now everything was ready; and Arabi and his men were awaiting the attack of Wolseley.

But what was the strength of the force under Arabi's command? Spies of course were available, as they always are, especially in Eastern lands; and from them Wolseley was able to glean some important facts. Within the lines there were two whole divisions, some twenty-four battalions, consisting in all of about twenty thousand men; also three regiments of cavalry, and about six or seven thousand irregulars.

About sixty guns were mounted, mostly in the redoubts. At Salahieh, which lay across the desert a few miles, there was a further force of five thousand men, with twenty-four guns, watching and guarding Arabi's left flank, but ready to march, at a moment's notice, to his aid.

The attack on such a position was not to be lightly enterprised. Wolseley, allowing for the force which he was compelled to detach to guard his base, and the long line of communications, could only throw forward about eleven thousand infantry, and two thousand cavalry. The odds therefore were great. And besides, the Egyptians who were contemptible in the open field were by no means a despicable foe behind entrenchments; and it was more than likely that they would stand well, and make a good fight of it. The result of the attack justified the prognostication.

After the stiff fight of Saturday, September the 9th, Sunday was a day of welcome rest to our weary fellows. I shall not soon forget that Sunday. It was the last that some were destined to spend on earth; and to many hundreds of others the next would come burdened with bitter pain. Our little Field Hospital tents were standing near the canal side, and here some of our poor fellows, who could not yet be moved even by the smooth transport of the boats, were still lying. A little quiet talk with them filled up the hours of the afternoon. Then towards evening, as the

sun was setting, we held our parade services;
and so the shadows closed in upon us, and
the Sabbath ended; one of the quietest that
I ever remember to have spent in any camp.

On Monday my friend Chapman, one of the
other chaplains, who had pluckily held out
till now, was compelled to give in. He had
been seedy for some time, and now dysentery
had seized him with virulence; and my
anxiety was to get him safely down to Ismailia,
and on board the hospital ship, the *Carthage*.

We actually had a train service now; a
primitive business enough, too! About noon
it came lumbering along, a string of open
waggons, many of them in a dilapidated condition, and drawn by a very ancient and
rusty locomotive, men of the Engineer corps
acting as drivers. The line was very badly
laid, and frequently in one and another spot
gave way; so progress was slow, and journeying tedious. Mile after mile we crept along,
my sick comrade groaning all the way, for his
pain was considerable, and the sun blazed
down on the unsheltered passengers. A

motley collection of sick men, and stores, odds and ends of all kinds, a few horses, and so on, were gathered aboard that train. At last, after more than three hours of jolting and stopping, the twenty miles or so were accomplished, and the little station of Ismailia was reached.

En route we had to stop at Mahsameh, where our cavalry fight had taken place a fortnight or so before. Here a part of a native regiment which I had known at Lucknow, the 7th Bengal Infantry, were encamped. The men gathered around me with sad words. They had heard that the *burra larai*, the big fight, was coming off in a day or two at Tel-el-Kebir; and here they were ten miles down the line, and not likely to be in it. Great stalwart fellows they were; and as they stood around me in their ordinary native undress, with brown muscular legs and arms, it seemed to me that any one of them could tackle half-a-dozen of the pusillanimous Egyptians. They almost had tears in their eyes, as they asked me to entreat Colonel Worsley, their commanding officer, to let his *baba log* come forward. They appeared to be only a detachment of the 7th N. I. who were on the line of communications. Whether these particular ones did get forward or not, I do not know; but certainly this gallant regiment, than which there is no better set-up body of men in the native army, was in the fight, and took its part right worthily.

At Ismailia I found that during the last week or so our hospital arrangements had been perfected, and everything now seemed in a thorough state of efficiency. The gorgeous palace of the Khedive, standing among the umbrageous trees of its Eastern garden, was still the main building. And within, everything was arranged with that perfectness of style and adaptation which may be seen in our military hospitals at home. The poor fellows, no longer made as comfortable as circumstances would allow on the bare hard floor, were now in the more restful cots, ranged with military regularity along the walls. When I was last in the building all the tending had to be done by the hospital orderlies, or almost all; though some of the devoted sisters of the neighbouring convent, always to the front with good works of charity, had come forward to lend their kindly aid. Some were French, some Italian, and some of negro race; but our suffering lads were deeply touched by their skilful and tender care. Now, however, a little band of military nurses had arrived from Netley. And as they moved quietly through the wards, doing their work with such gentle hand and such trained skill, their little red tippets flashing a gleam of bright colour over the sombre shadows of the hospital, the sick men watched them with brighter eye; new hope seemed enkindled now in their hearts, when they felt the touch of a woman's hand; and they grew better the more quickly.

Lying out in the harbour, the white hull of the *Carthage*, a big P. and O. boat, could be seen. This had been specially arranged internally for hospital work, and was most complete in every detail; it had only lately arrived from England. I went on board, and found here also a band of Netley nurses, a staff of doctors, and, alas! already most of the cots filled with sick and wounded. What would it be after the big battle?

In one of the wards of the Palace Hospital ashore I found poor Burton of the Rifles, the man who had lost both his legs a few days before. He greeted me with a bright smile as I went up to him. "Well," said I to him, "what about the arm that was injured too, and which the doctors thought would have to come off?" His answer was to stretch it out apparently whole as the other. He was a plucky fellow, and his pluck had carried him through bravely. Yet, alas! within two or three brief hours he was dead. I heard it as I was getting some food in one of the little hotels that evening, from a doctor who was sitting near. The poor lad had been too venturesome. Moving about in his cot, or actually trying to raise himself, an artery had given way, and he lay back and died before help could reach him. Indeed the cause was not discovered till the sheet was lifted and the blood found.

I found everyone in Ismailia and aboard the vessels in harbour were eager for news from the Front. They all knew that the great moment was drawing near. And all sorts of men, unattached, were endeavouring under various pretexts to get to the Front.

The Highland Brigade, under Sir Archibald Allison, had come up from the Suez side, and were now disembarked. Indeed, they were making the best of their way over the twenty miles or so of desert to Kassassin. The battalions which composed this brigade had been most carefully selected, and the men who marched in the ranks were for the most part veterans of some degree. A good deal was afterwards said about the young soldiers who formed the force under Wolseley in this campaign. As far as I could learn the men were distinguished rather by their length of service. It was well known that the various regiments had been carefully weeded, the young and weak soldiers being left behind at home, and their places filled by old " reservists ; " of whom, I suppose, some thousands in all marched with the colours ; while the Highland Brigade, upon whom, as we shall presently see, fell the heaviest brunt of the fighting, averaged over seven years' service. The 72nd Highlanders, fresh from India and Afghanistan, their breasts covered with medals and crosses, had numbers of grey-haired men in their ranks. It is well not to lose sight of these facts, because the time will never come when boy soldiers will be able to do what seasoned veterans can do. They will doubtless have the pluck and the dash for the charge, as English boys ever will have; but the stamina necessary for campaign severities, as well as the sturdy steadiness which is required of our lads in the actual "tug of war," will most certainly be lacking.

Having discreetly visited the street where the stores of the Greek traders were situated, and gathered up a few necessaries, among which, I remember, was a real loaf of bread, I proposed with one or two more to get back to the Front as quickly as possible. The dilapidated but useful railway train was to be our means of transport once more; and taking our seat, or, rather, perching ourselves on a heap of empty baskets which were being sent forward for some purpose or other, we jolted our way towards Kassassin, reaching it in about three hours.

A change had taken place in the appearance of things during the day that I had been away, and the camp had wonderfully extended its boundaries. The Guards were up from Tel-el-Mahuta, and the regular lines of their tents were now to be seen almost in the centre. The Highland Brigade were yonder on the outer fringe, the brawny Scotchmen not a bit the worse for their march over the desert, now that they had rested a few hours. The Indians were in full force, cavalry and infantry; far more at home with scant shelter and short rations than our own English lads. There was an air of buoyancy pervading the camp, for everyone knew that the tedious waiting which had been an element in all the preliminary work was about to end. The blow was to be struck in a few hours, for better or for worse, and the very prospect of fighting brought a thrill of enthusiasm to every heart. All were ready! Aye ready! I hurried off to my tent in the cavalry lines, and found that events had indeed hurried on apace while I had been away. No wonder there was a stir! The orders which had just come out were startling enough to cause some excitement.

CHAPTER XXIV.

The Battle of Tel-el-Kebir—The Lull before the Storm—Orders Out for an Advance—Last Letters—Fall In!—Disposition of our Forces—St. Vincent and his Final Fate—The Advance—Halt!—Onward March—Wyatt Rawson Steers by the Stars—Brookes of the "Gordons" goes in with a Spade—Silent March through the Darkness — Day Breaks—Terrible Opening Fire—Arabi's Arrangements—The Highlanders in First—Havelock-Allan Rushes the Ditch—A Narrow Shave—Egyptians Fight Steadily — Graham-Stirling and McNeill — The English and Irish Brigade at it together—The Marines Lose Heavily—Death of Strong—Wardell Falls: but is Avenged by Luke.

AT last the moment so eagerly longed for had come. The advance on Arabi's stronghold was to be made, and the attack delivered. How would it result? Would the position presently be in our hands, or should we be beaten back? The latter question occurred to only a very few probably, for the spirit of confidence which inspired our commander caught the hearts of the men generally.

Everybody, of course, had known before this that the critical moment was rapidly drawing near, and that the last scene in this drama of blood was about to be played; and like the ominous stillness which precedes the bursting of the fierce storm, so a great quietness had previously settled down upon our camp at Kassassin. The men were at high tension. Now, suddenly, the spell was broken; and all through the lines was the stir of eager preparation.

Wolseley had early in the day had his Divisional and Brigade Commanders in counsel, and had explained to them accurately and in detail his plan of attack; and at four o'clock in the afternoon general orders were out that a night march was to be made on the lines at Tel-el-Kebir. At six o'clock tents were to be struck, and the whole force was to advance soon after.

Amid all the excitement and bustle of preparation, the wild joy which came to many in the thought of the coming fight, the thoughts of most men veered homeward; and many letters were written, and mutual arrangements made between one and another "in case anything should happen to me, you know."

The red sun was sinking behind a high ridge of sand. It was the last sunset that many a gallant fellow was destined to see. The tents had been struck and packed, and the baggage of the various regiments was piled in order by the side of the railway line. The whole force was falling in—here the Guards, there the Highlanders, and yonder the Irish lads, with difficulty repressing their national jocosity; for a broad, humorous grin was even now flashing across the face of each "broth of a boy," and many a quip and crank dropped unconsciously almost from his lips.

Every man carried a hundred rounds of ammunition and a couple of day's rations, and the water bottles were filled with cold tea—a very capital arrangement. The march was to be made in order of attack. On our extreme right, what might be called the English and Irish Brigade, united now in common brotherhood under General Graham. This consisted of the Marine Light Infantry —a splendid battalion of solid, well-set-up men, the 84th, or York and Lancaster regiment, the 87th Royal Irish Fusiliers, and the 2-18th Royal Irish. They were to dash in on the left corner of the enemy's front line of defence. Next in order in our line were our forty-two field guns, seven batteries massed, under Goodenough. Then lower down, just about our centre, and consequently to rush at the middle of Arabi's lines, where his works and redoubts were strongest, marched our magnificent Highland Brigade, under the one-armed General, whom they all loved, Archibald Alison. How grand those sturdy Scotsmen did look as they proudly formed up under the keen eye of their leader! The Brigade consisted of four picked battalions—the 74th Highland Light Infantry, the 79th Camerons, the

75th Gordons, and the 42nd Royal Highlanders, better known as the celebrated Black Watch.

On the line of railway the ironclad train, which had already done such capital service, was brought along by some of our Naval Brigade, the main body of which, under Captain Fitzroy, of the *Orion*, marched with the Indian Contingent on the other side of the canal. Sir Herbert Macpherson, with whom I had served in Afghanistan, held in hand the Indians. His brigade was only in part native, for it consisted of one joint battalion made up from the three Indian regiments, a Mountain Battery, and the 72nd Highlanders.

General Wolseley very cautiously held, as a reserve line, the Guards' Brigade, under the Duke of Connaught, and a small force under Colonel Ashburnham, consisting of the 3-60th Rifles and the 46th Cornish Light Infantry; the former to march in a position somewhat between Graham's Brigade and the guns, and about a thousand yards farther back; the latter to take position behind the Highlanders. This was a wise precaution; as in the dire event of our front line being beaten back, matters would not be beyond recovery.

The English Cavalry were to sweep around on our right, and the Indian Cavalry on our left, to complete the work which was to be done by the brigades in their front attack.

Thus Wolseley disposed his force. The 50th West Kent Regiment, the 19th Hussars, and two companies of the Royal Engineers were detailed to guard our camp at Kassassin; while the 63rd Manchester Regiment and a portion of the native troops looked after the line of communications down to Ismailia.

The cavalry was not to march for some hours after the others. My tent was in their lines, and Lord St. Vincent, who was acting in some staff capacity, put his head in to tell me of the arrangements, his face lighted up with keen anticipation. Poor fellow! it was not his last fight; yet the deserts of Africa were to be his resting-place after all; for he was struck down in one of the desperate fights which took place in the ill-fated Nile Expedition. To my mind an incident connected with his last moments, and which came to me long afterwards through one of the surgeons who was tending him then, was singularly beautiful; the spirit and pluck which characterised him in life being with him even in the darkness of his last hour. When he fell, sore stricken indeed, and was carried to the doctors who were at work in the square, he said to them, "Examine me, and tell me if there is any chance." They did so, and then told him that he could not recover. "Very well," he said, "that is all I want; go and attend to the others who need your help, and leave me at peace." And so crossing his hands and closing his eyes, he waited there calmly for death to release him from his sufferings.

But now the men had formed up, each brigade in position, and awaiting the word to move forward. As the shadows of the night fell, the march was commenced; but when about a mile and a half on the way the men were halted, and there remained till half-past one in the morning. Then the advance was continued. There was no moon, but the stars were clear; and by the light of the stars the gallant Wyatt Rawson, the naval lieutenant, marching with the Highland Brigade about the centre of the line, steered the force, as he would have steered his ship, with marvellous precision. Scarce a sound broke the stillness. Just a whispered word now and again, or perhaps a command in low muttered tone, and the dull, steady tramp, tramp, tramp of the advancing host was all that could be heard.

Young Brookes, of the "Gordons," when the men were halted, in some way mislaid and lost his claymore. In the darkness search was difficult and without result. "Never mind," said the plucky fellow, seizing a pioneer's spade that was handy, "I'm going right in with this; and Arabi has no bullet that will touch me to-day." Alas! it was a false presentiment. A few hours after, just inside the trenches, among the thick of the dead, his body was found, the locked fingers still clutching the shovel, bent and dented, telling of the deadly work it had done, but himself pierced with no less than five bullets.

On marched the men, ever nearing the enemy's stronghold. Terribly long seemed those seven miles or so. It was wearisome toiling through the soft sand, and difficult, above all things, to keep the long line intact, though by means of connecting files this was done in part. The darkness revealed nothing. At any moment we might have happed upon scouting horsemen; or even marched right into the entrenchments. The question that was uppermost in many minds was whether we should reach them before the dawn broke; or, on the other hand, should be too late, and the light enable the foe to discern us from afar. Either mistake would involve possible failure. But Wyatt Rawson, with his eye on the unfailing stars, moved steadily on in front of the Highlanders. Anxiety and anticipation kindled into intensity. Every man waited with almost painful tension for what the next moment might develop.

Suddenly, as it does on those lands, the first faint gleam of coming dawn flashed across the Eastern sky. The day was breaking; and the cold grey light revealed, scarce three hundred yards ahead, the long line of solid earthworks. Aye, and more—an equally long line of dark-faced men who were waiting and watching for our advance and attack.

There was not one moment of pause. Just a few scattered shots from the enemy's pickets, and then the whole front burst into a line of flame from entrenchment and redoubt. With a mighty cheer, but with no answering shot, for it was to be cold steel, our men dashed forward towards the fringe of flame. The struggle was to be decided with the bayonet.

But here let me say that no troops in the world could, I believe, have stood against that fearful opening fire had it been in the most ordinary degree effective. We did not surprise Arabi. He was well posted up in our movements. Doubtless within an hour of our striking tents he was apprised of it. And all night long his men, in position, had watchfully waited for us. From end to end of his three miles at least of entrenchment, his soldiers were standing almost shoulder to shoulder, waiting to pull trigger. The very carefulness of their detail arrangements, humanly speaking, wrought their ruin. They had anticipated, no doubt, the possibility of seeing us from a fair distance, and every rifle was sighted carefully at eight hundred yards. Thus it was that when that terrible fire was opened upon us, the blast of the storm, the leaden hail, swept over the heads of the attacking line for the most part harmlessly. This was a contingency which could not, of course, have been counted on; and Wolseley's whole plan, involving the delivery of this front attack on a strong position held by a much superior force in point of numbers, has been very extensively criticised. And with reference even to the splendid final charge of our men into the very teeth of the fire, the old utterance has been requoted, *"c'est magnifique mais ce n'est pas la guerre."* But Wolseley's star shone clear on this night, and the result goes far to justify the means. A flank movement might have saved much life, but while the enemy would have been driven out of his position, he would probably have been able to take up another in the cultivated and broken country behind, with his army defeated, but not shattered. Wolseley desired to make this effort a final one, and when he once laid his hand on his foe, to crush him once and for ever.

It is beyond all doubt that the Highland Brigade came in touch first with the enemy. When the opening fire burst upon them and the line of flame flashed from end to end, a wild cheer broke from them; and, headed by their pipers, whose pibroch sounded shrilly above the battle din, they dashed forward. Gallantly Sir Archibald Alison led them against the very strongest point of the whole line. With them was a spectator, too; one whose keen eye watched every movement, and whose face was gleaming now with the battle light. Sir Henry Havelock-Allan rode with the Highland Brigade; for had he not had some of those very battalions under his command formerly? Surely the memories of Lucknow were upon him; memories reminding him of the day when he charged straight towards the rebel guns that were sweeping the Char Bagh bridge, and won the position and his V. C. a quarter of a century before. Now on his big chestnut charger, he went straight at the entrenchments. That chestnut was a hunter as well, and accustomed to fly its fences. So it made a dash at this. But ditch and earth-work were too much. It landed on the steep bank, and slid or toppled back into the ditch. For a moment its gallant rider, as he picked himself up, was filled with mortification; but the next instant that feeling gave place to thankfulness, for a gun was looking out from its embrasure in the very spot where the good horse had landed,

SIR HAVELOCK ALLAN AT TEL-EL-KEBIR.

and as it fell backwards that gun vomited forth its charge of grape shot. Soon Sir Henry was up and at it again, and this time more successfully. But he was too good a soldier to go in among the guns and bayonets with nothing but a hunting crop, as one legend records. I trow he had some better defence than that.

The Egyptian soldiers, and especially the Nubians, stood to their post with uncommon tenacity; when they were beaten back, occupying a second line, and filling the shelter trenches which were almost numberless.

Young Donald Cameron, of the Cameron Highlanders, appears to have been the first to mount the parapet, and he was the second to fall.

Between the first and second lines of defence our biggest losses were incurred. Here went down the gallant Wyatt Rawson, just as he had succeeded in getting over. A little to the right, where the big redoubt was, young Graham-Stirling fell shot through the head. And near to him the big Sergeant-

Major of the Black Watch, McNeill, one of the finest soldiers of the force. Six of the foe had he smitten down with his claymore when he fell covered with wounds. It was close-quarter work with the Highland Brigade.

On our right the English and Irish lads rushed on under Graham, the man, as Wolseley characterised him, "with the courage of a lion and the modesty of a young girl." Reginald Hart, a staff-officer who had won his V.C. in Afghanistan and might have been looking for one on this field too, went ahead of the Royal Irish, and they followed him at a rush, their characteristic yell ringing out. Very soon, at the bayonet's point, the Egyptian left flank defences were carried.

The Marines had a tough struggle. They advanced by companies and successive rushes till within a hundred yards or so of the ditch, and then charged to the parapet, where the Egyptians were plying their rifles fiercely. That last hundred yards was a pathway of blood. Down went Major Strong, shot through the heart while he was leading his men at a pace at which they could scarcely keep up with him. Then right in front of the parapet Captain Wardell fell, with a bullet through his brain. But his subaltern, Luke, speedily avenged him. Marking the Egyptian who had sped the fatal bullet, he rushed at him, and with one sweep of his sword severed his head from his body. Sandwith, of the same battalion, had a narrow escape, for a bullet pierced his helmet. Bayonet and clubbed rifle did their deadly work effectually in this part of the field.

CHAPTER XXV.

The Guards Peppered—Father Bellord Wounded—Forward! the Guns—Scotland for Ever!—First Gun Breaks Down—The Bridge—The Naval Brigade Work their Gatlings—The Indians and the Seaforths Shoulder to Shoulder—The Butcher's Bill—The Track of the Storm—Succouring the Wounded—Revolver or Water Bottle—Trenches Full of Dead—The Unread Letter—A Fatal Shell—Arabi's Army a Mixed Multitude—Words of Christian Burial in the Great Redoubt—Young Graham-Stirling—The Colonel's Promise—The Gallant McNeill—Scanty Dinner Rations—Wounded Egyptians—A Fierce Amazon—A Wounded Woman's Gratitude—Evening Burial—Strong and Kayes—A Smart Telegraph Trick—Wolseley's Wise Measures—A Dash on Zagazig and Cairo—Rout of the *Bedaween*—The Irish Lads' Love of Loot—I Sleep on the Field.

WHILE this fierce opening fire from rifles sighted at eight hundred yards passed over the heads of our advancing first line, for the most part harmlessly, it dropped pretty warmly upon the Guards' Brigade, who were a thousand yards behind them. The

Duke of Connaught's trumpeter was shot at his side, and others were struck down here and there. But the steady line of the Guards, like an unbroken wall, advanced in accordance with their best traditions; hastening to succour their comrades, if they needed succour; or in any case to have a hand in the fighting themselves.

Father Bellord, one of the Roman Catholic chaplains, was in their vicinity at the time, at least twelve hundred yards from the entrenchments. He was calmly regarding the onward rush of our men through his field glass, when he felt a slight blow on his leg. He imagined that a bullet had struck the ground near and knocked up a handful of sand against him; but on glancing down, the streaming blood soon revealed the fact that the bullet had passed clean through his leg; and he had to retire from further observations.

At this moment up came the guns, the whole seven batteries, which had been waiting for the opportune moment. With wild hurrahs they came thundering forward over the sand—the men of the Scottish Divisional Battery saluting part of the Highland Brigade, as they swept past them, with loud cries of "Scotland for ever!"

As they neared the entrenchments there was a momentary pause. The order was for them to go over somehow and get to work inside the first line. But how were they to do it? How could the heavy guns negotiate first the ditch, and then the steep earthwork? General Goodenough, who commanded them, a smart soldier, who is "good enough" for any military task that is left to him, never paused to ask how it was to be done. "Go right at it," he shouted. And with a mighty cheer the first gun went at the earthworks. But it was a forlorn hope, as it appeared, for a moment. Into the ditch it went—but out of the ditch it never came. The great strong gun carriage was broken, the stout wheels were shattered, and there at the bottom of the ditch lay the wreck of the first gun. But this was not enough to discourage British gunners. The guns were to go over, and over they should go, even if they had to be lifted on their own brawny backs. A sudden inspiration seized them. They saw in the wrecked gun a strong foundation for a path of safety across the ditch. So with another hurrah they leaped or scrambled to the top of the earthwork, and began to shovel down the earth and sand on the top of the dismounted gun and shattered carriage, as they lay there at the bottom of the ditch. For a few moments the rest of the guns were halted, but only for a brief breathing time. Soon the ditch was bridged, and over the bridge went the second gun at a gallop, and the rest followed; and a mighty cheer went up as they slewed round and unlimbered, and got to work inside the first line of entrenchments.

The Naval Brigade, except that portion of it which brought up the ironclad train on the railway, marched on the other side of the canal with the Indian contingent and the 72nd Seaforth Highlanders. They took with them their Gatling guns; and though the wheels sank deeply in the soft sand, with cheery words of encouragement to one another they set their shoulders to the wheels to heave the guns along. As the enemy's artillery thundered forth on our right at the dawn of day, the Jack Tars raised a shout, and fixing cutlasses, prepared to go in, when suddenly a body of Egyptian cavalry appeared through the dim morning light immediately in front of them. In a moment they got the Gatlings around; and then with the horrible grinding of the lever was mingled the whistling of many bullets, as the ground in front was swept by the leaden hail, and horse and rider went down before the storm.

Splendidly did the Indians, with the "Seaforths," do their work on the left flank of the Egyptians. Here there was less of the rush which characterised the front attack of our Highland and Anglo-Saxon brigades; there was rather the steady and persistent advance of seasoned warriors. The "Seaforths" had not forgotten lessons learnt in Afghanistan. The leading company was commanded by an ex-musketry-instructor, who allowed no independent firing, but only by volleys, he himself naming the ranges. Thus their fire was most deadly. The enemy could not appear at the embrasures. In front of their points of attack lay more than seven hundred dead, and thirteen captured guns. It was felt that our gallant Indians merited more than the scant praise they received afterwards.

Arabi had long since fled the field on a swift horse, and the bulk of his men were now in full retreat. The swarthy Nubians stood well for a time; but as the cavalry were seen sweeping around, they too joined the throng of fugitives, and very soon our men were in full possession.

When our losses were counted up, it was found that nine officers and forty-eight non-commissioned officers and men had been struck down fatally, and twenty-seven officers and three hundred and fifty-three non-commissioned officers and men were wounded; twenty-two also were missing. It was a big butcher's bill for half-an-hour's fighting! The heaviest losses were of course incurred by the Highland Brigade, who had been hurled at the strongest point of the entrenchments, and had the heaviest fighting just inside the first line. The Egyptian loss in killed and wounded was nearly three thousand.

The tide of battle had rolled on ahead as I passed across the trenches. Outside I had already come upon the track of the storm. Here, some fifty yards away from the ditch, lay a handsome bearded sergeant of the "Gordons." It was poor Fitzgerald, who had made an exchange with another sergeant that he might take part in the fight, for he had been detailed to remain behind at Kassassin. One of the first to fall, he lay there with calm, placid face, having died apparently without pain. Some poor wounded fellows were already limping along, or were being conveyed in stretchers to the rear, groaning in strong agony, or setting their teeth resolutely to bear the pain without sign.

Over the scene presented inside the line of

entrenchments one would fain drop a veil; but while memory lives it will bring back many a sad scene which I then beheld.

My first work consisted in doing what I could to succour the wounded, who lay thickly strewing the ground. It was a strange and horrible sight to see; as far as one's eye could reach, a line of bodies lying, or kneeling, or reclining against the parapet, from end to end. There they had stood till the rush of our men was upon them, and there they had fallen, most of them under the bayonet. The sufferings of those who still lived was evidently intense. To help them at first was most hazardous, for they had been taught that if they fell into the hands of the English they would be butchered at once. Several of our people, doctors and others, were deliberately fired at by those who lay on the field while they were engaged in deeds of mercy.

So it happened that to the first wounded Arab whom I wished to help I went with my revolver in one hand and my water bottle in the other. I could see a score of eyes fixed upon me from those who lay around. Was I going to slay or succour? As soon as my *bona fides* was assured to them, their fears vanished, and my peril too, and from all parts of the field the cry arose piteously, "*Moya! Moya!*" "Water! Water!" My own stock was of course soon exhausted. But it was easily replenished from the water bottles of the dead Egyptians who were lying thickly around. If I could read aright the faces of these poor creatures, and the gestures they made towards Heaven, many a devout thanksgiving went up to *Allah* for the draught of water which came to them in their misery by the hand of the infidel.

The shelter trenches inside the works were full of dead bodies. It was a horrible sight. I had the curiosity roughly to measure one. It wanted something of twenty paces, yet within it I counted over fifty bodies—one that of a woman—heaped together in horrid death. Thickly enough they lay all over the field; in the redoubts perhaps most of all. Here was a field gun overturned, its limber shattered, and its team of mules all killed. Some of the gunners had evidently taken refuge between the wheels below; but in vain Camels even were here and there lying wounded or slain outright. At the lower end of the field some of the Egyptian tents were still standing, of the better kind; perhaps belonging to members of the Staff. I entered one. At the very door an Egyptian officer lay dead—the presumptive occupier formerly. On the ground inside there lay a letter unsealed. It had apparently just arrived, and had never yet been opened. I felt free to take possession of this epistle, and afterwards had it read to me. It was from an affectionate son, who seemed to have been an officer in the Kafr Dawar army, to his father at Tel-el-Kebir; full of Eastern symbolism and figure, speaking of the calamities of the war, but praying for sunshine in the coming year. Alas! for the battle sound which called the father forth to his death, and left the unsealed letter to be read only by the infidel. I keep that Arabic letter by me still.

Passing along I came upon a group of dead Highlanders. They lay in a kind of circle: doubtless all struck down by one shell which exploded in their midst, and yet scarce any mutilation or gaping wounds were visible.

The heterogeneous character of Arabi's army was sufficiently apparent when one looked over the slain. Men fair as Circassians lay side by side with black Nubians. Here were true *Bedaween* of the desert, and there crowds of the poor *Fellaheen* of Egypt, who had been pressed into the army, so many of them against their will.

In one place I picked up a bundle of telegraphic tape, some of which had passed through the machine. What messages, I wondered, had it brought to Arabi! In another, a soldier's discharge paper, exempting him long ago from further service; yet here he probably had fought again, and perhaps fallen. As indicating, too, the distance from which Arabi's recruits had been drawn, I found one paper belonging to a man who had come down from the Soudan provinces. It was an army document, carrying the seals of the governors of the various provinces through which the man had travelled in order to join the standard.

But there were duties to the dead, as well as to the wounded, which required to be done. The poor bodies must be laid away to rest with Christian prayer as far as possible. At the corner of the big redoubt, where the fighting had been fiercest, we gathered some of them together, Highlanders all, and in the trench itself their comrades laid them reverently, covering them with an Egyptian cloth, while I stood on the earth-work above, and repeated the words of our beautiful Burial Service over them.

The men had already dug a grave in the centre of the redoubt for Graham-Stirling, the young officer of the Black Watch who had been shot through the head as he led on his men. "You will come out to Egypt after the fighting is over, and bring me home again, Colonel, won't you?" he had said to a friend of the family who was seeing him away from his home in bonnie Scotland. "Aye, that I will," said the Colonel, as he looked into the bright face of the young warrior, anticipating with such keen joyousness his first campaign. I believe the Colonel's promise was fulfilled, though with a sadness that was all unforeseen, when the body was removed later on to be re-interred near his Scottish home. By the side of Graham-Stirling they dug yet another grave, and there placed the gigantic sergeant-major of the Black Watch, McNeill, a right gallant soldier, a true man, and a most affectionate son, who had watched over his widowed mother with tender solicitude. He had lived unmarried for her sake, and by his death she lost her sole support. The bravest of the brave, smiting down with his claymore to right and left those who ventured to oppose him, he had at last fallen covered with wounds. Here, again, by the side of the two graves I stood, and offered words of prayer.

So the day wore on. In the afternoon I reached the bottom of the field, where a few tents hastily put up formed a little Field Hospital. Half a cup of tea, and another half-cup of beef essence, with some sago dissolved in it, which some of the doctors got for me, were most welcome, for I was almost fainting from fatigue and the heat of the sun; and this was all the dinner I got that day. I found that most of the wounded had been brought down hither. Some had already been despatched by boat to Ismailia, but still the tents were crowded. Some major operations were being carried out there and then as a last chance for some of the poor fellows; and the surgeons, with sleeves turned up, were hard at work. Not only were our own men attended to, but no less than five hundred and thirty-five of the Egyptians were cared for with all the skill and tenderness that were possible. Sitting in rows outside, some who were suffering from comparatively slight wounds were waiting their turn. As I mingled with them I saw that one was a woman—a young, handsome creature. She had stood beside her husband in the fighting, and when he fell had fiercely attacked one of our men with a sword. Parrying the strokes, he was pressing on his way, but she flew at him again, and he, hard pressed, gave her a slight wound with the point of his bayonet. The touch of steel cowed her, and here she was among those who were calmly waiting to be attended to. Passing across the entrenchments near the hospital, I found one poor creature lying on the ground groaning from a bullet wound in the leg. A diminutive person, it seemed to me, and ill-fitted for soldier work. I had some strips of linen with me, and I proceeded to bandage the wound as well as I could, for the bullet had gone right through. As I finished the little surgical work, my patient bent over and kissed my hand in true Oriental fashion, and then I perceived that this also was a woman.

Near the hospital tents many of the bodies of the dead also had been gathered. Here was Strong, of the Marines, his calm, handsome face untouched and undistorted in death, for he had been shot through the heart. Dudley Kayes, of the Highland

Light Infantry, too, lay there quiet and placid, and several others. As the rays of the evening sun were sloping down on the sandy waste we buried them in one grave, I reading the service from a tiny prayer-book which was found in Strong's pocket, and which we afterwards forwarded to his young wife in England.

While we were thus busied on the field itself, Wolseley had been perfecting his victory. Riding through with his Staff, he halted on the bridge and wrote his despatches. At Salahieh, a few miles off in the desert, a force, computed at five thousand, were awaiting orders to march down and take part in the fight. But the little telegraph station was seized and the signalling clerk captured bodily. And by a judicious use of telegraph and operator they were informed that they " were not wanted at present." Nor were they; yet had they suddenly appeared in force and shown fight, they would have given our men more work to do; and surely the work of death was already sufficient.

As it was, with cavalry sweeping around both right and left on the wretched fugitives, Wolseley also sent the Indian contingent, with the Seaforth Highlanders, across the field in hot pursuit. Pressing on without a halt, that afternoon they occupied Zagazig, a most important railway junction some fourteen miles off. Subsequently, also, the Naval Brigade was sent forward to join them. The cavalry made their way swiftly towards Cairo itself. Wolseley knew not what further stand might be made. The capital certainly was garrisoned by a very large force, and a swift and immediate advance might awe them into submission, and obviate any possible danger to Cairo itself. A wise forethought it proved to be. Under a burning sun the Cavalry Brigade, under Drury Lowe, pushed on, Sir Henry Havelock-Allan accompanying them. Now and again halting for their guns to come up, for it was terrible going for them in the heavy sand, they reached Abbassiyeh the next day, and saved Cairo from threatened destruction.

During the day of the battle a swoop was made on the camp at Kassassin by several thousand *Bedaween*. They thought to find it unguarded. But the West Kent men were on the alert, and pouring heavy volleys into them, sent them quickly to the right about.

When darkness set in on the field of fight a small detachment of our Irish lads marched in as a guard, for the *Bedaween* were about here also. They first proceeded to loot my knapsack, which lay in their way, entirely by mistake, for they took it for an Egyptian's, and returned the various articles subsequently by the hand of their sergeant. And then, wearied out, I lay down on the field, wrapped in an Egyptian rug, which I found in one of the tents, for I had no other shelter, and lulled to sleep by the sad moanings of the wounded Egyptians, who had crawled down, and were lying near me. In the morning, alas! they were most of them beyond pain. The sun had set with them, never to rise again.

CHAPTER XXVI.

After the Battle—Dash on Zagazig by the Indians and 72nd—The Cavalry Ride to Cairo—Surrender of the Citadel—Arabi Pasha a Prisoner—Wolseley Arrives—Scenes in Hospital and on Board the *Carthage*—The Tainted Battlefield—Strewn with Dead and Debris—I go on to Cairo in a Cattle Truck—The Donkey Boy at Midnight — Luxury of a "Square" Meal and a Bed—Mosquito Pests—Return of the Khedive—Illuminations and Rejoicings—The Fête at Ghezireh—*Bedaween* seek Wives among the Highlanders—A Little Blunder—The "Holy Carpet" Procession—Explosion at the Cairo Railway Station—Arabi's Trial and Sentence—What We Learned from the Trial—England's Mission in Egypt—My Meeting with Gordon—Is He Dead?—Testimony of Two Campaigns to the Pluck of Our Soldiers, and the Splendid Work of the Medical Department—The Chaplains' Department—The Echo of Wyatt Rawson's Words—The Call of Stern Duty to Every Man.

THE main body of the English forces after the battle of Tel-el-Kebir quietly settled down in camp for a few days of rest, occupying the tents which Arabi Pasha had left standing about a mile beyond the line of entrenchments. But in the smartest fashion the Indian contingent, with their comrades of the 72nd Highlanders, as well as the united cavalry, dashed on towards Cairo. "When once the Oriental has been put to flight, he must not be allowed to rest;" and swift action on the lines of this maxim was at once taken. The Indians and the "Seaforths" pushed forward by way of Zagazig, the cavalry by Belbeis. Zagazig was a most important railway centre, and at this time was crowded with fugitive troops. Its capture was initiated by a deed of daring which ought not to be forgotten. Lieutenant Burn Murdoch of the Engineers was ahead with five troopers of the 6th Bengal Cavalry. Dashing into the station, he found four crowded trains, with steam up, just preparing to make off. Reining up in front of the foremost, he ordered the driver to dismount, but he refused, and had to be shot. After this there was a general stampede on the part of both soldiers and civilian passengers, thousands of whom fled across the country. Half an hour later the main body of our men came up, and Zagazig was in our hands towards evening. A march of nearly twenty miles across the burning desert, after the terrible work of the morning, preceded by the night march from Kassassin, was a splendid testimony to the pluck and endurance of our native troops and the Seaforth men.

Drury Lowe, with the cavalry numbering a bare fifteen hundred sabres, and a battery of Horse Artillery, seized Belbeis after a slight skirmish. The next day, the 14th of September, they pushed on to Cairo. Outside Abbassiyeh, some three miles from the citadel, they were met by an Egyptian officer with a squadron of horse, each man fluttering a white flag. He announced that the garrison and city would surrender. This, however, was not deemed sufficient. It was without doubt that Arabi intended further resistance, if possible; and swift measures were necessary to allay all danger. The population was hostile, and the garrison, consisting of ten thousand men, were massed and under arms. Drury Lowe replied that Arabi, who was known to be in the city, must at once be given up. Meanwhile a small detachment of cavalry, accompanied by Captain Watson, of the Intelligence Department, making a detour around the city, rode up to the citadel, and demanded the instant surrender of Suleiman Effendi, the commandant of that fortress. It was a critical moment, where indomitable British pluck alone carried our men through. As Lawrence, who commanded the Mounted Infantry, and did such splendid service, afterwards told me, our men were utterly exhausted, and a force armed with sticks could almost have knocked them off their horses. But they attempted nothing of the kind. After consultation, Suleiman ordered the great gates to be thrown back, and the men of the garrison, to the number of some thousands, marched out, piling arms, in the sight of the little handful of weary troopers who thus dominated them.

About ten o'clock Arabi Pasha arrived,

accompanied by Toulba Pasha, the official Governor of Cairo, and gave up his sword to Drury Lowe. He carried himself with great dignity.

The next day Wolseley and his Staff, with the Duke of Connaught, arrived in Cairo by the railway; thus marching in on the very date that he had fixed as likely to terminate the campaign, the 15th of September.

The day following the battle we were busy enough at Tel-el-Kebir getting away the remnant of our poor fellows who had been wounded. The railway was now available, and this served as well as the canal boats. I went down myself to Ismailia, and, of course, found the Base Hospital crowded with our lads. On the *Carthage* it was much the same. My friend Chapman, the chaplain, who had broken down awhile since, was here, not a great deal better. Father Bellord, too, who had a bullet through his leg at the battle, was as cheerful as a man who had suddenly received a fortune. And so he might be, for he got his "step" through it, an appropriate reward for a wound in the leg. Colonel Richardson, of the Cornish Light Infantry, who had received a bullet in his mouth, was on board also, lively enough. He did not swallow the indigestible morsel as it sped through, and it came out somewhere behind his neck, fortunately doing no great damage. Poor Allan Park, who had been fatally struck, expired on board almost at once; and the gallant Wyatt Rawson, while the ship was making its way to Malta.

In a few days I went back to Tel-el-Kebir. The troops were still encamped here; but the horrible smell from the battlefield made it a most undesirable place of rest. Our own men, together with the Egyptian prisoners and the villagers, had been burying away the corpses, but the work had not been completed; and in many cases the bodies rested under only a few inches of sand, which did nothing to deodorize. As I rode from point to point I found bodies of men and horses, mules and camels, strewn everywhere. Overturned guns, smashed limbers, thousands of Remington rifles and sword bayonets, and numberless boxes of cartridges covered a vast stretch of desert. Not only within the lines, and especially in the redoubts, but far out into the sandy wilderness, the track of the fugitives was thus marked.

By slow degrees our men were being sent forward to Cairo. How they managed to live and keep free from fever in that pestiferous spot I never could tell. The horrible smell quickly drove me away. And one day about noon, finding that a cranky train of waggons, much the worse for wear, was going forward, I got on board, leaving my horse to follow, under the care of my Irish soldier servant.

It was a strange journey. Four of us, a cavalry officer on the Staff, a Guardsman, a Brigade surgeon, and myself found ourselves located in an open truck, much dilapidated; together with a horse, and some bags of grain. The doctor had a kettle and spirit lamp; and as the locomotive crawled along he made us some tea. It was a godsend, for we never reached Cairo till past midnight; accomplishing thus a railway journey of perhaps eighty miles at the rate of some seven miles an hour.

Arriving in the metropolis at that hour, what was one to do? Fortunately, one of the ubiquitous donkey boys of Cairo was near at hand, even at that unearthly hour; and he, in his wonderfully fluent mixture of English, French, and Arabic, promised to guide me to a hotel, which he averred would open its doors and let me in. Oh! those donkey boys, truly they are a *genus* by themselves! Nowhere else in this wide world to be matched for Mephistophelian cunning, for side-splitting drollery, and for infinite endurance. In this case the boy proved his usefulness by guiding me safely through tortuous streets to the Hôtel Royale; and after much knocking, very cautiously a *Boâb* peeped forth, and was persuaded to allow me to enter. It was a great thing for this or any other hotel to be open at all. The inhabitants had weeks ago shut up their shops, and most of those peaceably inclined had gone elsewhere to escape the troubles which were impending. The Hôtel Royale reaped its own reward in a golden harvest for the next month; for everyone who could among the Staff and Departmental men crowded in.

The sense of supreme luxury which came to me as I sat down to a "square" meal, and still more, when soon after I stretched myself on a decently-appointed bed, I shall never forget, despite the presence of my old Indian friends, the mosquitoes, who were here in hugher and more ferocious shape than ever. Some of the men fresh from England were in a sad way; and the picture of one of the young officers of the Cornish Light Infantry, who, most airily clad, was walking up and down the corridor in a state of intense physical irritation, after lying down on the lounge in his bedroom, does not fade from my memory. I had to take him into his room and show him the utility of his mosquito curtains; finally tucking him in, as his nurse might have done twenty years before.

The events which swiftly followed the close of the campaign are facts of public history. In a few days the Khedive, Muhammad Tewfik, returned to his capital, and was received with, at any rate, outward demonstrations of rejoicing. The streets lined with our troops were crowded, too, with the populace; and the shrill *lululus* of the women sounded above the hoarse roar of the multitude, and the clang of the Egyptian bands, as they toned forth the Khedivial Hymn.

For three nights the whole city, and especially the Esbekiyeh quarter, were illuminated, and strings of carriages passed along the bright streets. Everyone was *en fête*. To the officers of the Force the Khedive gave a most charming garden entertainment at Ghezireh Palace; where the darkness of night was chased away by lines of bright lamps hung along the garden paths; and on the river close at hand *Dahabiyehs*, brilliantly gay, floated quietly down the tide. In the big hall Tewfik received us with all graciousness, as indeed well he might. The whole scene was truly Oriental.

Soon after this I went into camp quarters again myself on the sandy plain of Ghezireh, just across the Nile. The Highland Brigade and part of the English were here. The former in their kilts were a perpetual puzzle to the inhabitants, among whom the tale had been diligently disseminated that the British forces had been almost annihilated, and the women had been sent out to aid their husbands, or replace them. This yarn had actually been largely accepted by the wild *Bedaween;* and one night, stealing in from the desert, they made a swoop on the Highland lines at Ghezireh, intending to repeat the Rape of the Sabines, and win for themselves British brides. Alas! for the poor Arabs, when the Scotsmen turned out, kilts and all, and with rapid volleys laid forty of them low.

About this time occurred the "Procession of the Holy Carpet," as it was called; when the consecrated cloth which was destined to cover the Prophet's tomb at Mecca was solemnly borne along the streets and around the Citadel Square, ere it was despatched on its journey across the desert. It made me thrill with shame when I saw our British soldiers paraded to do honour at this Mohammedan ceremony, and actually to present arms in general salute, as the camel bearing the sacred cloth passed by. No policy or necessity, it seems to me, could justify such a step; and the general outcry in England, added to the protest on the part of officers and chaplains in Cairo, will no doubt prevent any repetition in the future.

Quietly we were settling down to the work of occupation when the frightful explosion at the Cairo Railway Station brought further casualties and horrors. Whether accidental or incendiary could never be clearly ascertained. Waggon-loads of ammunition were ignited; and as I rode up the explosion of shells and the crackling of thousands of rifle cartridges reminded one of a very warm battle-field. Several men were killed outright, and numerous wounds, as well as marvellous escapes, were incurred.

All this time Arabi Pasha had been kept in close confinement; and in December his trial was to take place. Mr. A. M. Broadley and the Hon. Mark Napier had been retained for his defence. Others of his colleagues were to be tried at the same time, before a Council of Notables. Whether the trial was a *bona-fide* one or a farce was never sufficiently clear. Certain it is that Arabi for treason was condemned to death. Equally certain that this judgment was at once cancelled and that of exile substituted. I sat quite close to him at the time of his sentence, and had opportunity of studying the face and the man. A broad, and, for an Oriental, an honest face, there was something which appealed to your sympathy a good deal. He looked crushed by his misfortunes, yet there was still a dignity of bearing, which compared favourably with his judges. Certainly the facts which were opened up at the trial dispelled many delusions. We had gone to war, not with the Egyptian nation, but to crush a rebel movement which had thrown the country into a state of anarchy, and which threatened the safety of our highway to India. The facts which transpired at that trial showed this rebel movement to have been really a national protest against the tyranny of a government, with a weak Viceroy at its head, and men alien to the country as its Ministers. Arabi showed singleness of purpose in his aims. He truly had the nation at his back. No participation in, or approval of, the Alexandrian massacres could be brought home to him. He was a poor man when he began his movement; he was no richer when he ended—a strange fact, indeed, had he been nothing but an adventurer. Had he succeeded he would have been an Oliver Cromwell—his failure made him a rebel.

But if ever England is to do anything really worthy of her great name as a lover of liberty and righteousness, she must no longer palter with a government which is corrupt and rotten to its very core. The members of this government, Turks, Armenians, Circassians, Italians, anything but native Egyptians, have been satisfying their greed at the expense of the degraded *Fellaheen* for many a year. Let them be swept away. And though these so-called ministers would curse the name of England, yet a nation of slaves would rise up from the dust of their oppression to call her blessed.

. . . .

As is almost always the case after a campaign closes, we had a great deal of severe sickness among the men, and our hospitals were full. Exposure in the field infallibly tells upon the strongest constitutions; and though the excitement of the time carries men through the actual experience, there is many a collapse subsequently when they settle down to quieter life. My own work in hospital was consequently heavy, and at last, after several months in Cairo, I broke down myself, and was carried from my quarters to the citadel hospital with severe inflamation, which well nigh proved fatal. The skill of the doctors, by the good mercy of Providence, however, pulled me through; and as soon as I was convalescent, instead of accepting the Nile trip which the Government was good enough to provide for all its sick officers, I got permission to visit Palestine. It had been a dream of my life, and I was eager to grasp the opportunity which now presented. Half-a-dozen or so of us made up a party, and in due course reached Jerusalem. The details of our delightful visit I do not need to dilate upon, but it brought to me what I regard as one of the greatest honours of my life. As we sat at lunch one day I observed a stranger seated next but one to me. "Who is he?" said I to Wood of the Engineers. "It's Chinese Gordon," said he. He, the great Christian hero of the nineteenth century, and indeed of a succession of centuries, was here, seeking in solitude, nigh to the Holy City, knowledge as to his next great work; he was waiting to know whither his Master would send him. He was with us a good deal, for some of our party were known to him. Little did any of us foresee what was then drawing near to him. Had he himself any prevision? As I used to look at the sharp, keen face, the grey eyes kindly, yet flashing with a strange gleam, it almost seemed to me, in that far-away look of his, that he saw many things which were hidden from our grosser vision. The page of shame, blotted with the tears of a nation, which records his abandonment by his brother countrymen, after that defence of his post which was characterised by an almost superhuman skill, gallantry, and self-sacrifice, it boots us not to record again. The solitary figure standing there alone amid the gathering hordes, grand in his oneness, and dying there in his fidelity, with no brother's hand to clasp his in the dimness of the falling shadow, is a picture that will never fade, a memory which will abide in the hearts of his countrymen through all future ages.

But is it known with infallible certainty that he is really dead? I for one refuse to relinquish the last fragmentary hope that even to-day, in some far-away land beneath the Equator, he is fulfilling his heaven-appointed mission to lift up the degraded peoples of Central Africa. True! it is but a dim, shadowy hope, a bare possibility—nothing more. Yet I cling to it. The man who was faithful to all duty was also infinite in resource. When his post fell, his duty to remain there ended. Would he not have provided some pathway of escape to meet this last extremity? Gordon had eight steamers. Seven are accounted for; where is the eighth? It was not seen off Khartoum when our men swept the river front with their glasses ere they turned back to Metemmeh. Is it half-a-dozen or more *authentic* accounts of his death by eye-witnesses that we have received from time to time? And every one such account has strangely differed from every other.

But whether he be living and toiling among the tribes to-day, or his body lying among the sands of the solitary desert, the picture of this true knight, who lived for duty and for

God, will be for ever bright in the vision of his countrymen.

. . . .

After having thus followed the wanderings and the deeds of our soldier lads through two campaigns, it would be easy to develop the many lessons which one cannot have failed to learn from personal observation. The unfailing pluck and endurance of our men were always and everywhere apparent. The true British heart still lives in the British body as in days of old.

I may be permitted one word expressive of my admiration of the splendid work which was constantly done by our medical officers. In labours they are literally " more abundant," while in skill and tenderness they are beyond all praise. The Department seems to an outsider to labour under many defects of system, for which, however, the doctors are not themselves responsible; and never till these defects are remedied, can the work be thoroughly effective. Meanwhile one cannot but note with thankfulness the earnestness and capability of both officers and men of the A.M.D.

As to the men of the Chaplains' Department, I can only say that my colleagues with myself were deeply thankful for the honour accorded us in being permitted to do some little in alleviating the sufferings of our poor fellows when sick or wounded. It is a work that is very dear to us, and from it we gather many lessons and many encouragements. And as the words of the dying Wyatt Rawson ring in my ears, " Didn't I lead them straight, General ? " it seems to me as if those words should find an echo in the hearts of all true Englishmen. Whether as ministers leading people, or teachers pupils, or parents children, it is for us so to guide and lead for the Great Captain, as that when the greater march of life is ended, and the mightier conflict crowned with victory, He may greet us with a smile of welcome, and a " Well done ! " as those who have been " faithful unto death."

Every man is a soldier if he live truly. And before each one stern Duty stands to lead him forward to things higher and nobler. And

> " He that ever following Her commands,
> On with toil of heart and knee and hands,
> Through the low gorge to the far height,
> Hath won his way upward and prevailed,
> Shall find, the toppling crags of duty scaled,
> Are close upon the shining tableland
> To which our God Himself is Moon and Sun."

FINIS.

Cowan & Co., Limited, Printers, Perth.

AT ALL LIBRARIES AND BOOKSELLERS.

Handsomely Bound, Price 6s.

SOUVENIRS OF THE SECOND EMPIRE,
OR,
The Last Days of the Court of Napoleon,
BY THE
COMTE DE MAUGNY (formerly Minister for Foreign Affairs).

This interesting volume of the reminiscences of a Cabinet Minister is full of anecdotes relating to all that passed amongst the Court and Society, the Clubs and the Theatres, in the reign of Napoleon III. It contains, also, numerous particulars as to the lives of all the Celebrities of the period, with portraits, including the Emperor, General Fleury, the Prince and Princess de Metternich, Baron Hausmann, Von Moltke, Thiers, Guizot, &c., &c.

Third Edition. Just Published, Price 6s.

My Mistress, the Empress Eugenie;
OR,
COURT LIFE AT THE TUILERIES,
BY HER PRIVATE READER,
MADAME CARETTE (*née* BOUVET),
AUTHORISED TRANSLATION.

The *Daily News* of September 18th, 1889, says:—Madame Carette has written an agreeable book on her recollections of the Court life of the Second Empire. Madame Carette, the daughter of an officer, came to the Tuileries in her girlhood, and was attached to the Empress as a kind of companion and literary factotum. She saw the brilliant scene of the closing years of the Empire, and she relates what she saw in a lively and unaffected style; and she writes of the indoor rather than the inner life of the Tuileries. The household had a way of divining the secret of Imperial movements which is suggestive of the infinitely little Court life. Under this lady's guidance we walk through the Empress's apartments and see the private sitting-room, where objects especially dear to her were stored.

Just Published, Price 10s. 6d.

Intimate Recollections of the Court of the Tuileries.
THE EVE OF AN EMPIRE'S FALL.
BY
MADAME CARETTE (*née* BOUVET),
PRIVATE READER TO THE EMPRESS EUGÉNIE.
Authoress of "My Mistress, The Empress Eugénie; or, Court Life at the Tuileries."
AUTHORISED TRANSLATION.

The volume contains attractive portraits of Prince Bismarck, the late Emperor Frederick, M. Thiers, General Trochu, and Marshal Macmahon, and much interesting information relative to these celebrities.

Personal details about the Empress Eugénie, which formed the charm of Madame Carette's first work, are continued in the present volume, which includes an interesting account of her escape from the mob, and flight from the Tuileries, and the actual circumstances leading up to it. We also gain further facts as to the careers of the Emperor Napoleon, the Prince Imperial, Marshal Bazaine, and, in short, of every noted Frenchman of the period.

LONDON: DEAN & SON, 160A FLEET STREET, E.C.

Just ready, handsomely bound in cloth gilt, Crown 8vo, Price 6s.

BISMARCK INTIME.

By A FELLOW STUDENT.

EDITED BY H. HAYWARD

With Photo-Portrait of PRINCE BISMARCK and full-page Portraits of the EMPERORS WILLIAM I. and II., VON MOLTKE, and BISMARCK.

Illustrated by many Characteristic Anecdotes of—

BISMARCK AS A STUDENT.
BISMARCK AS A YOUNG MAN.
BISMARCK'S MARRIAGE.
BISMARCK'S HOME.
BISMARCK'S CHARACTER.
BISMARCK IN THE REICHSTAG.
BISMARCK'S POPULARITY.
BISMARCK'S WITTY SAYINGS.

"This volume extends to nearly three hundred pages, and all are full of interest, information, anecdote and shrewd observation, and the work holds one fascinated from beginning to end. It is THE BOOK OF THE DAY, and one that everyone must read, for it is a book that will be *the talk of Society*."—*Public Opinion.*

Earl Granville, in writing to the author, says: "I am reading 'Bismarck Intime' with great interest."

Handsomely Bound, Price 10s. 6d.

HOW

FRENCH SOLDIERS

FARED IN

GERMAN PRISONS AND HOSPITALS.

Being the Reminiscences of a French Army Chaplain during and after the Franco-German War.

By CANON E. GUERS, *Army Chaplain to the French Forces.*

This captivating volume, consisting of realistic descriptions from the graphic pen of an eye-witness, should especially appeal to all those who are interested in the welfare of our soldiers, in Hospital Work, in Ambulance Corps, and in the recent political and military history of France and Gemany.

The work contains excellent portraits of the AUTHOR, and of NAPOLEON III., MARSHAL MACMAHON, MARSHAL BAZAINE, WIMPFEN, THE EMPRESS AUGUSTA, VON MOLTKE, PRINCE BISMARCK, and other leading actors in the terrible scenes of twenty years ago. The thrilling narrative helps one to realise the self-denial and heroism, not only of the common soldiers, but of ladies of most exalted rank, who gave up much of the comfort of this life to tend the sufferings of the sick, wounded, and helpless soldiers suddenly interred in Fortress and Hospital.

LONDON: DEAN & SON, 160A FLEET STREET, E.C.,
Office of "Debrett's Peerage, Baronetage, &c."

www.ingramcontent.com/pod-product-compliance
Lightning Source LLC
Chambersburg PA
CBHW021954160426
43197CB00007B/126